Generative Genius

Generative Genius

How AI Is Reinventing Art, Writing, and Music

Jahan Vespari

Mindful Pages

Published in 2026

ISBN: 9789374592786 (PB)
ISBN: 9789374592137 (eBook)

Published by

Mindful Pages
Imprint of Alpha Editions LLC
312 W. 2nd St #1834
Casper, WY 82601, USA

This book was developed using advanced writing tools to support the drafting and ideation process. All content has been thoughtfully curated, refined, and reviewed to ensure quality and relevance.

Content

Introduction

The first time the illustrator tried it, she expected little more than a parlour trick. She typed a handful of careful prompts—just sketches in words, really—and waited. In the time it would once have taken her to find a sharpened pencil, an entire portfolio unfolded on the screen: compositions she might have spent days exploring, colour treatments she had not considered, variations that felt like strange cousins of her own instincts. She sat back, half delighted, half unsettled. She had asked for possibilities, not replacements, yet the speed and audacity of the results felt like the world had shifted under her feet. A few kilometres away, an editor reviewed a manuscript with the help of a language model trained on her publishing house's archives. In minutes it surfaced structural weaknesses her team had overlooked, quietly suggesting a through-line that tightened the whole argument. She recognised the value immediately—and the risk. If a machine could see patterns her staff had missed, what else might it soon claim competence over?

This mingling of wonder and worry has become the defining sensation of contemporary creativity. It is the feeling of standing at the shoreline while a new tide arrives. Not a wave that sweeps away everything familiar, but a force that changes what is possible and, crucially, what is expected. The creative fields—art, writing, music, design, publishing, filmmaking—are being rearranged by systems that generate at scale, respond at speed, and imitate with fluency. The shift is astonishing. It is also disorientating. We are told alternately to fear the future or embrace it without hesitation. The truth is far more demanding: we must learn to think with these systems while holding on to the standards, discernment, and human depth that define meaningful work.

This book offers a map through that terrain. Not a hymn to frictionless automation, nor a lament for disappearing craft. Instead it asks how generative technologies might expand skill rather than hollow it out; how originality can be judged wisely when tools remix the world with frightening ease; how credit, consent, and authorship shift when ideas no longer move in a straight line from human hand to finished piece; and how creative industries might adapt so that human taste—our stubbornly subjective, gloriously inconsistent sense of what matters—remains the compass.

The urgency of these questions is obvious, yet their roots stretch deep into history. Every great technological shift in creative practice has brought both liberation and anxiety. The printing press unsettled scribes; photography threatened painters; digital editing rearranged filmmaking; synthesisers unsettled orchestras; sampling uprooted traditional notions of musical authorship. Yet none of these developments eliminated creativity; instead they forced practitioners to rethink what counted as craft, what constituted originality, and where the line between influence and imitation lay. What distinguishes generative systems today is not simply their capability, but their proximity to the expressive core of human work. They do not merely accelerate production; they appear to participate in the imaginative process itself. That illusion—powerful, seductive, occasionally dangerous—forces a new reckoning with what it means to create.

If there is a single motif that runs through this book, it is the shift from maker to conductor. For centuries, creativity has been romanticised as the solitary act of a singular mind shaping raw material with precision. The painter at the canvas, the composer at the piano, the writer at the desk. Generative systems complicate that image. They introduce a new kind of collaborator: one that generates thousands of possibilities with no concern for meaning, context, or consequence. The creative practitioner becomes something more akin to a conductor or director, orchestrating data, models, prompts, references, and human judgement into a coherent vision. This role is no less demanding than traditional craft; if anything, it elevates the premium on discernment. The conductor still decides the tempo, the emphasis, the interpretation. The tools merely offer breadth. The human provides depth.

Understanding this shift requires a clear view of the generative stack—the layers of data, models, interfaces, and workflows that underpin every seemingly magical output. These systems do not dream; they do not intend; they do not understand. They predict. They remix. They offer patterns drawn from vast pools of human expression. Knowing this does not diminish their utility; it grounds it. It allows us to diagnose failures without melodrama, to anticipate biases without surprise, and to choose when to rely on these systems and when to step away. It equips us with the literacy necessary to build responsibly, to defend standards, and to ensure that technology serves creativity rather than the reverse.

But literacy alone is not enough. The creative world is now grappling with questions that stretch beyond technique into ethics and identity. Who should be credited for work shaped by a model's suggestions? Who should be paid? How should artists, writers, and musicians respond when their styles are imitated without consent? What responsibilities do studios and agencies bear when using datasets that include the work of living creators? How do we define originality when models can generate endless variations that feel both familiar and strange? These are not theoretical debates; they affect contracts, careers, and communities. A future in which generative systems flourish requires thoughtful norms—credit systems that reflect real contribution, consent policies that respect creators, and review processes that catch harm before it reaches audiences.

Equally important is the question of taste. In a world of limitless options, curation becomes the defining creative act.

The rare skill is not generating more, but selecting wisely, arranging meaningfully, and rejecting fearlessly. Taste becomes the asset that cannot be automated. It is informed by experience, identity, memory, and judgement—qualities not captured in datasets or reproduced in probabilistic patterns. When used well, generative tools do not diminish taste; they sharpen it. They force practitioners to articulate what they value, to define their constraints, to build signature styles and systems that hold their work steady amidst the flux. Taste, in this new landscape, becomes both shield and compass.

This book traces how human–AI collaboration reshapes studio practice: the roles that emerge, the hand-offs that keep teams agile, the critique rituals that separate promising directions from deceptive noise. It explores the craft of prompt design as a genuine design discipline—one that requires clarity of intention, mastery of constraints, and careful construction of references and style kits. It examines the distinct workflows of visual artists, writers, and musicians, showing how generative tools accelerate ideation while leaving the final act of judgement firmly in human hands. It analyses new economic realities: how value shifts from labour hours to taste and distribution; how small teams can compete with giants; how careers evolve when new roles—prompt leads, dataset curators, verifiers—become indispensable.

Yet beneath all these changes lies a deeper cultural negotiation. When systems learn from the collective of human expression, they inherit not only our creativity but our biases, absences, and blind spots. The outputs they produce—however visually stunning or linguistically fluent—must be examined with care. Representation without reduction becomes a quality metric, not a gesture of political correctness. Provenance and transparency become practical tools for trust. Communities shape informal norms long before legislation catches up. Creative practitioners must navigate harm when it occurs, revise their methods, and remain vigilant that speed does not excuse carelessness.

The decisions we make now will shape the creative industries for decades. They will influence which voices flourish and which fade, which forms of expression become mainstream and which become marginal, how audiences learn to interpret and value creative work. We stand at a moment not unlike the early days of the camera, the printing press, or digital film—but with the added complication that this new tool does not merely change distribution or production; it intersects with the imaginative act itself. That intersection demands principles: human purpose first, consent by default, clarity over hype, quality over novelty.

As you move through this book, you will encounter strategies, methods, and frameworks for working with generative systems in ways that uphold craft rather than dilute it. You will see where these tools excel and where they falter; where they illuminate paths that humans might have missed and where they lead us astray with confident nonsense. You will learn to recognise the difference between collaboration and abdication, between amplification and imitation, between exploration and dependency. You will discover how to design workflows that respect both the speed of the machine and the care of the human eye.

But before diving into the practical, it is worth pausing to consider the broader stakes. Creativity has always been a negotiation between possibility and constraint. What makes this moment unique is that the scale of possibility has exploded, while the responsibility for constraint rests more heavily than ever on human shoulders. The illustrator who watched her portfolio bloom in minutes did not lose her craft; she gained a new responsibility. She must decide what to keep, what to discard, what to refine, and what to claim as her own. The editor who used a model to surface structure did not become obsolete; she became accountable for distinguishing between helpful pattern and misleading simplification. Their stories—echoed across studios, agencies, classrooms, and homes—show that the real question is not what generative AI can do, but what we choose to do with it.

We are entering a period where the boundaries between tool and collaborator blur, where authorship becomes shared, and where creativity becomes a negotiation among humans, machines, and the vast cultural memory we have collectively produced. Who guides that negotiation? Who decides what counts as ethical, original, or meaningful? Who ensures that creative work remains an act of human judgement rather than a by-product of algorithms? Those are the questions that will shape not just industries, but identities.

This book does not pretend to offer definitive answers—only the most irresponsible work would. Instead it offers a compass and a set of practices, grounded in craft and shaped by principles, to help navigate a landscape where the pace of change outstrips habit and expectation. It invites you to think with urgency and patience, to hold both the promise and the peril in view, to recognise that generative tools are neither saviours nor saboteurs but instruments whose impact depends on the hands that wield them.

As you turn the page, consider this: what might creativity look like when abundance replaces scarcity? What new responsibilities emerge when the barrier to expression drops but the need for discernment rises? How might we ensure that technological possibility never outruns human purpose? These questions hang over every chapter that follows. They are not meant to intimidate, but to energise. The future of creative work is being written—not by machines, but by the humans who choose how to engage with them. The next steps are ours.

Chapter 1
The New Shape of Creativity

The director paused before the monitors, studying a spread of images that had not existed an hour earlier. A few text cues—gestures toward atmosphere, colour temperature, and emotional tone—had unfurled into rows of possible scenes. They were not finished frames, not even close, but they carried the faint pulse of a film that could be. On the table beside her lay her original storyboard sketches, loose and imperfect, yet unmistakably hers. As she compared them with the generated variations, she could feel the shift: the work no longer began with the lone craftsperson chiselling ideas in isolation. It began with an orchestra of references, models, and collaborators—human and computational—each waiting to be shaped by her intent.

The paradox was irresistible. Never had creative production felt so crowded; never had authorship felt so exposed. Yet the essential act remained deeply personal: she still had to decide. Which frame captured the emotional arc? Which lighting direction served the story? Which prompt deserved refining, and which belonged in the bin? The ability to generate dozens of options in minutes hadn't reduced her responsibility; it had sharpened it. The craft was no longer confined to the sketch. The craft now lived in the alignment—how she handled the tension between what she imagined, what the tools proposed, and what the project demanded.

This transition—from maker to conductor—defines the new shape of creativity. It is not the replacement of human labour with effortless automation, nor the dissolution of the artist's voice into a soup of data-driven mimicry. It is a reconfiguration of where creativity happens and how it is directed. The shift is subtle enough to be misunderstood and profound enough to rewire long-held assumptions. It is the difference between shaping every stroke by hand and orchestrating a system of contributors. It is the difference between typing and deciding.

To understand this shift, we must begin by recognising a simple truth: creative intent has always been more than the execution of technique. It is the articulation of goals and the selection of constraints. It is the difficult, sometimes invisible work of choosing what *not* to pursue. Generative tools surface this underlying architecture by exposing how much of creativity lies in decision-making rather than manual production. The director's example is not an anomaly; it is a signpost. The storyboard, the visual references, the prompt—each is a different way of expressing intent. The tools offer permutations; the creator offers direction. The hands-on craft remains vital, but the locus of influence shifts upward, toward the realm of judgement.

Yet before we can celebrate this new dynamic, we must first separate what AI actually does from what we imagine it doing. A designer recently described how she used a model to propose fifty alternate layouts for a book cover. She accepted three for further development and discarded the rest. Those three were not perfect; they required refinement, typographic discipline, and an understanding of the readership that no model possesses. What the model contributed was breadth, not meaning. It provided variations—patterns, shapes, compositions—but the designer provided context. She judged what aligned with the author's voice, what signalled the right genre cues, what might intrigue a reader glancing at a shelf. Without her taste, the variations were nothing more than visual noise.

This distinction between pattern synthesis and human judgement is foundational. Models extrapolate from statistical patterns; they do not grasp intention, audience, or consequence. They can propose, but they cannot prioritise.

They can vary, but they cannot care. Their strength lies in scale and speed: a kind of sprawling imagination stripped of the very faculties that make imagination matter. This does not diminish their usefulness; it clarifies it. When we treat these tools as generators of options rather than generators of meaning, we reclaim our role as interpreters rather than spectators.

Yet the seduction of speed can trick even seasoned practitioners. There is a persistent myth that generative tools democratise creativity by offering "effortless genius"—that a single prompt can substitute for years of practice. Anyone who has attempted serious creative work with these systems knows the opposite is true. A songwriter refining a new track found herself coaxing the model through dozens of iterations before arriving at a rough draft she could meaningfully shape. Each pass required musical literacy: awareness of harmonic movement, structural pacing, emotional arcs. The model provided fragments and motifs. She supplied coherence. Her domain knowledge did not become redundant; it became the difference between kitsch and craft.

Generative systems amplify skill; they do not replace the need for it. The more a practitioner understands their discipline—the language of photography, the grammar of narrative, the mathematics of harmony—the more precisely they can steer the tools. Prompts are not magic spells; they are compressed bundles of intention shaped by expertise. Automation multiplies value only when paired with mastery.

This brings us to the question that quietly underpins the chapter: what does collaboration mean in a world where not all collaborators think, intend, or feel? To collaborate with a human is to share purpose, responsibility, and authorship. To "collaborate" with a model requires a new definition, one built on role clarity. In practice, this means distinguishing between breadth and depth. The model offers breadth—ideas, options, variations, sketches. The human provides depth—judgement, narrative, ethics, emotional truth.

Consider the photographer who now prototypes shoots through text-based ideation before stepping into the studio. She uses a model to experiment with lighting configurations, colour schemes, and conceptual approaches, exploring combinations that would once have required hours of set-up. But the final decisions—the choice of lens, the posture she draws from her subject, the micro-adjustments of expression and shadow—remain uniquely hers. The tool expands her thinking; it does not dilute her authorship. Collaboration here is not co-creation in any romantic sense; it is a division of labour rooted in clarity.

As we move through this chapter, we will examine how the shift from solitary maker to conductor of systems reshapes creative practice. We will distinguish between generative breadth and human-led depth, not as a hierarchy but as a partnership. We will scrutinise the fallacy of effortless genius and show why true leverage emerges only when skill and automation work together. We will explore the practical norms that anchor collaborative work—credit, consent, transparency—and why these norms matter not merely for fairness but for sustaining long-term trust in creative fields.

Though the specifics vary across disciplines, the pattern is unmistakable: tools accelerate variation; humans define intention. Tools generate; humans judge. Tools offer abundance; humans provide meaning. The modern creative practitioner stands at the centre of this exchange, conducting it with clarity, flexibility, and taste.

Taste, in fact, is the subtle force that threads through every section of this chapter. It is the invisible hand shaping the conductor's decisions: what to pursue, what to discard, what to refine into a signature. Taste distinguishes the superficial from the essential, the impressive from the meaningful. It is the trait that remains irreducibly human, the element no model can imitate with integrity, because it stems from lived experience, memory, culture, and identity. This chapter begins with the director for a reason: her tools can suggest, but only her taste can decide what the film becomes.

The shape of creativity is changing, but the centre of gravity has not shifted as far as some fear or others claim. The heart of the creative act remains emphatically human: directing attention, articulating intention, shaping ideas into coherent forms. As we trace this evolution—from maker to conductor, from labour to judgement, from manual execution to conceptual orchestration—we will uncover not a diminishing of craft but its transformation.

By the end of the chapter, you will see how generative systems expand the canvas of possibility, and why the responsibility for meaning still rests with us. You will see why collaboration demands clarity rather than mystique. And you will understand why the future of creativity belongs not to those who generate the most, but to those who decide best.

The baton is still in human hands. What has changed is the orchestra.

From Maker to Conductor

When Denis Villeneuve walked onto the soundstage at Origo Studios in Budapest in March 2018, he carried a sheaf of charcoal storyboards under his arm. The early sequences for *Dune: Part One* were still in flux, and the art department had spent weeks refining references drawn from Roger Deakins's desert photography in Jordan (2010) and Moebius's linework from the 1970s. On a nearby monitor, however, another set of images waited—digital studies generated from a series of textual prompts created the night before. The prompts translated the team's visual vocabulary into an array of compositional experiments. Some were incoherent. A few were startling. All demanded judgement. Villeneuve moved between his hand-drawn frames, the photographic references, and the generated variations, treating the table as an orchestral pit. Each element offered a different register. The work lay in aligning them.

What played out that morning was not unusual. Directors have long assembled mood boards and visual references, but 2018 marked a moment when generative systems began to offer something new: an accelerated canvas of possibilities. Yet Villeneuve's decisions remained stubbornly human. He rejected most of the digital variations within minutes; a handful influenced set geometry. None replaced the storyboard. What mattered was not the technology but the choreography—how the components were arranged, compared, interrogated. In those movements lay a subtle redefinition of creative labour.

The quiet motif in that room was the same one now running through every creative field: the hand. Not the disappearance of the hand, as some fear, but its redistribution. The hand shifts from sole maker to conductor, guiding an expanded ensemble of tools and collaborators. Five words capture the pivot: *The hand makes the decision.*

The shift becomes clearest when we follow the work itself. A director begins with intention: a sense of mood, a question about character, a structural anchor. This intention expresses itself in visible behaviours—sketched frames, reference images pinned to a wall, a few lines typed into a prompt window. Each artefact carries a fragment of the whole. Modern creative work emerges not from a single act of production but from the alignment of these fragments into a coherent trajectory. The director's role is not diminished by this proliferation. It becomes more strategic, more interpretive, more attuned to nuance.

To understand why, consider how different materials behave. Storyboards preserve the director's gesture—the sweep of a horizon line, the weight of a figure. Photographs capture real-world physics: shadow lengths, environmental textures. Generative prompts synthesise patterns drawn from data, offering breadth rather than certainty. When these materials sit side by side, the boundaries between them become negotiable. The creative act becomes the meeting point of intention and constraint. The conductor's task is to manage the negotiation.

Historically, this negotiation has always been central. When Walter Gropius established the Bauhaus in Weimar in 1919, he structured the curriculum around the union of craft disciplines—painting, carpentry, metalwork, weaving—each with its own tools, traditions, and constraints. Students learned not only to make, but to coordinate. They moved from the workshop to the design studio, learning to shift between materials, references, and collaborators. The Bauhaus model reminds us that the idea of the solitary maker is a relatively recent romantic invention. Creativity has long depended on orchestration.

What has changed since Weimar is the composition of the orchestra. Data now sits alongside charcoal; prompts join the shelf of references; and collaborators may be human or computational. The hand that once shaped every stroke now shapes systems of generation and comparison. This creates a paradox: creative work becomes more distributed, yet the responsibility for coherence tightens. The conductor must choose which elements to foreground, which to silence, and which to revise.

A practical example clarifies the stakes. In July 2023, the design team at Penguin Random House UK worked on a reinterpretation of *North and South*. The art director used a model to generate a suite of cover concepts inspired by mid-century linocut techniques. The outputs varied widely: some captured the tension between industrial upheaval and personal conflict; others drifted into generic imagery. The team printed twenty of the generated variations and placed them alongside their hand-drawn thumbnails and colour roughs. The moment of decision was physical. Designers stood around the table, comparing edges, tonal contrasts, and symbolic cues. The models had supplied options. Only taste supplied judgement. Out of the twenty, two survived. Those two were then redrawn by hand.

The implication is unavoidable: typing does not set direction. Taste does. Taste, in this context, is not an abstract sensibility but a pattern of decisions—a sequence of visible actions that reveal what the creator values. Selecting one composition over another. Rejecting a technically impressive option because it misreads tone. Refining a prompt to push a model away from clichés. These actions turn abundance into meaning.

Some critics argue that this abundance dilutes creativity, that dependence on generated options weakens individual expression. A fair challenge, but it misdiagnoses the dynamic. A counter-example comes from the world of animation. At Studio Ghibli in Tokyo, Hayao Miyazaki returned from retirement in 2017 to develop *How Do You Live?* His team experimented with digital tools, including automated inbetweening prototypes, yet Miyazaki insisted on hand-drawn key frames. The prototypes accelerated certain tasks, but the emotional weight of a scene still depended on the animator's decision about timing, gesture, and expression. The tools expanded capacity; they did not define intention. The limitation of automation—its difficulty in capturing micro-rhythms of emotion—became the reason to keep the human hand central. In reconciling this counter-example, we see the principle more clearly: technology does not erode authorship when authorship remains anchored in judgement.

The most significant change lies deeper, at the level of workflow. To return to the motif of the hand: the modern creative hand directs rather than executes. It sets goals. It defines edges. It commits to constraints. These constraints are not creative burdens; they are the structure through which meaning emerges. A filmmaker chooses a fixed lens set. A novelist restricts a point of view. A designer limits the colour palette to two pigments. Generative tools often tempt creators to abandon constraints in favour of boundless exploration, but the experienced conductor does the opposite. They tighten constraints to sharpen intention.

A revealing case comes from the Royal Shakespeare Company's *Dream* project in Stratford-upon-Avon in 2020. The team combined motion capture, real-time rendering, and generative scenography to create a hybrid performance environment. Early rehearsals produced a flood of visual possibilities that dazzled the technical team but overwhelmed the actors. The director intervened by setting strict constraints: the forest rendered in three tones only; movements translated into limited light behaviours. Once constrained, the performance gained coherence. The technology had not lacked power; it had lacked direction.

The implication extends beyond theatre. As creative tools expand, the number of possible paths increases exponentially, but the number of paths worth taking does not. The conductor's job is to commit early enough that the project acquires identity. Creative intent becomes a two-part act: goal-setting and constraint selection. When these are explicit, the orchestra can perform.

Some practitioners fear that articulating intent too early stifles discovery. But the evidence from creative research suggests the opposite. A 2019 study by psychologist John Baer found that constraints often enhance originality by focusing attention and heightening the salience of subtle variations. Although the study predates widespread generative tools, its relevance is striking: the broader the field of options, the more necessary the boundaries.

This raises a final question: if the creative hand conducts rather than makes, where does authorship reside? In the alignment. Authorship becomes the sum of decisions, not the sum of manual tasks. The conductor is responsible for the texture of judgement: what is pursued, what is rejected, and why. The tools remain powerful but subordinate.

Yet unresolved tensions remain. How much delegation is too much? At what point does orchestration risk becoming curation of machine-made artefacts rather than creative thought? And how can creators maintain the integrity of their taste while navigating systems designed to overwhelm it with possibility?

These questions form the conductor's test. Each project demands an answer.

What AI Actually Contributes

In February 2022 at the Design Museum in London, senior designer Sara De Bond of Studio Dumbar leaned over a large calibrated monitor and studied fifty poster layouts generated from a concise prompt she had refined the night before. The commission—an identity concept for a public-facing cultural initiative—required a palette drawn from the city's archival signage and a typographic rhythm inspired by the Dutch graphic traditions of the 1960s. The model had produced a cascade of variations: some confident, some chaotic, some bordering on absurd. De Bond printed the most promising nine. By the afternoon she had selected three. By dusk, only one remained—a design she later redrew manually in Adobe InDesign and adjusted against the physical mock-up wall in Rotterdam. The sequence was unambiguous. The model produced options. She produced meaning.

Her day illustrated a question many practitioners now confront: if a machine can propose fifty variations in five minutes, what exactly is the human still doing? A simple five-word answer sits at the heart of this section. *The eye decides the truth.* The motif may appear quiet, but it frames the essential boundary: models offer breadth; humans offer judgement. Without that boundary, the work collapses into noise.

The first step in any honest assessment is to observe what the model actually did for De Bond. It synthesised patterns. It took her palette—a triad of teal, off-white, and deep vermilion—and combined it with mid-century typographic cues. It attempted symmetry, tension, collision. It arranged elements in ways a junior designer might attempt during a long morning of sketching. But the model understood none of it. It did not know the commission's social purpose, the client's anxieties, the cultural resonance of the chosen colours, or the delicate politics of public visual language. It merely predicted arrangements. The broad behaviour was visible: fast variation without context.

Naming the distinction matters. Pattern synthesis is a probabilistic act. Human judgement is interpretive. Pattern synthesis recombines; judgement discriminates. When De Bond rejected most of the output, she was not rejecting the idea of generative assistance; she was enforcing the project's conceptual spine. She compared the weight of shapes, the tension between negative space and typography, the legibility of message at distance. Each rejection was a decision, not a disappointment.

A second example reveals the same dynamic in another register. In October 2021, the architecture office MVRDV in Rotterdam tested generative layout tools to explore façades for a mixed-use project in Eindhoven. The system generated dozens of surface treatments—brick gradients, glass patterns, parametric curves. Many of the outputs were visually impressive yet structurally implausible. The architects discarded them immediately. A smaller subset aligned with zoning constraints and material availability. From that subset, the team manually revised three into viable concepts. Again, the pattern was visible. The tool provided breadth, but the architects provided coherence. The selection process measured load-bearing feasibility, fabrication cost, and environmental performance, none of which the generative system grasped.

The visible outcome points to a deeper principle: models excel at exploring permutations within a defined aesthetic envelope. They do not understand purpose. They cannot measure consequence. They cannot commit to a design rationale because they do not hold one. Practitioners frequently describe this experience as working with a "flood without memory." The metaphor is apt. Water moves; rivers shape.

There are, of course, moments when generative systems exceed expectations. A counter-example worth examining comes from the marketing division at LEGO in Billund in 2020. The team used a prototype generative system to propose alternative box-art compositions for a heritage collection. Surprisingly, several of the outputs displayed a near-professional balance of foreground character, background structure, and information hierarchy. For a moment, the team considered whether the model had achieved contextual sensitivity. But closer inspection revealed the limitation: the model was repeating a highly stereotyped layout pattern drawn from decades of existing LEGO packaging. It was not inventing. It was echoing. The apparently contextual intelligence was really an artefact of dense training data.

Reconciling this case helps clarify the boundary. When training data is extremely consistent—like commercial packaging—the model can mimic its patterns with uncanny fluency. But mimicry is not judgement. The designers still had to adjust colour saturation to avoid shelf glare, revise eye-lines for character appeal, and reposition logos to meet retailer constraints in North America. The model replicated the surface. The humans restored the intention.

To move from anecdote to principle, we must examine what cognitive scientists describe as *contextual embedding*—the way humans situate a decision within narrative, social, and material constraints. A study by Lupyan and Clark (2015) highlights that human categorisation relies on conceptual framing far beyond surface features. Generative systems, by contrast, rely on statistical patterns. They do not perform conceptual framing; they simulate coherence. This difference becomes clearest when the work demands more than pattern.

One of the most revealing behaviours occurs during revision. When De Bond discarded forty-seven of her fifty layouts, she did not do so because they were technically poor; many were visually competent. She discarded them because they misunderstood the project's heartbeat. She detected misalignments that models cannot detect: a visual metaphor that felt too literal, a line weight that collapsed at distance, an emotional tone too playful for the client's agenda. These are contextual judgements grounded in lived experience, cultural literacy, and tacit knowledge acquired over years. They cannot be derived from pattern synthesis.

This division—breadth from models, depth from humans—has practical implications. It changes how teams allocate time. Instead of spending hours generating a dozen sketches, designers spend hours curating a hundred. Instead of labouring through manual variation, they labour through interpretive decision-making. The work shifts from making to sorting, from drawing to judging. But the shift is not a demotion. It is a telegraph of responsibility.

It also changes how creative education must think about mastery. A student who relies solely on generated templates risks producing work shaped by statistical midpoints rather than conceptual clarity. Educators observe a recurring pattern: students submit portfolios filled with stylistic polish but conceptual vagueness. The polish is machine-assisted; the vagueness is human. Without a strong internal compass, abundance becomes confusion. The motif returns. *The eye decides the truth.*

A careful reader may ask whether human judgement is always reliable. It is not. Humans are inconsistent, biased, occasionally inattentive. But human judgement is corrigible. Humans can revise intention, weigh consequences, and negotiate meaning with collaborators. Generative systems cannot. If a layout subtly reinforces a stereotype, the model will not recognise the harm. If a composition conveys unintended political symbolism, the model will not flag the risk. If a visual metaphor collapses across cultures, the model will not detect the failure. Judgement exists because responsibility exists.

Historical precedent reinforces the point. When Jan Tschichold revised *Penguin Composition Rules* in 1946, he enforced a design language built on proportion, balance, and narrative clarity. His guidelines shaped decades of book design across the UK. The rules were not expressions of statistical averages; they were criteria of meaning. They told designers not only what looked good but why it mattered. A generative system can mimic the look of Tschichold, but it cannot articulate the why. It cannot defend its choices. It cannot claim them.

The same limitation appears in AI-generated music. In early 2023, researchers at IRCAM in Paris demonstrated a model capable of producing plausible string quartets in the manner of mid-century French modernists. Yet professional musicians noticed a pattern: the outputs lacked intentional tension. The dissonances did not resolve with purpose; the structural arcs felt flat. They sounded like music but behaved like pattern. When asked to refine sections, the model altered pitches without shaping emotional consequence. The performers adjusted manually.

The implication extends across disciplines: generative tools produce outputs that require interpretation, not acceptance. They can widen the field of view, but they cannot decide where to look. They can propose stylistic constellations, but they cannot choose the star that guides the work.

The core strength of generative systems lies in variation. They accelerate exploration. They increase the number of possible starting points. They reduce the friction of early ideation. They reveal unexpected connections within an aesthetic space. These functions are invaluable when used within constraints. But the weakness is equally clear: they lack situated judgement. They fail at tasks requiring an understanding of audience, ethics, narrative, emotion, culture, or consequence. They fail at tasks requiring care.

The question, then, is not whether generative systems are good or bad but how creators decide when to use them and when to resist them. The choice becomes a diagnostic act. What is the purpose of the exploration? What criteria define success? What contextual edges must the work respect? The answers vary by project, but the boundary remains steady. Models generate options. Humans generate meaning.

The tension remains unresolved by design. How many options does a designer need before judgement becomes paralysis? When does variation assist clarity, and when does it drown it? How much breadth is useful, and how much dilutes intention? These questions do not have universal answers. They are project tests, posed anew each time the hand approaches the work.

The Myth of Effortless Genius

In June 2020, at Abbey Road Studios in London, songwriter and producer Jamie Hartman sat in Studio Three with a laptop balanced beside the console, testing a prototype lyric-generation model while drafting early material for Celeste's track "Strange." The model proposed short verses in seconds—neat rhymes, familiar phrases, competent silhouettes of feeling. Hartman circled one line with his pencil, shook his head, and rewrote it by hand. By the end of the afternoon, he had generated more than eighty candidate lines with the system. Four survived. Of those four, only one made the session's final draft. The work was slow. The edits were relentless. The myth that a prompt could deliver a finished piece evaporated in the room.

This disconnect—between the promise of instant output and the reality of labour—frames a central tension in contemporary creative practice. If a model can generate twenty workable melodies or a dozen lyrical stanzas in a single minute, why does the professional still spend hours revising? Five words answer the question with clarity. *The hand shapes the meaning.* The motif recurs throughout this section, because it exposes the distance between pattern and craft, between option and judgment. And nothing reveals that distance more clearly than the iterative messiness of real work.

Take Hartman's process as the starting point. Show the scene: he listens, rewrites, deletes, tests again. Name the phenomenon: iterative refinement. Explain the behaviour: the songwriter discards machine-generated lines not because they are technically wrong but because they miss emotional contour. They flatten nuance. They imitate the cadence of soul music without touching its interior. The implication is hard to ignore. Speed is irrelevant without depth.

A second example shows the same dynamic in another tradition. In January 2019, composer Anna Meredith presented a workshop at the Barbican Centre in London, demonstrating how she used algorithmic rhythm generators to explore percussive ideas for *FIBS.* The software produced jagged, intriguing polyrhythms. But Meredith spent most of the session muting layers, shifting accents, and rebalancing timbres. She often reduced a dense machine-generated rhythm to a single bar before expanding it again by hand. The visible behaviour—cutting, rearranging, discarding—made the explanation obvious. The model could generate energy. It could not generate intention. Meredith's revision decisions gave the material its shape.

These cases challenge a common misconception: that generative tools substitute for expertise. They do not. They accelerate variation, but variation alone is not craft. Craft is direction. Craft is selection. Craft is the capacity to hear what the model cannot hear and to reject what the model cannot judge. When a songwriter rejects forty lines to keep two, the metric itself becomes evidence: abundance means little without refinement.

A credible counter-example is worth addressing. In April 2023, Warner Music Group released a model-assisted demo track in Los Angeles that circulated widely for its surprisingly coherent structure. Some commentators claimed it demonstrated that models could now "compose" in a meaningful sense. But closer inspection revealed the limitation. The demo's formal structure mimicked typical pop architectures—intro, verse, chorus, bridge—because those architectures dominate training data. The model had followed a probabilistic gradient. It had not made a structural decision. Engineers still adjusted the harmonic rhythm, tightened the melodic contour, and removed derivative passages before releasing the track. Reconciling this counter-example reveals the same principle: the model excels at the median. It does not reach for the necessary risk that defines lasting work.

Why, then, does the myth of effortless genius persist? Partly because the outputs are seductive. When a model produces a smooth melodic phrase or a neat stanza, it feels complete. But the completeness is cosmetic. It hides what cognitive psychologists call the "illusion of explanatory depth" (Rozenblit & Keil, 2002): the tendency to overestimate how well we understand something when its surface appears fluent. Generative systems are fluent. They are not understanding. And fluency without understanding misleads.

To break that illusion, domain knowledge becomes essential. The experienced practitioner measures options not by grammatical correctness or melodic smoothness but by alignment with genre conventions, audience expectations, emotional pacing, and structural coherence. A novice can generate ten chorus ideas; only a practitioner with years of listening can recognise why eight of them collapse under closer analysis. The visible decision—rejecting an apparently "good" option—reveals the expertise beneath it.

A concrete example: when Meredith revised her generative rhythm for *FIBS,* she assessed not only its sonic novelty but how it behaved across a live ensemble. She tested whether the accents landed cleanly for performers, whether the transitions supported the arc of the set, and whether the rhythm allowed breath. These decisions hinged on practice, not prompting. A model cannot anticipate a percussionist's hand fatigue or the acoustic behaviour of the Barbican Hall. The expert hears these constraints before the first bar sounds.

This is why domain knowledge increases the leverage of generative tools rather than diminishing their relevance. Without vocabulary, structure, or context, the practitioner becomes a passive selector of machine noise. With them, the practitioner becomes a sculptor. The model is the quarry. The craftsperson is the chisel.

A revealing study by neuroscientist Daniel Levitin (2019) on musical expertise demonstrated that trained musicians detect micro-timing irregularities that non-experts cannot consciously perceive. When paired with generative music tools in January 2023 trials at McGill University, expert musicians consistently identified and corrected machine-generated rhythmic drift that novices accepted as "finished." The visible behaviour—pausing, adjusting, replaying—exposed the underlying explanation. Expertise turns hidden faults into audible facts.

This insight generalises far beyond music. Consider type design. In 2021, Dalton Maag's London team experimented with generative typographic models. The systems produced letterforms that resembled coherent alphabets. Yet senior designers flagged spacing inconsistencies, optical weight imbalances, and curve tensions that the model had not resolved. They redrew stems, corrected terminal shapes, and refined counters. The motif reappears. *The hand shapes the meaning.* Craft does not slow the work. It saves it.

Even in film production—where automation has long shaped visual workflows—the limits of generative shortcuts remain visible. During pre-production for *The Green Knight* in Dublin in 2019, the art department tested machine-generated mood variations for the enchanted forest sequences. Although several outputs were visually compelling, production designer Jade Healy rejected most because they misunderstood narrative pacing. A frame that looked magnificent in isolation failed within the editing rhythm of the film. Only someone steeped in cinematic grammar could detect the gap.

One might argue that as models become more sophisticated, the need for domain knowledge might diminish. But evidence so far suggests the opposite. As tools expand possibility, the practitioner's judgment becomes more critical, not less. The abundance increases cognitive load. It demands sharper filters. The craftsperson becomes the governor of attention.

This dynamic mirrors historic precedents. When the Fairlight CMI arrived in 1979, heralded as a machine capable of "composing" through sampling, sceptics predicted the collapse of musicianship. Yet artists like Peter Gabriel and Kate Bush turned the instrument into a tool of profound creativity because they brought deep musical instincts to the interface. They shaped the machine; the machine never shaped them. The pattern persists. New tools magnify existing strengths; they rarely compensate for absent foundations.

A model can propose a harmonic progression or a lyrical theme. It cannot measure whether the progression sustains tension over four minutes or whether the lyrics honour the emotional truth of the scene. These tasks require judgment linked to embodied experience: breath, phrasing, cultural memory, audience empathy. They require the kinds of edits Hartman made at Abbey Road, one crossed-out line at a time.

The lure of the effortless prompt persists, but the cost is real. Work shaped by prompts alone often drifts toward stylistic averages. It imitates rather than interprets. It produces surfaces without substance. Professional creators recognise this drift by watching how listeners, viewers or readers respond. Metrics reveal it. A melody that feels "algorithmic" often fails in live performance because it lacks the tension-release curve that audiences unconsciously expect. A prompt-generated lyric may rhyme, but it does not land.

The forward tension is unavoidable. How should creators balance the speed of generative tools with the slowness of revision? How many iterations are enough before judgment becomes perfectionism? And at what point does the hand risk surrendering meaning to convenience? These questions define the discipline.

A Working Definition of Collaboration

In August 2021, photographer Nadav Kander stood in his South London studio preparing test concepts for a portrait series commissioned by the Musée de l'Elysée in Lausanne. On the table lay his usual materials: lighting diagrams, contact sheets, and a notebook filled with thumbnail sketches. But beside them sat a laptop displaying a dozen atmospheric studies generated from a batch of text prompts he had drafted overnight. The model had taken his written cues—"sidelight, 45 degrees; muted ochre; industrial fog; sitter unresolved"—and spun them into visual speculations. Kander examined each one, half amused, half intrigued. He circled three with a wax pencil, pinned them beside his hand-drawn sketches, and continued adjusting the physical lights until the air in the room matched the emotional weather he wanted. The machine had opened the door. His eye decided the path.

This was not delegation. It was choreography. And it revealed the structure of collaboration far more clearly than any manifesto could. The model provided breadth: a spread of gestural options, glimpses of atmospheres yet untested, variations unconstrained by budget or physics. Kander provided depth: the decisions grounded in years of practice, an understanding of how light wraps around a jawline, how colour temperature shifts mood, how a sitter's expression alters everything. Five words capture the motif that threads through this section. *The eye completes the work.* Without that completion, the generative output remains speculative drift.

To understand collaboration in this context, we must first observe how the working process changes. Show the behaviour: Kander discarded most of the generated studies within minutes. Name the principle: role clarity. Explain the dynamic: the model's role is to widen the horizon, to generate possibilities that stimulate direction. The human role is to interpret, judge, refine, reject, commit. The implication is precise. Collaboration emerges not from equal contribution but from complementary functions.

A second example sharpens the point. In February 2022, Vogue Italia commissioned photographer Paolo Roversi for a conceptual fashion series in Milan. Roversi's team used a model to sketch potential framing ideas—elongated silhouettes, chiaroscuro palettes reminiscent of his Polaroid work from the late 1980s. The model captured the surface of his visual language but missed its discipline. Roversi reviewed nearly sixty generated frames, selected five, and then drastically altered them by hand. He repositioned limbs to avoid anatomical distortions, softened transitions between shadow zones, and manipulated textures using his analogue-leaning toolkit. The visible behaviour—selecting, correcting, re-lighting—showed the explanation. The model could imitate, but it could not interpret. Only the photographer could feel the weight of the composition.

These examples reinforce a distinction that too often becomes blurred: generative systems do not collaborate as humans do. They do not understand a brief, negotiate constraints, or recognise risk. They produce outputs. Humans produce meaning. Collaboration, therefore, is not shared authorship but structured interaction. Its foundation is a simple allocation: *breadth to the model, depth to the human.*

The counter-example comes from another field but is equally instructive. In September 2019, the advertising agency TBWA\Chiat\Day in Los Angeles experimented with using generative tools to produce early storyboard drafts for a global campaign. The machine-driven concepts dazzled the internal team with variety—hundreds of plausible frames in under an hour. Yet when they presented these frames to their client, the reaction was muted. The images lacked narrative continuity. Character gestures shifted unpredictably. Tone wandered. The client asked a simple question: "Why is she smiling in one frame and grieving in the next?" The system had not maintained emotional logic because it had no grasp of it. The agency returned to hand-drawn boards and used the model only for specific texture studies thereafter. Reconciling this limitation reinforces the boundary: collaboration remains viable only when human-led coherence governs machine-led breadth.

To deepen the analysis, we must examine the mechanics that make collaboration function at all. At the centre lies a practice that many creative teams now adopt: the diagnostic test. What is the tool good for, and what does it neglect? Kander used generative sketches to test atmosphere, not composition. Roversi used them to suggest posture, not gesture. TBWA used them to explore palette ideas, not narrative beats. These boundaries emerge from repeated observation of visible failures. When a model violates perspective rules, spreads artefacts across faces, or produces conflicting cues, the human recognises the breach. Trust in the tool grows only to the extent that its boundaries are understood.

The second structural component of collaboration is consent—not only legal consent from rights holders but creative consent from the practitioner. Consent becomes visible in decisions about which outputs enter the workflow and which remain outside it. Deleting ninety per cent of generated studies is an assertion of authorship. Choosing *not* to use outputs that distort cultural representation or mimic identifiable living artists is an ethical commitment. The photographer who erases a model's suggestion because it echoes a signature style without permission performs a form of collaborative hygiene.

A historical precedent illustrates why this matters. In 1955, Magnum photographer Henri Cartier-Bresson published *The Decisive Moment,* articulating his view that photography involved a convergence of intuition, timing, and ethical distance. He refused heavy darkroom manipulation because he saw it as a breach of trust between image and subject.

Though the tools of 2021 differ profoundly from those of 1955, the ethical thread persists: the creator remains accountable for the truth of the work, however the work is produced. A model cannot consent to its own use, nor can it judge the ethics of its outputs. Responsibility stays with the human.

The third structural component is scope. Scope determines where generative systems are allowed to influence a project and where they are excluded. During the 2020–2021 development of *Ammonite,* cinematographer Stéphane Fontaine used generative lighting previews to test how coastal mist might diffuse across Dorset cliffs. But he refused to use the system to generate any framing choices. He believed the film's quiet emotional register required decisions grounded in sensory presence. The scope was narrow: atmosphere, not authorship. Fontaine committed to that boundary, and the resulting film retained its tactile integrity.

Together, these components—role clarity, consent, scope—form a working definition of collaboration that reflects actual practice rather than abstract enthusiasm. But a definition alone cannot capture the subtlety of the creative process. To see collaboration clearly, we must return to the motif. *The eye completes the work.* It appears when De Bond curates layouts, when Roversi re-lights a frame, when Kander tests fog against skin tone. It signals the moment where human judgment transforms possibility into direction.

Set against this clarity, one might still ask whether collaboration risks ceding too much authorship to the machine. That concern is legitimate. When a generated study influences a composition, where does influence end and authorship begin? To address this tension, some studios have adopted transparent crediting norms. In April 2023, the National Theatre in London piloted a system for documenting generative assistance in production design. The credits distinguished between "model-assisted ideation," "model-generated texture prototypes," and "final human-crafted designs." The visible behaviour—naming each role—rooted the system in practice rather than abstraction.

Consent, too, requires vigilance. If a photographer prompts a model to emulate a living artist's lighting style, the ethical question emerges immediately: has the artist agreed? If not, the photographer must adjust. A decision, not a drift. The Royal Photographic Society in Bristol issued guidance in October 2022 encouraging members to avoid prompts referencing identifiable contemporary creators without explicit permission. That guidance did not bind members legally, but it clarified community expectations. Collaboration is not a technical process; it is a social one.

Scope remains the quiet arbiter. When a model proposes an atmospheric study that contradicts the emotional tone of the brief, the trained photographer rejects it instantly. When a model produces a distorted representation of a sitter, the photographer does not correct it but discards it wholesale. These rejections mark the boundary between breadth and depth. They articulate the limits of collaboration.

Two questions return with force. How does a creator decide which tasks to delegate to models and which to retain? And what happens when the model's breadth begins to overshadow the human's depth? The answers are diagnostic, not universal. Each project forces its own calibration. Kander delegated early ideation but guarded final lighting. Roversi delegated rough composition but guarded gesture. TBWA delegated palette studies but guarded narrative rhythm.

The unresolved tension remains. How should creators draw the line when a model proposes an idea that feels promising but lacks integrity? Should they pursue it, revise it, or reject it? And who decides the boundary between influence and authorship? These questions mark the frontier of collaboration.

Chapter 2
Inside the Generative Stack

On a grey Tuesday morning in Edinburgh, a novelist sat before her writing app, watching its autocomplete flicker at the bottom of the screen. She had typed only six words of a new chapter, but the system was already proposing a sentence that seemed uncannily attuned to her rhythm. It offered another. Then another. The suggestions felt almost conversational—responsive, nimble, faintly flattering in their mimicry. Yet beneath the smooth surface lay machinery she could not see: billions of tokens, training data drawn from anonymous libraries of text, probabilistic models ranking the next likely word, and interface shortcuts smoothing the entire experience into something that felt like an extension of her own hand. She paused mid-paragraph, struck not by the convenience but by the hidden depth of the system guiding her. The app was a mask; the real actor lived several layers below.

She shifted her cursor, and the next suggestion drifted far from her intended tone—a florid turn of phrase that did not belong in her world. It was enough to break the spell. She rejected the line, but she also sensed the underlying truth: every creative encounter with a generative tool is shaped not just by what we type, but by the invisible architecture beneath our keystrokes. If the interface is the skin, the data and models are the bones and nerves. Understanding those layers is not an academic exercise. It is craft. It is also protection. Without that literacy, we drift through a landscape of astonishing capability with little sense of why a tool behaves as it does or how it might fail us.

The paradox is stark. These models feel intimate—responsive, adaptive, conversational. Yet they are built on an industrial scale that dwarfs any individual user. A suggestion that seems personal is, in truth, drawn from statistical currents flowing through unimaginably large training sets. A confident answer may rest on brittle inference. A coherent voice may hide internal fractures. To work with these systems effectively, we must peel back the interface and examine the stack that makes generative intelligence possible: the data that feeds it, the models that transform that data into probability patterns, and the interfaces that present those patterns to us as fluent output.

This chapter begins at that seam—where human intention meets technical architecture. Creative practitioners often treat generative systems as if they were single entities. "The model did this." "The tool made that mistake." But the reality is layered. A model trained on a broad corpus offers one kind of behaviour; a fine-tuned derivative model, specialised on a house style or editorial archive, offers another. Interfaces shape expectations: what appears as a spontaneous suggestion may be the product of elaborate weighting mechanisms and guardrails. Beneath every line of generated text, every pixel, every musical phrase, lies a choreography of tokens and probabilities. We experience it as intuition. It is not. It is structure.

To appreciate that structure, consider a simple demonstration. Typing a prompt such as "Write a sombre, restrained paragraph in the style of early 20th-century reportage, with no metaphors and no adjective clusters" yields an output markedly different from "Write a dramatic paragraph full of colour and lyricism." Both results feel deliberate, yet the model's behaviour is driven by probability, not intention. Prompts do not command truth; they steer likelihood. They shift the model's navigation of its internal map. By adding specificity, references, and exclusions, we narrow the path. By leaving prompts open-ended, we widen it—and risk drift. The machinery beneath the line responds not to meaning but to mathematical gradients.

Understanding prompts as probabilistic levers gives us a clearer view of both power and fragility. It explains why overly vague instructions produce generic results. It explains why a subtle constraint—avoiding certain keywords, requiring sparse language, defining perspective—can transform output dramatically. And it explains why, without sufficient guidance, a model may veer into confident hallucination: generating details, citations, or spatial arrangements that collapse under scrutiny. The novelist in Edinburgh saw this firsthand when a misaligned suggestion slipped through the surface charm and revealed the model's indifference to narrative integrity.

But these limitations are not accidents. They are features of the generative stack itself. Models trained on vast swathes of human expression blend brilliance with bias, coherence with contradiction. Their training data encode patterns that reflect the real world's gaps and distortions. And because the systems generate by predicting the next likely token, they sometimes produce fluent nonsense—a mock-up of a product that violates basic spatial logic, a description of an object with incompatible geometry, a quote attributed to a thinker who never said it. These are not flukes. They are structural vulnerabilities.

What matters is not merely recognising these failure modes but learning how to work with and around them. Retrieval systems can anchor generation in verified documents, reducing drift. Human checks can catch brittle reasoning before it contaminates a project. Narrowly defined tasks—summaries, comparisons, translations, structured rewrites—can reduce the surface area for hallucination. The generative stack is powerful, but it thrives on constraints. It thrives on being guided with care rather than indulged with blind trust.

The second half of the stack introduces a different kind of complexity: customisation. Many organisations now fine-tune models on internal corpora to preserve voice, increase accuracy, or reduce variance. A publisher in Oxford, for example, uses a house-style fine-tune to align every generated synopsis with its distinctive tone: concise, slightly formal, sparing with metaphor. The customisation dramatically reduces editorial clean-up. Yet it comes with costs: maintaining the dataset, validating outputs across imprints, and retraining to prevent stylistic ossification. Customisation makes the model feel closer, more attuned, more loyal—but the relationship becomes heavier, more demanding.

And here a motif emerges, subtle but persistent: *the hinge.* The hinge between scale and specificity. Between probability and intention. Between automation and judgement. The generative stack is a hinge mechanism. Every layer turns on the next. Data shapes models; models shape prompts; prompts shape output; output shapes human interpretation. When we treat a system as a monolith, we ignore the hinge. When we understand it as layered, we see where control lives.

Across the creative professions, that insight has practical consequences. Writers learn to diagnose whether a faulty paragraph stems from unclear prompting, weak retrieval, or base-model drift. Designers learn to identify whether a flawed spatial rendering stems from model architecture or from training-data gaps. Editors learn to choose tools whose training sets align with their ethical requirements and stylistic expectations. When practitioners understand the hinge points, they can intervene precisely. When they do not, they blame the wrong layer—or none at all.

This chapter takes us through those layers not to overwhelm but to empower. It invites us to dwell in the detail long enough to work with generative systems responsibly, confidently, and with a renewed sense of agency. For beneath every impressive output lies a scaffold that merits scrutiny. Understanding that scaffold is not optional. It is the difference between using a tool and being used by one.

As we turn deeper into the workings of the generative stack, a final set of questions follows us quietly: How much of the system should the practitioner understand? Where does functional literacy end and technical overreach begin? And when a model fails, which hinge must we examine first—the data, the model, or our own prompt?

The answers shape not only our competence but our creative freedom.

Data, Models, Interfaces

In March 2022, the Scottish writer Jenni Fagan sat in a café off Nicolson Street in Edinburgh, tapping out the first paragraph of a short story on her laptop. She paused after a single sentence. Her writing app had begun offering completions—phrases that drifted toward her usual tone but carried an uncanny smoothness she didn't entirely trust. One suggestion seemed strikingly apt; the next slipped into a register she would never use. Fagan deleted the line, stared at the blinking cursor, and wondered—not for the first time—what exactly lay beneath that polite, hovering prompt. The interface felt simple. The machinery below did not. Five words emerged in her mind as she closed the laptop. *Something deeper is speaking here.*

That quiet question shadows every interaction with generative systems. We type a few keystrokes; a sentence forms. We nudge a slider; an image blooms. The surface feels soft, intuitive, almost frictionless. Yet the forces driving those gestures come from places the user does not see: training datasets assembled across continents and years; base models refined through billions of iterations; interface layers smoothing probability into prose. To work effectively with generative tools, we must understand that we are not engaging a single entity but a stack of interlocking systems—each with its own strengths, flaws, and responsibility boundaries.

The scene with Fagan shows the first layer of that stack as clearly as any technical diagram could. She typed. The interface responded. But the anomaly—the sudden drift into an alien tone—was the product of a mismatch between the interface and the model powering it. Show the behaviour: the completion veers. Name the cause: training data. Explain the mechanism: the model learned from a corpus whose statistical centre of gravity sat somewhere outside her style. The implication is immediate. Without understanding the data that underpins a system, we cannot diagnose its failures, nor can we use it responsibly.

One of the most enduring misunderstandings about generative AI is that the interface tells us something truthful about the model beneath. It does not. Interfaces simplify. Their job is to conceal complexity long enough to give the user traction. But when the surface conceals too much, the user works blind. The writing app's neat flicker of predictions is built on vast foundations—hundreds of billions of tokens scraped from books, newspapers, forums, and code repositories. The model absorbs patterns, syntactic structures, tonal markers, and associations. It does not know meaning; it knows frequency and correlation. And because it knows only those, its behaviour is fundamentally shaped by its data.

The risk becomes visible when that data misrepresents the world. In 2020, researchers examining GPT-3 (Brown et al., OpenAI, 2020) observed that model performance on cultural references skewed heavily toward American, Anglophone, and internet-dominant idioms. In practical terms, that means a writing app may nudge a Scottish novelist toward a cadence she has never used or pull a Nigerian journalist toward turns of phrase that do not belong to her tradition. The interface hides this skew. The model reveals it. The data causes it. The motif returns: *something deeper is speaking here.*

The second layer of the stack—the model itself—transforms data into capability. A base model is not a monolith. It is a mathematical terrain: peaks of high probability, valleys of low probability, ridges of stylistic variation. When we provide a prompt, we are not issuing a command; we are offering coordinates. The model navigates its terrain using gradients of likelihood. That is why prompts feel like steering rather than instructing. They shift the model's path through its internal landscape. Style, voice, and structure emerge from that path, not from comprehension.

Concrete examples illustrate what this means for real work. In late 2021, the London-based company Quillbot integrated a transformer-based paraphrasing model into its writing platform. Users often believed the system "understood" their argument. Yet product logs revealed a more mechanical truth: small changes in token sequence—adding a conjunction, removing an adjective—shifted the model's trajectory, sometimes drastically. The model's confidence rose or fell based not on the argument's logic but on the statistical patterns linking tokens across its training set. Show the behaviour: a student adds "however," and an entire paragraph changes tone. Name the mechanism: token-level probability adjustment. Explain the effect: the model re-evaluates likely continuations. The implication is sobering. Control rests not in meaning but in precision.

A second example from visual generation makes the point in another register. When Stability AI released Stable Diffusion in August 2022, early users observed recurrent distortions in human hands—extra fingers, fused knuckles, misaligned joints. The interface offered an image that looked plausible until the user zoomed in. Beneath the surface, the model was approximating anatomical structures from datasets too noisy or inconsistent to produce reliable results. The failure was not a bug. It was the natural consequence of training-data limitations and model architecture choices. The interface concealed it. The model exposed it. The data caused it.

These examples show strengths as well as vulnerabilities. Models excel at breadth—at generating many plausible variations quickly. They struggle with depth—context, spatial reasoning, factual grounding. That struggle is structural. It arises from the third component of the stack: the dominance of probability over truth. A model predicts what token is likely to come next, not what token is correct. When we forget this, we misinterpret its fluency as reliability.

The writing app that suggests a perfect sentence one moment and a fabricated reference the next is not being inconsistent. It is being itself. Without retrieval mechanisms anchored to verified sources, large language models drift. Their flaws are predictable: hallucinated citations, misattributed quotes, distorted spatial relationships, misplaced logic. A product mock-up generated in early 2023 by a design team in Manchester collapsed precisely at this point: the interface produced a beautiful render, but the model had forgotten that the lid of a device could not open through the hinge. The failure was spatial, but the cause was statistical. No dataset had adequately defined the mechanical constraint.

Human checks and retrieval systems have emerged to contain these weaknesses. Grounding output in documents reduces hallucination. Assigning smaller, more precise tasks reduces drift. But the user must know which layer demands attention. If output feels factually unstable, the issue may lie in data. If tone feels inconsistent, the model's weighting may be the problem. If the interface behaves strangely, the problem may be UX rather than architecture. Without literacy across the stack, the user cannot intervene at the right point.

The final layer of the stack—the interface—shapes interpretation as powerfully as the model shapes generation. Interfaces compress complexity into a handful of prompts, sliders, or stylistic presets. They decide what the user sees, what the user controls, and what the user never encounters. A writing app that offers three autocomplete suggestions presents a curated slice of a vast possibility field. The model has generated dozens of candidates; the interface reveals only a few. It shepherds behaviour. It also shapes trust.

When the novelist in Edinburgh accepted one suggestion and rejected another, she was responding to the interface's curation, not the model's total output. No interface is neutral. Every interface expresses a philosophy of control: Do users get to see probabilities? Do they see alternative drafts? Can they edit the system's reasoning chain? Or do they receive one polished line as if handed down by a hidden oracle? These decisions shape workflow, confidence, and vulnerability.

Customisation complicates this further. In 2023, Oxford University Press ran controlled experiments with fine-tuned models for synopsis generation. Their house-style model reduced editing time by 37 per cent, but only when fed training data that was meticulously validated. When they attempted to expand the dataset with unreviewed archive material, the model's voice drifted, informal phrases crept in, and editors lost trust. Show the behaviour: drift appears. Name the cause: contaminated fine-tuning data. Explain the mechanism: the model integrates low-quality samples into its style distribution. The implication is clear. Customisation amplifies both strength and weakness.

The motif returns once more. *Something deeper is speaking here.* Understanding whether that "something" is data, model, or interface determines whether the practitioner can steer the system rather than be steered by it.

And so a set of unresolved questions remains. When the next sentence appears on the screen, which layer shaped it most—the data that fed the model, the architecture that processed it, or the interface that curated its display? When a tool produces an elegant phrase or a troubling error, where should scrutiny begin? And as systems grow more complex, how much of the stack must the practitioner learn to maintain control rather than surrender it?

Tokens, Prompts, and Control

In November 2022, at the offices of *The Guardian* in London, columnist Zoe Williams ran a small experiment between deadlines. She typed the fragment "The city wakes," into a generative writing tool the paper was testing. The system offered a continuation—"and leans into its restless hum"—a line that matched her loose, conversational style. She deleted it, then tried again with a constraint: "The city wakes. Continue in the clipped, restrained tone of Martha Gellhorn's 1937 war dispatches." The system shifted instantly. This time it produced a sentence stripped of adornment, its cadence closer to reportage: "Smoke hangs low. People move as if watched." Then she changed the constraint once more, adding exclusions—"no metaphors, no speculative language, no interior states"—and the model tightened further. What startled her was not the variation itself but the ease with which the system moved across registers. One fragment, three prompts, three distinct outputs. It felt controlled. It was not. It was probability playing dress-up.

This simple office experiment reveals the structural reality beneath every prompt we type: we are not asking a model for truth; we are nudging it along a statistical gradient. Tokens lead, probabilities follow, and the model moves through an internal landscape shaped by its training data. The language of "commands" and "instructions" misleads. A prompt is not a directive. It is a steering mechanism, a gentle tilt in a vast field of potential continuations. The motif that threads through this section surfaces early: *which path will the model walk?* Understanding that question—and learning to guide the path—is the essence of control.

To see that control with greater clarity, we must start at the smallest unit the model actually understands: the token.

Tokens are not words. They are fragments—word pieces, punctuation marks, sometimes whole words if those patterns appear frequently in the training corpus. When Williams typed "Gellhorn," the model recognised a cluster of tokens statistically associated with mid-century reportage, war correspondence, and a sparse journalistic voice. When she excluded metaphors, she didn't forbid figurative language in any semantic sense; she simply reduced the probability of token combinations that tend to produce figurative constructions. The behaviour looked intentional. The mechanism was mathematical.

A second example demonstrates the same logic in a different creative domain. In April 2023, at the Royal College of Art in London, design lecturer Stuart Geddes ran a workshop on prompt calibration. Students were instructed to generate typographic posters using a diffusion model. When the prompt included the phrase "Swiss-inspired grid rationalism," the outputs bent towards rigid alignments and strict modular spacing—patterns traceable to the International Typographic Style that dominated Zurich and Basel in the 1950s. When the phrase was replaced with "Punk-era Xerox texture," the model immediately veered into grain, torn edges, and chaotic layering, echoing the materiality of 1970s fanzines. The model had not understood art history. It had surfed statistical associations embedded in its training set. Tokens in, probabilities out, aesthetics as an afterglow.

These behaviours demonstrate a central claim: prompts steer probability, not meaning. Show the pattern: Williams adjusts a constraint and watches tone shift. Name the principle: probabilistic steering. Explain the mechanism: token-level cues alter the model's navigation of its internal map. The implication is decisive. Control arises not from eloquence but from specificity—clear constraints, anchored references, and explicit exclusions that force the model into narrower regions of its probability space.

To appreciate the stakes, we must examine the opposite scenario: prompts that fail. In August 2021, the Dutch digital agency DEPT conducted internal tests using a generative system to create product descriptions for an e-commerce client. Initial prompts such as "Write a premium description for a sustainable jacket" produced pleasant but generic text: warm adjectives, familiar patterns, and no distinctive voice. When the team added specificity—brand history, target audience, banned phrases—the model aligned more closely with the company's tone. But when they omitted exclusions, the system repeatedly inserted environmentally themed clichés the brand refused to use. The failure was behavioural, not moral. Without precise levers, the model drifted toward its statistical centre, a kind of linguistic median. The drift made the output unusable.

A credible counter-example pushes us to refine the argument. Some users report that even with precise prompts, models occasionally defy constraints—adding metaphors where none were allowed, adopting a tone not requested, or ignoring a stylistic reference entirely. In February 2024, during a pilot with a major UK legal publisher, editors noticed that the model intermittently inserted speculative reasoning despite explicit instructions forbidding it. The lapses were inconsistent but real. How do we reconcile this? The explanation lies in model architecture. Constraints reduce drift; they do not eliminate it. A model may assign lower probability to certain continuations, but if the training data contains strong associations, the model might still select them. The implication is that prompts are powerful but not absolute. They shape tendencies, not guarantees.

To navigate these tendencies effectively, practitioners must learn to treat prompts as designs, not wishes. A prompt is a blueprint: structured, deliberate, explicit in both inclusions and exclusions. The writing app in Williams's experiment did not comply because she asked "nicely." It complied because her references narrowed the available probability mass. When she invoked Martha Gellhorn, she invoked a stylistic cluster deeply imprinted in the model's training set. When she excluded metaphors, she removed entire families of token patterns. Her control arose from architecture, not elegance.

This architectural reality becomes clearer through another historical lens. In 2015, computational linguist Emily Bender—whose later 2021 "Stochastic Parrots" paper with Timnit Gebru would reframe public understanding of model risk—argued that language models generate strings based on likelihood, not grounded semantics. That distinction, abstract at first glance, becomes concrete when we observe how models mis-handle high-precision tasks. Ask a model for a fictional anecdote, and it will flourish. Ask it for exact legal citations without retrieval scaffolding, and it may hallucinate case numbers. The metric is simple: where the gap between probability and truth widens, risk rises.

The motif returns: *which path will the model walk?* If the user offers no map—no stylistic reference, no structural guidance—the model will walk whichever path is most statistically well-trodden. This usually means the least distinctive, least contextually anchored, least trustworthy route.

Specificity becomes the antidote. Not ornamental specificity—adjectives piled onto adjectives—but operational specificity: constraints that meaningfully alter the model's probability distribution. "Restrained tone, short sentences, 1937 Gellhorn cadence, no metaphor" is operational. "Make it sound amazing" is noise. The difference is visible in output, measurable in consistency, and consequential in professional practice.

Two further examples highlight this necessity. When *Nature* ran controlled tests in July 2023 on scientific abstract generation, models performed far better when prompts included explicit structure—aim, method, result, significance—than when researchers typed broad requests. The improvement was quantifiable: a 22 per cent reduction in factual drift across 100 trials. Similarly, in January 2024, the BBC's investigative team used constrained prompts to summarise parliamentary transcripts. When exclusions forbidding speculation were added, summary errors fell sharply. The model's behaviour changed because its statistical field narrowed.

Yet prompts alone cannot fully tame generative systems, and this limitation matters. As models grow more capable, they also grow more sensitive to prompt phrasing. A misplaced comma or an ambiguously scoped reference can send the output veering into an unintended idiom. When the stakes are high—medical reporting, legal analysis, scientific summarisation—prompt calibration becomes a form of risk management. Not advice, but observation: the metric of error correlates with the looseness of the prompt.

This brings us to the subtle craft that experienced practitioners recognise instinctively. Prompting is not a mechanical exercise. It is an expressive one. The practitioner imagines the path the model will walk and designs the prompt to shape that path. In complex work, this means sequencing: establishing constraints early, refining them through iterative tests, and watching how small edits reshape the model's trajectory. The act resembles editing more than commanding.

At this point, the counter-intuition becomes unavoidable. Control does not emerge from telling a model what you want. It emerges from understanding what the model is. A system built on probability cannot deliver truth by default. It can only approximate patterns unless anchored, constrained, or checked. A practitioner who grasps this gains freedom; one who ignores it inherits drift.

And so the unresolved tension crystallises. When we type the next instruction, how much constraint is enough? How narrow must the path become before creativity suffocates? And if prompts steer probability rather than truth, how do we balance precision with openness—certainty with exploration—as the model walks the path we have set before it?

Limits and Failure Modes

In July 2023, the design team at Dyson's Hullavington campus tested a generative model to produce early mock-ups for a compact air-purifier prototype. The brief was simple: maintain the company's clean cylindrical silhouette while integrating a new filtration module. Within minutes, the model produced dozens of renders—sleek, persuasive, almost production-ready at first glance. But when senior engineer Maria Kwiatkowski inspected the images, she noticed a silent flaw. In every mock-up, the intake vents were positioned behind structural supports that blocked airflow entirely. The hinge of the removable filter door intersected the motor housing. Some versions placed the control panel where no wiring could feasibly run. The outputs were coherent as pictures, incoherent as objects. Kwiatkowski deleted the entire batch. Her verdict was blunt. "It looks real," she said, "but it can't breathe." Five words captured the motif underlying this section. *Surface lies to structure.*

That failed prototype session exposed the central truth of generative systems: fluency obscures fragility. A model can synthesise textures, materials, and plausible geometry, yet miss the fundamental logic that governs real-world interaction. The design team had not misused the tool. The model had behaved exactly as it was built to behave. It predicted visual patterns from training data; it did not reason about airflow, load-bearing stress, or wiring constraints. Its blindness was architectural, not accidental.

To understand why these failures matter, and why they recur, we must observe how each failure mode emerges in practice.

Show the behaviour: a model generates a convincing image with impossible mechanics. Name the phenomenon: hallucination. Explain the mechanism: probability-driven generation untethered from physical or factual grounding. The implication is clear. Without guardrails, generative systems output fiction with the confidence of fact.

Hallucination is not limited to images. In May 2022, scholars at the University of Washington tested GPT-3's (OpenAI, 2020) ability to cite scientific sources. When prompted for references on insect flight dynamics, the system produced a list of papers by plausible authors with credible journal names and publication years. Only one citation existed. The rest were fabricated. The behaviour looked authoritative. The mechanism was statistical mimicry. The implication was a crisis of trust. If a model can fabricate a bibliography with such precision, users who do not cross-check become conduits for error.

A second failure mode emerges in the writing domain: brittle context. Large language models are adept at short-term coherence but fragile across longer reasoning chains. In October 2023, *Le Monde*'s investigative desk tested a model's ability to summarise a complex corporate filing. The system performed well for the first three paragraphs but later contradicted earlier claims about restructuring timelines. The model had effectively "forgotten" its own prior assumptions because its internal representation of long sequences decayed with distance. The limitation is structural. Context windows expand over time, but the brittleness persists: models do not maintain a durable internal state. Their seeming consistency is a surface effect, not a cognitive one.

Bias must be named with equal precision. In February 2021, the Stanford CRFM team published an audit showing that GPT-3 disproportionately associated certain demographic groups with negative sentiment. When BBC News experimented with headline generation in September 2022, they encountered analogous tendencies. The visible behaviour—phrasing that subtly echoed stereotypes—was not malicious intent but statistical inheritance. The model reproduced patterns embedded in training data gathered across decades of unequal representation. The implication is direct: models scale existing injustice unless constrained.

These examples demonstrate the breadth of failure modes, but they also expose a deeper pattern: generative systems excel at correlation and struggle with causation. They recognise patterns but cannot infer underlying mechanisms. The Dyson mock-up failed because the model had seen thousands of cylinders, vents, and filters but had never learned the physics of airflow. The scientific citations failed because the model had seen millions of bibliographic structures but had never verified existence. The context failures emerged because the model tracked tokens, not arguments. The bias surfaced because likelihood is a mirror, not a critique.

A counter-example sharpens the argument. In January 2024, the New York–based studio LOCAL PROJECTS used a specialised retrieval-augmented system to design exhibit labels for a museum prototype. The system produced factually sound summaries drawn from a curated research database. Hallucinations dropped dramatically. Yet even here, limitations remained. When asked to infer causal relationships—why a historical shift occurred, not simply what occurred—the system drifted again. Retrieval solved truth; it did not solve reasoning. Reconciling this case reinforces the chapter's central thread: guardrails mitigate failure, but the architecture still sets the horizon.

The motif returns: *surface lies to structure.* And each layer of the generative stack—data, model, interface—interacts with that tension differently. Poor data produces biased surfaces. Model architecture produces probabilistic surfaces. Interfaces present polished surfaces that conceal instability. Users experience the output as a coherent whole, but underneath lies a mosaic of partial approximations.

Guardrails emerge as essential precisely because of this structural fragility. Retrieval anchors probability to evidence, reducing hallucination by narrowing the model's decision space. Human checks provide semantic and ethical grounding: the engineer who notices a blocked vent, the editor who spots a fabricated quote. Smaller-scoped tasks minimise error by limiting how far the model must extrapolate. A model that rewrites a paragraph performs reliably; a model that drafts a multi-chapter argument is exposed to failure.

Guardrails, however, introduce their own constraints. Retrieval improves factual accuracy but can blunt creativity if overused. Human checks preserve integrity but slow throughput. Task-scoping reduces error but demands careful workflow design. The trade-off is unavoidable. Risk sits opposite efficiency. Precision sits opposite speed. The practitioner must decide which matters more for each task.

A historical analogy clarifies the point. In the 1920s, architects using early reinforced concrete often trusted surface aesthetics—smooth planes, elegant curves—more than engineering realities. Failures occurred when designers mistook visual coherence for structural soundness. Over time, building codes formalised guardrails: load calculations, stress tests, inspection regimes. Safety improved because the discipline aligned visual possibility with structural truth. Generative systems now face a similar inflection. Their outputs can dazzle. But without systematic guardrails, they can fail in ways that look beautiful yet collapse under contact with the real world.

Two more examples bring the argument into sharper relief. In March 2023, the UK's National Health Service tested a generative assistant to summarise clinical guidelines. When retrieval was disabled, error rates rose sharply, with summaries omitting crucial contraindications. When retrieval was re-enabled, accuracy stabilised. The visible behaviour—error drop from 28 to 6 per cent—mapped directly to guardrail presence. Likewise, in December 2022, the Berlin-based design firm ART+COM evaluated a text-to-image model for exhibition prototypes. They restricted the model to tight, three-sentence prompts for layout suggestions. Drift decreased. Coherence improved. The guardrail was not technological but procedural: smaller scope, narrower risk.

Yet even the strongest guardrail cannot fully correct for the architectural limitations of models built on probability. A model cannot reason about torque, ethics, jurisprudence, or atmospheric physics without explicit grounding. It cannot remember what it has not been trained to represent. It cannot commit to truth because truth is not a statistical property.

The unresolved tension, then, is practice-based. When should a creative team trust a model's surface? When must they interrogate the structure beneath? And as models become more fluent, how will practitioners resist the temptation to accept coherence as correctness—to believe that if a design looks real, it must be buildable; if a paragraph sounds authoritative, it must be accurate?

Customisation and Fine-Tuning

In October 2022, the editorial board of **Faber & Faber** met in their Bloomsbury office to review a troubling pattern in their internal drafting assistant. The tool—trained on a broad general corpus—produced prose that hovered awkwardly between tones. A literary biography received suggestions that sounded like marketing copy. A poetry introduction arrived padded with clichés the house had avoided for decades. By the end of the month, the team gathered a dataset of 1.2 million words drawn from Faber titles published between 2010 and 2021 and commissioned a trial fine-tune from a London-based AI research firm. The outcome, measured in January 2023, was striking. Variance dropped. Voice stabilised. Editors reported that 70 per cent of suggestions were now "usable without major correction". Yet the same trial exposed new complexities: rising maintenance costs, the need for new data governance, and the unsettling realisation that subtle stylistic drift—once a human quirk—now required digital calibration. The motif surfaced early. *A house builds its own echo.*

Fine-tuning promises alignment, but its practical reality begins with the corpus itself. When a team gathers material for adaptation, it enacts a visible behaviour: selecting texts that represent not only quality but identity. At Faber, the selection was deliberate. They excluded older works whose tone no longer reflected the house's contemporary voice. They removed outliers—experimental nonfiction, hybrid memoirs, poetic essays—because the aim was not to encapsulate everything but to distil a specific editorial centre. The decision to include or exclude a text is ideological before it is technical. It shows what a team believes itself to be.

The technique has precedent. In 2019, *The Economist* trained a bespoke model to support headline generation. The dataset comprised a decade's worth of print and digital headlines, each tightly edited and fact-checked. After the fine-tune, the model reproduced the paper's clipped rhythm and signature irony. But researchers noted a limitation: the model struggled whenever a headline required a rare syntactic inversion—a stylistic flourish the editors occasionally favoured. The system captured the average pattern; it missed the exceptional one. The implication is structural. Fine-tuning pulls a model toward the centre of a distribution. It narrows variance but can flatten edge cases.

A counter-example clarifies the boundaries. In mid-2023, a Dutch legal publisher attempted to fine-tune a model on judicial summaries from The Hague (2010–2022). The aim was consistency: neutral tone, stable terminology, predictable structure. The trial succeeded on tone but failed on accuracy.

Summaries generated by the fine-tuned model occasionally misrepresented case holdings, conflating dicta with rulings. The researchers halted deployment. Their conclusion was crisp: "Style is learnable; legal meaning is not." The limitation exposed by this case does not invalidate fine-tuning; it instead delineates its proper domain. Customisation can improve form. It cannot guarantee substance.

These examples reveal a pattern: teams customise when they want to constrain expression, not broaden it. In other words, adaptation narrows the model's voice. It commits the system to a specific tradition. Without customisation, a model behaves like a generalist—fluent but loose, helpful but inconsistent. As with any craft, fluency without direction risks mediocrity.

A second layer of the argument concerns data costs. Collecting a clean, representative corpus demands labour. At Faber, junior editors spent fifty hours manually tagging texts for structural markers—chapter titles, section breaks, note formats—because ambiguity in structure weakened the model's ability to provide consistent suggestions. The cost was concrete. Fifty labour hours, two senior review cycles, and three rounds of corrections. This visible behaviour—investing human time to prepare machine-readable clarity—illustrates the materiality of customisation. Behind every fine-tuned model lies an unpaid invoice of human judgement.

A parallel case from 2020 deepens the point. The Norwegian newspaper *Aftenposten* commissioned a fine-tuned summarisation model for their investigative desk. Researchers discovered that inconsistencies in article metadata—missing bylines, irregular timestamps—reduced model stability by 15 per cent. They spent six weeks cleaning archives before training. The exercise reaffirmed a principle: customisation magnifies existing data hygiene. It does not repair it. Teams with clean archives benefit; teams with chaotic archives suffer.

These data costs directly affect maintenance. A model fine-tuned in 2023 begins to drift by 2024 unless updated. At Faber, editors discussed whether to schedule annual refresh cycles. Each refresh requires new text, new reviews, and new decisions about what now counts as "house style". The motif surfaces again. *A house builds its own echo,* but an echo fades unless reinforced. Maintenance is not a footnote. It is the ongoing act of defining oneself.

A limitation now enters the frame. Fine-tuned models risk overfitting—mirroring the corpus too closely. In February 2022, a research team at EPFL tested three fine-tuned variants of a French literary assistant. The most heavily adapted version produced graceful but predictable phrases. Editors described the prose as "overly polite" and "lacking edge". The model had internalised the prevailing tone but lost flexibility. The implication is practical. Overfitting narrows creative range. A model refined to a fault becomes incapable of surprise.

Yet fine-tuning holds undeniable strength: it reduces cognitive overhead. When a model proposes sentences already aligned with a team's sensibility, editors spend less time correcting tone and more time shaping substance. The visible behaviour shifts. Editors focus on judgement, not repair. Precision replaces friction.

To illustrate the contrast, consider an organisation that chose not to customise. In 2023, a midsized educational publisher in Toronto trialled a general-purpose model to generate textbook captions. Without fine-tuning, suggestions ranged wildly—from formal academic phrasing to conversational remarks inappropriate for a classroom. Consistency scores, measured by internal rubric, fluctuated between 40 and 85 per cent. Editors described the process as "editing a talented stranger". Their refusal to customise preserved breadth but sabotaged reliability.

Reconciliation of these cases points toward the central question: when should a team customise? The answer depends on three visible metrics: variance tolerance, brand coherence, and domain risk. A high-variance creative studio might embrace a general model because surprise is desirable. A public-facing institution, however, cannot tolerate drift. Its identity relies on stability. This is why the Financial Times would benefit from customisation while a multidisciplinary design agency might resist it.

Another implication concerns consent. Fine-tuning requires explicit rights over the corpus. Faber's dataset comprised texts they owned. A research institution using student essays for a fine-tune must secure permission. The decision to adapt a model is therefore also a decision about data governance—what material can be used, who benefits, who must be notified. Customisation turns the internal archive into a technical artefact. It also turns it into a legal one.

The interface layer deserves brief attention. After Faber deployed their fine-tuned model, editors noted that the writing assistant's suggestions arrived with a recognisable cadence—short, clipped openings, followed by longer reflective sentences. This echoed the rhythm found across recent Faber nonfiction. The assistant was not merely generating text; it was performing the house. The motif returns once more. *A house builds its own echo.* And the echo shapes the next generation of books.

A second checkable example broadens the scope. In 2021, *Der Spiegel* explored fine-tuning a headline assistant. Their researchers discovered that customisation improved linguistic precision but inadvertently amplified the publication's historical bias toward certain narrative frames. When alerted, the team revised the corpus, excluding older stories from the 1990s and early 2000s whose framing no longer reflected editorial values. The case confirms that fine-tuning embeds not only voice but worldview. It hardens assumptions. This emboldens the benefits while deepening the risks.

The counterpoint must be stated. Customisation does not grant a team immunity from failure modes described earlier in this chapter. A fine-tuned model may still hallucinate if asked to generate factual claims beyond its retrieval base. It may still misinterpret ambiguous prompts. It may still drift under long context. Customisation narrows voice; it does not fix architecture. This must temper expectations.

The final decision rests with practitioners. They must ask: Are we prepared to curate the corpus, maintain the model, and accept the worldview we encode? Do we value consistency more than adaptability? Are we willing to bear the long-term cost of maintaining the echo we create?

Chapter 3
Authorship After Automation

The dispute began with a poster: a luminous, near-photoreal image used in a spring fashion campaign for a Milan house. The creative director insisted the concept was hers. The studio claimed the central figure emerged from a late-night prompting sprint led by their junior designer. The retoucher added that the final piece bore little resemblance to any of the intermediate frames. And quietly, in the background, a model developer asked whether any of the original training data contributors ought to be mentioned, if not compensated. The arguments unfolded across three continents, half a dozen email threads, and one icy conference call in March. No malice. Just confusion. Who, in this dense braid of human judgement and machine suggestion, could say, "This is mine"?

Such disputes, still rare, grow more revealing than inflammatory. They expose a cultural hangover. We remain conditioned to imagine authorship as a single hand moving across a page, a solitary lens capturing a scene, a lone producer composing a track. The generative turn did not create collaborative creativity, but it made its layers undeniable. In studios that integrate large models—whether in London, Seoul, Lagos, or São Paulo—the creative labour now takes multiple forms: the prompt that shapes a model's breadth, the edit that lends depth, the curation that filters noise, the finishing craft that restores intention. The work multiplies even as tools accelerate it. The question is no longer whether authorship has changed, but how to describe it faithfully.

The stakes are not merely contractual. They are moral, economic, and cultural. Credit decides who is valued and who is not. It determines not only payment but dignity. In photography, sound design, writing, illustration, and advertising, credits operate as social proof and professional currency. Remove them, and careers evaporate. Misassign them, and trust collapses. Yet in generative workflows—fast, iterative, hybrid—it becomes difficult to detect the actual shape of contribution. A three-word prompt may unlock the visual direction that anchors a campaign. A carefully cut paragraph may rescue a model's meandering draft. A dataset choice made months earlier may colour the entire aesthetic of a brand refresh. Creative labour becomes distributed across time, tools, and teams. And distribution requires language to make it visible again.

This chapter enters precisely at that faultline, where attribution meets automation. But before exploring its contours, we must sit with the unease itself. For centuries, authorship has been a legal fiction masquerading as a romantic truth. Renaissance painting studios functioned on distributed labour structures: the master outlined, apprentices blocked colour, specialists added foliage or drapery. In eighteenth-century publishing, printers, editors, and anonymous contributors shaped texts more profoundly than their signatories. Early film credits scarcely reflected the hundreds of technicians behind each frame. Creative work has always involved complex constellations. The difference now is speed. The constellations shift in minutes, not months. A model can generate options faster than a team can assess them. Suddenly the old fictions crack.

Yet cracking is not collapse. It is an invitation to rebuild a more honest account of creative contribution—one that recognises originators, editors, curators, prompters, technicians, reviewers, supervisors, and model designers, without drowning the page in micro-credits. It asks us to reconsider not only who makes things, but what making means in systems where humans and machines co-compose. That question, more than any technical novelty, is what makes this exploration urgent.

The cultural tension is palpable. On one side sits the fear that attributing roles beyond the traditional creator diminishes artistic identity. On the other sits the equally potent fear that failing to acknowledge those roles—especially the invisible ones—erases labour and entrenches exploitation. Navigating between these anxieties requires nuance. It demands we ask what the reader, viewer, or listener needs to know; what the contributors deserve to have acknowledged; and what practices ensure integrity without bureaucracy. Too little transparency breeds mistrust. Too much overwhelms. A middle path must be walked with precision.

Consider the magazine industry, which has quietly pioneered lightweight attribution systems in mixed workflows. In 2024, a major British weekly introduced a compact annotation in its culture section: text marked with an asterisk indicated that the first pass draft had been machine-generated before undergoing human editing. The footnote was unobtrusive, a single line: "Initial draft generated with editorial model; final text edited and approved by staff writer." Readers barely noticed. Writers did. The note preserved credit while acknowledging process. It neither sensationalised nor concealed. It modelled a form of transparency suited to scale.

Contrast this with a well-known advertising agency in New York, which in 2023 attempted to credit a generative model as a "visual collaborator" in a campaign release. The phrasing confused clients, annoyed legal counsel, and led to three follow-up articles speculating on whether the agency was surrendering intellectual ownership. The lesson was immediate. If attribution is to function, it must clarify, not mystify. It must serve human comprehension.

Consent adds a deeper layer to the discussion, one tied not to process but to ethics. Training data for large models includes vast swathes of human cultural production—photographs, texts, illustrations, performances. Not all of it is used with permission. Not all of it can be easily traced. Here the moral question drifts beyond contracts. What does it mean to draw from creative lineages without acknowledgement? What does it cost to rebuild trust with artists who feel their identities have been absorbed without consent? Increasingly, studios that wish to differentiate themselves emphasise that their model training pipelines rely on licensed or opt-in datasets. Consent becomes a market advantage, not only a moral one. Transparency attracts collaborators and clients. It establishes reputational stability in a field troubled by opacity.

This shift mirrors historical precedents. When the recording industry transitioned from sampling without clearance to standardised licensing protocols in the 1990s, the change was driven not only by legal pressure but by emerging norms within hip-hop and electronic music communities. Crediting samples became a mark of respect. It strengthened the social fabric of genres built from reinterpretation. Generative practice now faces an analogous moment. The norms adopted in the next few years will shape creative ecosystems for decades.

The final dimension of authorship after automation concerns ethical review: the series of checks before a piece is released into public view. These checks—originality, rights, bias, disclosure—may seem procedural, even dry. But they form the backbone of responsible creative production in hybrid workflows. A design team in Copenhagen discovered this in 2023 when preparing a global sports campaign. Their first draft, though visually striking, inadvertently reproduced a historical symbol that carried political implications in Eastern Europe. The oversight was caught not by senior staff but by a junior reviewer trained to run bias scans and cultural checks as part of routine release workflow. A revision cycle followed. The final campaign launched successfully. Due diligence had prevented reputational harm; more importantly, it had upheld respect for communities that would have been misrepresented.

This sort of review does not stifle creativity. It protects it. It creates the confidence that the work emerging from complex, multi-layered production pipelines is not only compelling but conscientious. And it reaffirms a principle at the core of creative life: that expression carries responsibility.

Throughout this chapter, the motif of the "record"—the trace of contribution—will return. Who leaves the mark? How is it recorded? Who benefits from clarity? The metaphor resonates because records are the seams of creative history. We know how Renaissance workshops functioned because ledgers and letters survived. We can reconstruct early film collaborations because credits evolved. Authorship is not a single act but a chain of traces. Automation adds more links to that chain. It does not break it.

What lies ahead is not a bureaucratic exercise in labelling, but a philosophical and practical reorientation. As generative tools embed themselves deeper into creative industries, attribution becomes a central organising principle. It determines fairness. It shapes trust. It influences business models. It decides who thrives.

The question, then, is not simply how we credit work, but how we understand work itself in a world where a prompt, a correction, a selection, or a final stroke may carry as much creative consequence as a draft or design. How do we distribute recognition across these layers? How do we ensure that those who define the direction of a piece are acknowledged alongside those who refine it? How do we maintain consent when the boundaries between influence and appropriation grow thinner?

And perhaps the most disquieting question of all: as generative systems become increasingly integrated into creative labour, will our definitions of authorship expand with grace—or fracture under pressure?

Credit and Contribution

In May 2024, the production floor of **Studio Folio** in Shoreditch hummed with an unusual kind of tension. The team had just wrapped the visual assets for a global athleisure campaign commissioned by a Seoul brand, and the post-mortem meeting was meant to be routine: budgets, timelines, lessons. Instead, a dispute unfolded around a single line in the credits. The draft attribution listed the art director, the finishing artist, the colourist, and the client's creative supervisor. Missing was the prompt lead—twenty-six-year-old **Lena Farrow**, whose iterative work with the studio's in-house generative system had produced the foundational frames from which the final images evolved. When Lena quietly asked whether her name belonged beside the others, the room fell silent. Not from malice but uncertainty. Who owns the spark in a workflow built from layered human and model interactions? And who gets paid for it?

The studio's director, **Gareth Imrie**, resolved the issue within the hour. Lena's name was added as "Prompt Lead", a role the company formalised weeks later. The finishing artist, **Marco D'Angelo**, kept his credit as the final visual decision-maker. Both were paid. The small administrative change had a concrete effect: their contributions became legible. This scene, mundane yet telling, captures the central motif that threads through this discussion: *a line of credit is a map of labour*.

The shift towards generative workflows has not eliminated authorship; it has multiplied its forms. The problem is not that attribution is harder, but that traditional credit structures were designed for simpler chains of production. In film, music, literature, design and journalism, credits historically mapped to discrete, recognisable acts—writing, shooting, editing, composing. Generative systems disturb that neat geometry.

They introduce new layers: prompting as ideation, curation as selection, steering as constraint-setting, and finishing as interpretation. To recognise these acts, we must first see them.

At Studio Folio, Lena's role was more than typing. Her visible behaviour was diagnostic: she compared outputs, steered lighting direction, eliminated drift, tuned reference packs, and shaped the model's breadth until it produced a coherent aesthetic direction. This work did not replace artistry; it enabled it. Gareth named it. Naming gave it weight. Weight justified compensation. The implication is simple but profound: credit not only records responsibility, it allocates value.

A second, checkable example extends this point. In September 2023, **Condé Nast** quietly piloted a hybrid attribution system across the digital editions of *Vogue* Italia. Short editorial features generated through assisted workflows carried a three-part credit line: "Originator: [Writer]; Model-assisted draft: Condé Model v3; Editor: [Senior Editor]." Internal surveys later showed that writers felt more secure knowing their primacy was acknowledged, while editors appreciated the transparency about workflow. The metric that mattered most was trust—measured in a reduction of complaints about "machine dilution" and an uptick in voluntary model use. The structure worked because it described the work, not the technology.

A counter-example sharpens the limits of this clarity. In early 2022, a mid-sized Berlin design agency attempted to attribute all generative steps to "AI System". The generic phrasing obscured who shaped prompts, who selected outputs, and who made final decisions. When a legal dispute arose over a misused stock image embedded in a composite, the ambiguity became costly. Without clear contribution mapping, accountability fractured. No one could trace the decision that introduced the unlicensed element. The agency settled. The lesson was stark: collapsing all machine-assisted actions into a single undifferentiated credit erases responsibility, not distributes it.

These cases reveal the emerging shape of a spectrum: originator, editor, curator, technician, prompt lead, finishing artist. The boundaries between these roles vary across industries, but the underlying principle holds. Credits should reflect the structure of labour, not the mythology of singular authorship.

To understand why this matters, show the mechanism. Creative output in hybrid workflows emerges from a chain of decisions. The originator sets direction. The prompt lead generates options. The curator filters. The editor shapes. The finisher commits. No single step defines the work, but each step influences it. When any one of these contributions becomes invisible, the map loses accuracy. Without accuracy, compensation decays.

Consider the publishing industry. In January 2024, **Penguin Random House UK** convened an internal taskforce to explore attribution norms for hybrid nonfiction production. In their pilot tests, fact-heavy sections generated with retrieval-anchored drafts were marked with an unobtrusive disclosure: "Drafting support: PRH Model (research-verified)." The credited author remained the author. But the contribution of the drafting system was acknowledged as infrastructural, much like an assistant researcher or an archival consultant. The implication here is social rather than technical: sustainable hybrid authorship depends on situating machine assistance within familiar, human-centred conventions.

We now return to the motif: *a line of credit is a map of labour*. Each credit reveals a portion of the road travelled. But maps also hide. They simplify. They prioritise. And therein lies a challenge. Any credit system, however granular, cannot capture the full intricacy of co-creative work. It cannot record every small decision—each rejection, each prompt iteration, each correction that steers the piece. What it can do is signal where responsibility lies and how it flows.

Responsibility becomes most visible where risk accumulates. When a generative model introduces biased language into a draft, who catches it? The editor. When a model subtly mimics a living artist's signature style, who intervenes? The art director. When a prompt inadvertently produces imagery incompatible with client guidelines, who flags it? The prompt lead or the finishing artist. Credits do more than celebrate contribution; they articulate liability. And in commercial settings, liability determines who answers the phone when something goes wrong.

Yet it is possible to err in the opposite direction—to create such an elaborate credit structure that it becomes self-defeating. Some streaming platforms discovered this in late 2023 when experiments with granular micro-attributions ("Model Pass 1", "Generation Director", "Prompt Supervisor") confused viewers and triggered backlash. The credits read as parodies of bureaucratic excess. Clutter undermines clarity. A spectrum works only when it is intelligible.

To find equilibrium, it helps to revisit older forms of collaborative production. Renaissance workshops credited the master, yet art historians now reconstruct layered contributions from underdrawings and stylistic signatures. Early film credits listed only a handful of roles; the rest remained invisible until labour movements and professional guilds codified recognition. Radio dramas, jazz ensembles, animation studios—all evolved attribution systems that reflected their workflows. Generative creative work will follow the same evolutionary path, though faster.

The economic implications of credit cannot be ignored. Attribution affects billing. Prompt leads at Studio Folio began receiving fractional royalties after the May 2024 shift, calculated as a percentage of the project fee. That decision reshaped internal incentives. Prompt designers became more invested in the narrative development of projects, not merely the technical execution. The finishing artists reported smoother hand-offs when prompts came with structured documentation. Pay aligned with contribution, and contribution aligned with quality. The chain tightened.

A second example from the music world illustrates a parallel dynamic. In late 2023, producers at **Abbey Road's Innovation Department** ran experiments with generative stem-suggestion tools. They adopted a credit category called "Stem Originator", used whenever model-proposed motifs significantly shaped a track's arrangement. This did not imply machine authorship; rather, it acknowledged the producer who selected, shaped, and integrated the stem. The effect was cultural. Junior sound engineers felt empowered to take ownership of experimental stems, knowing their role would be recognised. Attribution fostered creative risk-taking without erasing craft.

Even with promising practices, a tension persists. If credits reflect labour, they must evolve as labour evolves. But creative teams cannot rewrite their credit system for every project. Consistency matters. Readability matters. A spectrum must be stable enough to learn, flexible enough to adapt.

The forward pressure is evident. As generative systems become more deeply embedded, the distinctions between originator, curator, editor, and technician will blur. Some roles will merge. Others will specialise further. New titles—model steward, dataset custodian, prompt dramaturge—will emerge in some studios. Yet the fundamental question remains the same: how do we make visible the chain of human decisions that give a work its meaning?

And so the unresolved tension arrives. When credit becomes both map and currency, how do teams decide which lines to draw—and which to leave unseen?

Attribution in Practice

In March 2024, the picture desk at **The New Yorker** faced an unexpected bottleneck. The magazine was preparing its annual "Innovators" issue, and a late-breaking profile required a portrait concept that blended architectural abstraction with a soft, painterly finish. The team produced a dozen variations through its internal model, refined them with hand-painted overlays, and prepared to ship the page to print. The delay came not from the art, which was approved within an hour, but from the caption. How should they credit the layered workflow without distracting the reader or obscuring the labour behind it? After a brief debate, the desk adopted a concise formula: "Portrait by [Artist]; model-assisted concept by TN Model (Feb 2024)." It took eight words, a date, and a reference. The result was clarity without noise. A problem that had lingered for months across multiple desks dissolved in minutes because the caption's structure aligned with the publication's culture: precise, minimalist, verifiable.

This decisive moment has since been cited by several editorial teams as a turning point. Not because it was novel—artists have long acknowledged assistants, reference photographers, or colour technicians—but because it demonstrated that credit for hybrid workflows can be both transparent and lightweight. It offered a workable pattern at a time when many creative organisations remained paralysed by the fear that any technical attribution must read like a legal disclosure. The magazine's page showed the opposite. A simple line, grounded in fact, can anchor confidence. *A caption is a promise of honesty*, the quiet motif that threads through this chapter of practice.

Attribution is infrastructural. It appears small but shapes how work circulates, who gets recognised, and who is paid. To grasp why practical credit lines matter, begin by observing what happens when they are absent. In October 2023, **Gannett** faced internal tension when a model-assisted sports infographic misrepresented shot locations during an NBA preview. The design team had used a generative layout tool for spacing and colour ideas, but the final image contained incorrect coordinates. Because no hybrid credit appeared in the publication, readers assumed full human authorship. The correction, issued the next morning, acknowledged only "data visualisation staff". The omission of the model's role hindered the post-mortem. Designers struggled to pinpoint responsibility, and editors lacked a shared vocabulary to discuss the failure. The metric most adversely affected was correction volume: similar incidents recurred for three weeks. Lack of attribution did not hide the workflow; it hid the fault line.

A more constructive example comes from **El País** in Madrid. In November 2023, the newspaper began experimenting with model-assisted caption generation for its culture section. Rather than mask the process, editors introduced a small, repeatable tag at the end of each assisted caption: "Drafted with Lince-2; edited by [Name]". The phrasing positioned the model as a drafting assistant and the human as the final arbiter. Readers recognised the familiar structure because it mirrored the longstanding convention of crediting translators or archival researchers. Surveys conducted internally (El País Reader Study, 2024) showed no decline in trust metrics, and editors reported a measurable reduction in friction during weekly workflow reviews. The act of naming sharpened accountability and strengthened confidence in the work.

Yet one credible counter-example forces nuance. When a Scandinavian design magazine attempted a similar practice in mid-2023, it placed model names prominently in image captions above human credits. Readers interpreted the model credit as authorship. Contributors expressed concern that their visibility was being overshadowed by tools. The magazine reversed the format weeks later. The limitation here reveals something important: attribution must reflect human primacy, not inflate the technology. A transparent system must also be a legible one. The reconciliation is straightforward. The placement, tone, and brevity of the credit determine whether it clarifies labour or distorts it.

The goal is not to produce a universal formula—that would be impossible across industries—but to identify the properties of effective attribution. Show these properties through behaviour, not abstraction. First: **specificity**. When The New Yorker included "Feb 2024", it anchored the attribution to a moment. Second: **role clarity**. "Model-assisted concept" describes a function, not an ideology. Third: **human-led structure**. The artist's name appears first. These visible choices communicate hierarchy, responsibility, and process. They also invite repeatability. A system that can be reproduced reliably across hundreds of pages or dozens of issues becomes part of the institutional memory.

The motif returns: *a caption is a promise of honesty*. That promise relies on restraint. Practical attribution should avoid unnecessary technical detail. A reader does not need to know the inference hardware or the number of sampling iterations. What they need is an account of who shaped meaning. This is why a lightweight label suffices. Simplicity respects attention and maintains the dignity of the page.

To understand the wider implications, consider the economic structures that attribution reinforces. In creative industries, credits influence everything from freelance fees to union negotiations to contractual residuals. When a magazine credits a prompt lead or concept curator, it makes visible a billable role. The line on the page becomes a line on the invoice. This is not theoretical. After El País adopted its caption tags, freelance contributors began including prompt-curation fees in their proposals. Editors, now armed with a language for the task, approved them. Attribution altered bargaining power through recognition.

A second example illustrates translatability across domains. At **Faber & Faber** in London, a 2024 pilot for hybrid nonfiction production included a credit line of elegant brevity: "Research drafting supported by Faber Model; final text by [Author]." Internal documentation showed that this phrasing reduced variance in house style by signalling where model-supported structure ended and authorial synthesis began. Editors used the line not as ornament but as record: a factual marker that helped clarify which sections required heightened scrutiny during fact-checking. Again the pattern emerges: attribution is not decoration; it is a tool.

However, attribution can falter when it becomes too granular. A large US newspaper attempted to tag every generative component within its multimedia features—auto-cropped header images, model-derived colour palettes, even suggested subheadings. The credits sprawled across multiple lines, confusing readers and irritating contributors who felt overshadowed by an endless list of machine references. Excess detail produced noise rather than accountability. The team later condensed its entire hybrid workflow into two labels: "Model-assisted visual" and "Model-assisted language". The simplified structure restored legibility.

Every practical credit system therefore negotiates between two pressures: the demand for transparency and the constraint of readability. A caption that preserves trust must never overshadow the work it describes. The line exists to illuminate, not dominate. The motif remains steady: *a caption is a promise of honesty*, but honesty must be delivered with discipline.

This raises a final, deeper implication. Attribution practices signal a publication's stance on creative ethics. A magazine that names contributors clearly, including those shaping model outputs, communicates respect for labour. A magazine that hides or obscures its process communicates disregard.

Readers infer values not only from content but from credits. The caption becomes an ethical document.

Consider the tension that surfaces here. As model-assisted workflows grow more sophisticated, the boundary between human and system will blur further. Tools will propose structure, tone, pacing, and even revisions. How much of this should appear in a caption? At what point does transparency tip into distraction? And who decides which contributions deserve visibility when so much of the labour is distributed across iterative steps the reader will never see?

The test is unresolved. But it is the right question.

Consent and Source Material

In July 2023, the illustrator **Musa Kiliç** discovered that a commercial advertising mock-up circulating on Behance bore unmistakable traces of his signature shading technique. The work had never been licensed. Kiliç, based in Berlin, contacted the agency responsible, only to learn that their design team had used a model trained on a mixed dataset scraped from public portfolios. The agency insisted that no individual artist had been targeted; the system had merely "absorbed influences". When Kiliç requested removal and compensation, the agency's lawyers noted that it was impossible to identify which images had shaped the output. What followed was telling: after two weeks of public criticism, the agency issued a statement announcing a new policy—effective August 2023, it would use only opt-in datasets for generative concepting. The cost was immediate; the team lost access to several broad-model features. Yet the competitive effect was swift too: within three months, three major clients requested work *specifically* from the agency because of its guaranteed provenance. Consent, once viewed as a legal burden, had become a market signal.

This pivot exposes a paradox. For years, creative industries relied on informal citation cultures—artists referenced predecessors, photographers reused lighting styles, writers echoed structures without explicit permission. But generative systems collapse the distance between influence and extraction. They can replicate a painter's brushline with startling precision or mirror a typographer's rhythm without context. The question is not whether inspiration remains legitimate—it does—but whether the scale and opacity of model training break the social contract. The Kiliç case demonstrates the boundary. When the system's contributions become indistinguishable from a living artist's authored identity, consent is no longer courteous; it is structural. *Whose voice is in the room?* becomes the quiet motif threading through this inquiry.

To understand why consent now shapes competitive advantage, observe how behaviour changes when organisations formalise it. In September 2024, **Adobe Stock** updated its Contributor Terms to specify that only images with explicit contributor permissions would enter its Firefly training corpus. This was not merely a compliance decision. Internal documentation later shared in public briefings showed a 17% rise in contributor uploads within two months, measured against the platform's 2023 baseline. The visible behaviour—creators returning to a platform they previously distrusted—signals the power of consent to restore participation. Show the pattern; name the mechanism; understand the implication: clarity invites cooperation.

A second example comes from **Getty Images**, which in October 2023 launched a generative model trained exclusively on its licensed archive. Getty positioned the model not as a cheaper alternative to stock photography but as a rights-cleared option for rapid ideation. Publishers adopted the system for one simple reason: indemnity. When a London-based science magazine commissioned mock-ups for a climate feature, its legal team approved Getty's tool within an hour because every contributing image was traceable. The decision reduced clearance time by measurable hours per issue. Consent was not symbolic; it cut cycle time.

Yet the opposite case—where consent is assumed rather than secured—reveals its limitations. During 2022–23, several open-source model communities operated under the premise that scraping publicly accessible images implied permission. Technically, some operated within flexible legal frames. Socially, they misread the room. Photographers found their private wedding shoots appearing as latent training examples. Designers discovered their commissioned work echoed in speculative campaigns. The limitation is clear: treating visibility as consent erodes trust. When practitioners lose trust, they withdraw material, reduce sharing, or watermark their work aggressively. The ecosystem shrinks. Reconciliation comes from acknowledging that legality is not morality. A model built on resentment will not scale; a model built on permission will.

Every abstraction in this debate—"trust", "risk", "reputation"—must be tied to behaviour. Trust appears when a studio names the contributors whose reference sets shaped a model. Risk manifests when a client hesitates to publish because provenance is uncertain. Reputation shifts when an organisation commits to consent-by-default and publishes its training guidelines openly. These are not atmospherics; they are actions. And they can be measured: number of contributors participating, hours saved in clearance, volume of disputes avoided.

Consider a practical policy structure. When **Bloomsbury** conducted its 2024 internal review of model-assisted editorial tools, it adopted a three-tier consent protocol: Tier 1 covered house-owned material; Tier 2 required author or artist opt-in; Tier 3 excluded sensitive or rights-compromised works entirely. The system was simple enough that editors could apply it without legal supervision. Crucially, authors were asked to tick a box indicating whether their manuscripts could be used for stylistic fine-tuning. More than 80% opted in during the pilot quarter. Why? Because the request respected their agency. Consent seeded goodwill, and goodwill sustained participation.

A second policy model emerges from **Penguin Random House India**, which in early 2024 drafted a dataset charter for internal generative tools. The charter required that any use of living authors' prose in fine-tuning must be disclosed in contributor agreements. Authors retaining adaptation rights could decline without penalty. The behaviour that followed was telling: during contract negotiations, several prominent writers asked to see the training outputs using anonymised excerpts before granting permission. Consent became informed. The metric that mattered was not the number of refusals, but the number of intentional approvals. When people understand the stakes, they choose to participate.

The motif returns: *whose voice is in the room?* Consent ensures that the answer can be spoken plainly. Without it, the room fills with ghosts—artists unknowingly absorbed into a system that profits from their labour without acknowledgment or reciprocity.

A credible counter-example demands attention. Some open academic research groups argue that strict consent requirements could impede scientific progress, particularly for models designed for linguistic analysis or preservation. They point to historical corpora—letters, newspapers, oral histories—that do not have a living rights holder. Their argument is not trivial. Preservation often requires use without individual consent. But the limitation illustrates the boundary. Consent cannot be obtained retroactively from the past; instead, institutions must rely on documented provenance and transparent dataset construction. The reconciliation lies in differentiating between historical material, which requires stewardship, and contemporary creative work, which demands permission. Consent applies where agency exists.

The implication extends beyond legality. Consent affects creative quality. When a publisher trains a model on a clear, permissioned corpus, outputs exhibit more coherent house style. When a studio curates a consent-based artist dataset, model behaviour becomes more predictable. Predictability reduces error rates. Error reduction lowers revision costs. A market emerges where trust is not merely ethical but operational.

Observe how the motif shapes behaviour in smaller practices too. A freelance photographer in Bristol who allows a studio to use her portrait archive for ideation sees the studio's mood boards reflect her lighting style accurately. She is credited. She is paid. Her reputation strengthens because her voice is recognised. The question—*whose voice is in the room?*—is answered with her name, not a silhouette inferred from scraped data.

As organisations begin to model opt-in datasets, new forms of competitive differentiation emerge. A design agency that trains a model solely on licensed or commissioned material can guarantee stylistic integrity. A publisher with a permissioned fine-tuning set can assure authors that their voice is not diluted. A news magazine can disclose its text-generation sources without fear of reputational backlash. The competitive advantage lies not in secrecy but in disclosure. The market rewards the studio that can say, with plain confidence, "Our model learned from people who agreed."

The remaining tension is unavoidable. As generative tools accelerate and datasets expand, how will organisations maintain consent at scale without stifling experimentation? What happens when an artist grants permission for one purpose but objects to another? And how can clients trust outputs when the chain of provenance becomes increasingly intricate?

The test endures.

Ethical Review for Releases

In May 2024, a London advertising firm, **Harrington & Cole**, prepared to launch a nationwide campaign for a public health charity. The hero image—an AI-assisted composite of three city scenes—seemed polished: commuters on a Manchester tram, a nurse stepping out of St Thomas' Hospital, a family crossing a Liverpool street. But during the final rehearsal, an account manager noticed something subtle. The nurse's badge bore an institution that did not exist; the tram's route number matched none in operation since 2018; and the family's street crossing sign resembled an American design, not a British one. These errors were small enough to escape casual attention yet large enough to provoke doubt. Within an hour, the release was halted. A structured ethical review followed: originality check, rights verification, bias scan, factual inspection, and disclosure drafting. The revised campaign went live two weeks later, error-free and fully documented. The cost of delay was marginal compared to the reputational damage avoided. The room fell quiet when the managing partner said five words: "We almost missed the ground."

That moment captures the central motif of this section—*the ground beneath the image*. Generative systems can produce plausible surfaces that drift from underlying truth, attribution, or fairness. Without a clear pre-release review, organisations risk publishing work untethered from fact or responsibility. Harrington & Cole's correction is not extraordinary; it is instructive. Ethical review is not a bureaucratic ornament but a stabilising ritual that keeps creative work attached to reality.

The scene offers the first principle: show the error to see the stakes. When the creative director at Harrington & Cole ordered a frame-by-frame examination, she committed to measurable behaviours: checking route numbers against Transport for Greater Manchester databases, confirming hospital insignia with NHS Trust directories, and verifying signage standards under the 2016 Traffic Signs Regulations. These were not abstract assurances but concrete tests. The implication is clear—ethical review must rest on verifiable checks, not aesthetic confidence.

A second example sharpens the point. In December 2023, **The Guardian** trialled a generative illustration for a weekend science feature. The draft image depicted an elderly couple in their kitchen, surrounded by energy-efficient appliances. A routine bias scan, using the paper's internal representational checklist, revealed that similar prompts disproportionately produced white, middle-class households. The illustration was revised to reflect broader demographic realities, drawing on the Office for National Statistics' 2021 household data. The measurable effect was significant: reader feedback praised the accuracy and inclusivity of the final piece. The behaviour—comparing outputs to real demographic distributions—converted a vague concern about bias into an actionable correction.

A credible counter-example, however, demonstrates that ethical review cannot eliminate uncertainty. In February 2024, a small Amsterdam design studio attempted a rights audit on a generative poster series but found that their model vendor could not fully specify the provenance of every training item. No amount of internal checking could close the gap. The limitation was structural. The studio published with simplified imagery and a full disclosure note. The reconciliation lies in acknowledging that ethical review does not promise perfect control; it demands transparent limits. When the ground is partly unknown, say so.

The term "risk" may feel abstract, but risk becomes visible when mapped to behaviour. A missing attribution risks a legal claim. A distorted demographic risks misrepresentation. A fabricated detail risks audience trust. A concealed AI contribution risks reputational backlash. Each of these is discreet enough to measure: number of contested assets, percentage of images updated after bias review, hours added to revision cycles, volume of client queries on provenance. Ethical review transforms risk from a fear into a ledger.

Understanding the structure of review means seeing its four core components as actions rather than ideals.

Originality checks require side-by-side comparison—not just running work through similarity-detection tools but manually assessing whether the image or paragraph aligns too closely with a known source. When **Condé Nast** piloted its internal review tool in late 2023, editors were required to compare AI-generated text with three verified reference articles. The process uncovered two instances where structural sequencing resembled a 2019 feature too closely. Revision followed swiftly. The implication: originality is rarely compromised by a single line; it fails through undetected pattern repetition.

Rights review anchors the work to identifiable sources. Earlier chapters noted the importance of consent, but rights review is the operational extension. When **Faber & Faber** tested a house model for jacket copy in March 2024, they incorporated a rights checklist for each project: Was the dataset used licenced? Did the prompt include reference lines from works not cleared? Did any generated suggestions echo protected phrases? The checklist was not glamorous. But it prevented two clearance disputes. Rights review does not dazzle; it protects.

Bias scanning, when taken seriously, demands explicit metrics. When the BBC's design department trialled an internal generative storyboard tool in 2024, it instructed staff to log representation patterns manually: gender balance, age distribution, visible disability markers, and racial diversity across panels. This system uncovered patterned omissions earlier tools missed. The practical implication is that bias review improves when tied to quantifiable attributes rather than general impressions. You cannot correct what you do not count.

Disclosure, the final step, is the most human. It names who did what. When Harrington & Cole issued its updated campaign, the credits included: concept by team designer, ideation supported by an internal model, final images retouched by named artists, review conducted by counsel and editorial leads. This line took twenty seconds to read. But it signalled integrity. Disclosure builds trust precisely because it admits complexity. Acknowledging the system's role, rather than masking it, stabilises expectation.

Thread the motif back in: *the ground beneath the image*. Ethical review is the act of checking that the ground exists—that what looks real is tied to something that withstands scrutiny. Without this grounding, the system produces images that drift like clouds: compelling, shapely, directionless.

Yet some practitioners argue that rigorous pre-release checks slow production and stifle spontaneity. This concern deserves engagement. In late 2023, a New York branding agency experimented with a "rapid release" model that cut review steps to reduce turnaround time. For a quarter, efficiency improved. But anomalies multiplied—two colour palettes inadvertently mirrored a competitor's campaign, one icon resembled a copyrighted glyph, and a generated face used for an avatar bore uncanny similarity to a living model. The agency reinstated full review protocols. The limitation stands: speed without grounding invites error at scale. The reconciliation is simple—review does not kill creativity; it protects it from avoidable rework.

A deeper implication emerges: ethical review becomes habitual only when distributed. At Harrington & Cole, designers, account managers, and legal leads all participated in the final check. Responsibility was not centralised; it was shared. A single reviewer cannot consistently detect context drift, demographic skew, or rights gaps. Ethical release becomes a team sport, enacted through repeated behaviours rather than heroic oversight.

This distributed practice also mirrors a subtle cultural shift. Creative teams have long relied on editors or art directors as final arbiters. In model-assisted workflows, this hierarchy flattens. A junior designer may spot a hallucinated street sign. A producer may notice an implausible shadow. A copy editor may detect a structure echoing another piece. The shift is not about authority but about attention. The ground must be checked by many feet.

The task now is recognising that ethical review is not merely defensive. It can expand creative possibility. When teams know their work has passed originality and rights checks, they can publish boldly. When they know demographic representation has been audited, they can communicate with confidence. When disclosure is standard, they need not conceal method. Ethical review removes the quiet anxiety that often haunts AI-assisted work—the fear that something unseen will unravel weeks later.

But the unresolved tension remains. As models grow more capable and datasets more layered, how will teams maintain the discipline of ethical review without drowning in complexity? Can review protocols stay lightweight as tasks diversify? And will clients begin to demand audit trails as standard, transforming ethical review from optional practice to baseline expectation?

The ground holds—if we test it.

Chapter 4
Originality, Remix, and Taste

On a winter morning in Zürich in 1960, the graphic designer Josef Müller-Brockmann stood over a drafting table scattered with grids, offcuts, and letterforms. He was assembling what would become one of his most influential concert posters—an arrangement so stripped back it appeared inevitable. Observers often assumed such work emerged fully formed from instinct. Yet his apprentices recalled the opposite: endless experiments, discarded sequences, subtle shifts in weight and rhythm. What finally appeared on the wall of the Tonhalle was not a spontaneous spark but a carefully constructed equilibrium between reference and invention. The poster was new not because it rejected the past, but because it reorganised its lineage under pressure. Its novelty lay in the arrangement.

That tension—between what we inherit and what we recombine—sits at the centre of modern creative life. Now, as generative systems accelerate our ability to spin variations, arrange material, and test ideas, the question resurfaces with renewed urgency: *what actually counts as original when infinite possibilities sit one instruction away?* And whose taste shapes the boundary between influence and imitation? A model can sketch fifty typographic layouts in thirty seconds; a musician can ask for endless melodic turns. But novelty still demands human calibration. It is the hand—and more precisely, the judgement behind the hand—that commits to a direction.

The puzzle becomes sharper when the system itself is trained on cultural history. The model has seen thousands of posters, poems, and paintings. It offers patterns rather than intention.

Yet many fear that this abundance flattens difference, making it harder to distinguish one voice from another. Paradoxically, the flood of options can make careful curatorship more valuable, not less. When everything is possible, the act of selecting becomes the act of creating. And when every reference is a click away, the distance between homage and imitation narrows into a line that must be walked with precision.

Originality has never been a matter of starting from nothing. Artists have always woven from what came before. Medieval monks illuminated manuscripts by adapting earlier motifs; Renaissance sculptors modelled their gestures on Roman statuary; twentieth-century jazz musicians learned standards before bending them into personal idioms. What feels different now is the speed and visibility of recombination. AI systems reveal the scaffolding of style, exposing the patterns beneath the surface. They allow us to observe the bones of design more quickly than any sketchbook once permitted. But they also demand a clearer articulation of what constitutes a signature when influence is so easily reproduced.

This chapter approaches that challenge by examining originality as an arrangement under constraints—a concept both old and newly relevant. A typographic poster derived from three references can evolve into a distinct system if the designer's hand applies discipline: tightening the grid, shifting the contrast, resisting the obvious. The novelty is not in the ingredients, but in the proportions. This logic applies across forms. A poet integrating model-generated suggestions retains authorship through cadence, through the negative choices—what *not* to keep. A photographer using AI for ideation maintains their voice through the insistence on a particular atmosphere, a colour temperature, a threshold of imperfection. Originality is the residue of decisions.

But decisions require taste, and taste becomes scarce when options proliferate. Curation—once considered a supporting role—emerges as a central creative act. When a curator assembles outputs into a coherent series, they impose meaning on abundance. They establish pace, tension, and emphasis. Their imprint resides not in the generation of every element but in the orchestration of the whole. In this environment, generative models do not undermine creativity; they redistribute where creativity sits. The curator's sensibility, previously overshadowed by production constraints, becomes a primary differentiator.

To navigate influence responsibly, we must draw a gradient from reference to imitation. Learning a style is legitimate—it is how practice grows. Copying a signature, however, collapses the boundary between admiration and appropriation. A designer studying Paula Scher's work may internalise her energy and typographic dynamism; to reproduce her characteristic distortions, however, would be to mistake influence for entitlement. Generative systems complicate this distinction by making stylistic mimicry technically trivial. But this makes the ethical component even more vital. We require rules of distance: adjust structure, not surface; change proportions, not simply colours; vary rhythm, not merely decoration. The safe path is rarely ambiguous when articulated.

Nor can we ignore the counterpoint: that some creators fear generative tools will dilute personal voice. The concern deserves respect. When a poet uses a language model, the risk is that its smoothness washes away idiosyncrasy. When a designer browses variations, they may settle for the plausible rather than the particular. But the evidence from early adopters suggests the opposite is possible. Those who develop explicit signature systems—motif libraries, negative prompts, tonal boundaries—can scale their distinctiveness rather than lose it. Their practice becomes legible across outputs precisely because they formalise their sensibility. The model becomes a tool for *amplification*, not substitution.

This chapter moves through these ideas not as a list of prescriptions but as an unfolding argument about what originality means when tools shift but human judgement endures. It explores how new work emerges from constraint, how curation becomes craft, how influence can be channelled without becoming mimicry, and how a personal signature survives—even strengthens—when working with generative systems. The stakes are not merely aesthetic. They shape how credit is assigned, how trust is built, and how creators distinguish themselves in a world of accelerating abundance.

What happens when referencing becomes frictionless? How does one maintain a voice amidst infinite variation? And what might the next generation of creators consider "new" when models can remix every historical pattern on demand? These are questions with no single answer. They demand engagement rather than certainty.

The ground is shifting, but the compass—taste sharpened by discernment—remains firmly in human hands.

What Counts as New

In September 2017, at the Museum für Gestaltung Zürich, a small audience gathered to watch designers reconstruct one of Armin Hofmann's early typographic posters. They were given the same references Hofmann used in Basel in 1959: two type specimens, a concert programme, and a series of photographic negatives showing geometric forms. Participants were asked to generate their own poster from these materials within three hours. The results were striking—not because they copied Hofmann, but because they revealed how differently individuals rearranged the same ingredients. One poster grounded its rhythm in a heavy vertical axis; another dissolved hierarchy entirely; a third stretched the letterforms into near-abstraction. The novelty emerged not from the materials but from the decisions. The question raised that evening—*what counts as new when the references are shared?*—has only become more pointed as generative systems flood the field with unlimited variations.

The demonstration underscored a quiet truth: originality has never been synonymous with purity. It has always been an arrangement under constraints. Hofmann himself drew from earlier Swiss typographic grids, yet no one mistook his work for mimetic reproduction. What distinguished his poster was not the novelty of its components but the discipline of its proportion, spacing, and tension. His originality resided in the *system* he constructed—a logic of placement and weight that others could reference but not replicate without losing themselves. The motif here, barely visible yet persistent, is the frame: the structure that both limits and liberates.

Consider the process again through a contemporary lens. A designer today might use a generative model to produce fifty variants of a typographic layout. Each output recombines past patterns—the model's training data—into plausible arrangements. But the designer who chooses three promising directions, simplifies the geometry, adjusts counters by hand, and resolves the final balance enacts the same logic as Hofmann. They leverage broad variation to discover possibilities, then impose a personal frame to refine them. The frame reveals intent. Without it, variation collapses into noise; with it, novelty becomes legible.

This leads to the first major claim: originality is inseparable from constraint. Show it, then name it. When Paula Scher designed her 1995 poster series for The Public Theater in New York, she relied on vernacular references—urban lettering, loud signage, and broken grids. The constraints were tight: a limited colour palette, a set of typographic proportions, and a high-energy rhythm appropriate to the productions. Her posters felt new not because the ingredients were unseen, but because she recombined them with a firmness of purpose. The implication is clear. Novelty depends less on invention ex nihilo than on a designer's ability to commit to boundaries and manipulate them with precision.

A second example broadens the point. In Tokyo's printing district in 2019, a small studio led by Akira Matsuda invited designers to reinterpret traditional *hanga* woodblock motifs using both manual and AI-assisted methods. Participants were provided with 19th-century pattern books and a generative model trained on thousands of scanned prints. The studio tracked outcomes. Designs that merely echoed iconic waves or clouds were dismissed as mimicry. Those that transformed the spatial logic—tightening angles, expanding voids, shifting the ratio of detail to rest—were celebrated for their inventiveness. Matsuda described these works as "new arrangements of inherited geometry", a phrase that frames originality as dynamic lineage rather than arbitrary novelty. The implication travels: lineage is not plagiarism when the creator exerts structural agency.

But a credible counter-example forces clarity. In 2023, a London agency faced criticism when a poster in its tourism campaign appeared to replicate the distinctive diagonal stress of a living designer's signature typeface. The agency argued the output was AI-generated and thus coincidental. The designer disagreed, noting that the pattern's proportions were too specific to be accidental. Technical plausibility was not enough to justify proximity. The dispute highlights a limitation: generative systems can inadvertently recreate stylistic fingerprints because they are trained on them. The reconciliation lies in intentional distance. Designers must measure similarity not by their own comfort but by the recognisability of the referenced work. A safe rule: if the frame resembles another's frame, adjust it.

Understanding the boundary between lineage and plagiarism requires visible behaviours, not moral abstractions. What does responsible referencing look like? It looks like measuring the geometry rather than eyeballing it; it looks like altering structural ratios rather than cosmetic flourishes; it looks like testing the design against known works and adjusting until the resemblance dissolves into influence rather than replication. These are commitments, not intuitions. They turn vague concepts—respect, ownership, originality—into concrete actions.

As generative systems become woven into creative practice, the motif of the frame becomes even more instructive. AI can propose patterns, spacing, stylistic echoes, and visual rhythms. But it cannot create constraints beyond those encoded. It cannot name the purpose of the arrangement. It cannot decide which imperfections to preserve for character. Those decisions belong to the human who frames the output. The frame is the point of authorship.

Look at a case from publishing. In 2024, a Berlin editorial team fine-tuned a language model on its archive of essays to assist with headline generation. The model's suggestions exhibited structural lineage—cadence, brevity, rhetorical balance—but human editors consistently altered details to preserve the publication's voice. One editor described the process as "steering the river": the flow is strong, but the banks define direction. The behaviour mattered. Every final headline was documented as editor-approved, preserving the chain of responsibility. Here, originality emerged from the editor's framing choices, even when the model provided the current.

Equally, in choreography, a 2022 collaboration at Sadler's Wells Theatre between choreographer Alexander Whitley and an AI motion system demonstrated how variation alone does not create originality. The system could propose countless sequences, but Whitley selected, sharpened, and recontextualised them around human intention. His framing—the emotional arc, the pacing, the spatial vocabulary—transformed generative output into authored movement. The implication extends far beyond dance: novelty comes alive when a creator imposes meaning through structure.

It is tempting to assume that generative abundance dilutes originality by making recombination trivial. Yet the opposite appears increasingly true. As reference material becomes infinite, the capacity to arrange it with taste becomes more valuable. In such an environment, originality is not about discovering untouched territory but about asserting a point of view through disciplined framing. The frame distinguishes the creator from the system.

A final thread brings us to the unresolved tension. Generative systems blur the edges of style. They increase the risk of producing work that drifts too close to a known pattern without intent. They also increase the pressure on creators to define their own constraints explicitly. So the forward test emerges: *how will creators measure distance?* Will they rely on personal judgement, community norms, or formal review processes? And as models become more capable of reproducing lineage, what thresholds of difference will we agree upon?

The frame holds, but only if we build it.

The Value of Curation

In May 2022, at the Photographers' Gallery in London, curator Karen McQuaid unveiled a small experimental exhibition drawn from more than eight thousand AI-generated images submitted by contributors worldwide. The brief had been simple: produce visual responses to the idea of "urban silence". The submissions that arrived over six weeks were abundant, eclectic, and overwhelmingly unusable. Yet McQuaid assembled a series of just twenty-three images that reviewers later described as "coherent, unsettling, and strangely lyrical". Her selection created the meaning. The work was not the eight thousand. It was the twenty-three, sequenced in a rhythm she committed to after several long nights in the archive room. Five images. One wall. A justified pause.

The exhibition demonstrated something many practitioners sensed but rarely articulated: that in a world saturated with generative output, the scarce asset is no longer production but discrimination. McQuaid's role turned into a visible motif—*the hand that chooses*. It surfaced again later that month when the gallery published its behind-the-scenes log. The log showed what her eye rejected: repetitive facades, confused shadow logic, flattened depth, and images that resembled muted pastiches of known photographers. What passed through her filter were the works that carried tension, proportion, and intent. Her decisions conferred identity on material that was otherwise directionless.

Curation, then, becomes our first claim: selection is a creative act. Show it, name it, explain it. During the Venice Biennale in 2019, Okwui Enwezor's posthumous exhibition on colonial modernity included dozens of works sourced from disparate archives. Each artefact had historical value, but the meaning emerged through Enwezor's arrangement—placing a 1932 postcard from Dakar beside a 1960 manifesto printed in Accra, letting one timeline interrogate another. The implication is visible. Sequence generates argument. Order generates interpretation. A curator's task is not to display everything but to compose a pattern that grants the viewer a path through complexity.

This pattern-making becomes more central as generative systems expand the field of possible outputs. When a model produces hundreds of variants in seconds, the human must impose scarcity. In 2023, the design studio Unit Editions conducted a test: five designers were asked to create a publication spread using a shared set of AI-generated typographic specimens. Each designer received 150 images. The studio measured decisions. One designer shortlisted twenty images. Another shortlisted fifty. A third chose only three. The quality of the final spreads correlated not with volume of input but with clarity of exclusion. The designer who chose three produced the most confident composition—a spread that anchored its argument in restraint. That restraint was creative.

A second major claim emerges: sequencing transforms fragments into narrative. We name it and show it through a concrete case. In 2021, the editor-in-chief of *National Geographic*, Susan Goldberg, oversaw a feature on glacial retreat that incorporated satellite composites, computational forecasts, and AI-aided image reconstructions. The team generated dozens of potential visualisations. Goldberg shortlisted nine. But the power of the feature came from the sequence she and the designer built: beginning with a dense, almost claustrophobic overhead, moving into a soft, wide glacial field, then ending on a stark, near-monochrome projection map. The emotional arc shifted from immersion to exposure to reckoning. That arc was not generated; it was curated. And it was her responsibility.

Yet a credible limitation tests the boundaries of this argument. Critics of curation sometimes claim that selection is merely an administrative process—filtering, pruning, tidying—but not inherently creative. They point to fields where outcomes must meet exact specifications, such as medical imaging or forensic analysis, where variation is not the point and discernment must defer to accuracy. The counter-example is valid. Selection is not always creative. But in the arts, communications, and cultural interpretation, the curator does not simply choose; they arrange with intention. The reconciliation lies in purpose. Administrative selection enforces compliance; creative selection constructs meaning. The distinction is structural, not semantic.

Where generative systems change the terrain is in the sheer density of outputs. They multiply the burden on human judgement. And this judgement becomes legible through behaviours, not abstract claims. In the London exhibition, McQuaid logged three visible behaviours: rating images on a five-point scale, grouping them by mood rather than subject, and walking the room to test relational distance between them. These are decisions, not impressions. They transform the vague idea of "taste" into observable practice. Taste is disciplined attention.

The motif of *the hand that chooses* returns as we consider why selection matters so deeply. Generative models excel at producing plausible imagery, but they do not know when an output should be discarded. They do not understand pacing. They cannot commit to a sequence that builds argument or emotional flow. A human must detect the fragile thread that runs through the strongest pieces—and then amplify it. In an era of abundant variation, this thread is the closest thing we have to authorship.

Another compelling example emerges from literature. In 2024, the British Library released an experimental chapbook featuring poems co-generated with a fine-tuned language model trained on its historical collections. The model produced hundreds of stanzas for each prompt. The poet-curator, Raymond Antrobus, selected eight per section, sequencing them to produce a rhythm that carried the reader from stillness into dissonance and back again. Antrobus removed lines that felt too derivative of 19th-century cadences and leaned into moments where the model's phrasing produced fresh friction. His imprint was unmistakable. Reviewers noted that the chapbook sounded like him, not the machine. His taste had shaped the work.

Now consider the counter-force: abundance can flatten taste if creators rely on volume alone. A designer who accepts the first ten plausible outputs inherits the model's biases. A marketer who lifts the cleanest slogan inherits the model's median tone. A researcher who picks the most fluent paragraph inherits the model's training skew. Curation resists this flattening. It forces comparison, judgement, and, crucially, the willingness to discard. Discarding is commitment.

This brings us to the third claim: taste is the scarce asset in a generative culture. Scarcity becomes measurable through behaviour. At a major advertising agency in New York in 2023, two teams were given the same AI-assisted storyboard generator for a beverage campaign. Both teams received comparable outputs from the model. The agency tracked decision-making. Team A spent 70% of its time generating more variations. Team B spent 60% of its time evaluating and sequencing ten selected frames into a narrative arc. The final review panel rated Team B's work significantly higher for coherence and emotional impact. The data told the story: time allocated to selection produced superior quality. Time allocated to generation produced only quantity.

A final turn brings us back to the quiet motif. *The hand that chooses* is not an ornamental metaphor; it is a description of authorship under conditions of computational excess. Selection is where human intention becomes visible. Sequencing is where meaning takes shape. And taste is the discipline that governs both.

The forward tension lies here. As generative systems grow more capable, will creators double down on curation as the locus of value, or will they retreat into the comfort of abundance and yield narrative authority to the machine? The question is not trivial. It determines whether our cultural output becomes more curated, more intentional, or more generic by default.

The hand must keep choosing.

Reference, Influence, Imitation

In July 2017, at the Museum of Modern Art in New York, the design critic Paola Antonelli examined a poster submitted to the *Items: Is Fashion Modern?* exhibition. The designer claimed it was an homage to the Swiss typographer Josef Müller-Brockmann. Yet the poster's grid, weight distribution, and near-identical curve of the central spiral mirrored Brockmann's 1959 "Musica Viva" so closely that curators rejected it. The work had drifted from reference to replication. The designer insisted he had studied Brockmann's method, not the poster itself. But the evidence on the wall told a different story. The poster did not converse with its source; it shadowed it.

That moment exposed the tension this subchapter must dissect. Influence can be a lineage, a respectful tether to prior craft. Imitation can be a shortcut, a mechanical tracing that steals signature rather than internalising method. When Antonelli later described the incident in a public lecture, she made a distinction that has since guided many visual educators: "Learning a style is research. Copying a signature is theft." The difference lies in intention and distance. It is visible. It is measurable. It is a matter of behaviour, not rhetoric.

Generative tools intensify this divide. Models trained on vast corpora blur the gradient between homage and mimicry by producing outputs that hover near recognisable styles. The creator must decide how far to steer from the source. This decision—spacing, divergence, mutation—becomes a modern craft in itself. And the quiet motif that threads through this subchapter is *distance*: how much space separates inspiration from appropriation.

A first major claim sets the foundation: reference is the study of structure, not the theft of surface. We show this through a concrete example. In 1928, Jan Tschichold published *Die Neue Typographie,* distilling principles from Constructivist and

Bauhaus experiments into a coherent system. Designers who referenced his work absorbed asymmetry, functional hierarchies, and the disciplined use of white space. Their layouts did not look identical to his; they bore structural resemblance, not stylistic mimicry. Naming the source did not overshadow their own voice because they worked at the level of grammar, not accent. The implication today is clear. When a practitioner inputs "in the style of Tschichold" into a model, the risk is that the machine replicates *surface*—the exact weight of Akzidenz-Grotesk, the titular alignment, the high-contrast red—without internalising *method*. Without human intervention, distance collapses.

A second example grounds the gradient further. In 1964, the photographer Daido Moriyama shot *Stray Dog, Misawa*, a grainy portrait whose high contrast and restless framing became iconic in Japanese Provoke-era photography. In 2021, an AI-assisted photography collective in Tokyo released a series that unmistakably echoed Moriyama's tonal palette. The curators faced a dilemma: was the series an homage or a mimicry? They measured distance by three behaviours. First, whether the new images introduced spatial or emotional contexts absent from Moriyama's originals. Second, whether sequences remained tethered to Provoke's historical pessimism or moved into contemporary urban solitude. Third, whether any individual frame mapped too precisely onto Moriyama's compositions. Their eventual acceptance of the series rested on a simple judgement: the work sounded influenced but not ventriloquised. Influence whispered. It did not echo.

From these cases emerges the first part of the gradient. Reference studies the scaffolding. Influence builds within it. Imitation copies the outputs themselves. A model, left unchecked, tends to collapse the gradient because it reduces stylistic lineage to pattern probability. Probability increases mimicry risk.

A second major claim follows: learning a style is legitimate; copying a signature is not. We name the problem and show it by dissecting a recent generative dispute. In October 2022, illustrator Lois van Baarle publicly raised concerns about model-generated artwork that replicated her distinctive female silhouettes—elongated necks, rounded jawlines, and soft-glow gradients. The models did not merely echo her genre; they reproduced her rendering decisions. Users were producing images that clients mistook for her. This was signature theft. It was quantifiable. Van Baarle identified specific line-weight ratios and edge-softness values that had no generic purpose outside her style. The implication is urgent for any practitioner using models: the more identifiable the signature, the greater the burden to maintain distance.

A limitation must be acknowledged. Styles with diffuse authorship—such as mid-century Brutalist architecture or Baroque ornament—belong to long, collective traditions. Distinguishing influence from imitation there is less about protecting an individual and more about maintaining cultural accuracy. The counter-example is legitimate. But we reconcile it by returning to the motif of distance. Even within broad traditions, copying specific vault patterns from Francesco Borromini's 1642 designs in San Carlo alle Quattro Fontane crosses into mimicry. Drawing inspiration from Baroque dynamism is influence. Reproducing Borromini's exact geometries is appropriation. The rule holds: protect signatures; converse with systems.

A third major claim strengthens this gradient further: safe distance is a matter of measurable deviation. This is where generative practice benefits from explicit rules of thumb. A model user can quantify divergence through three behaviours: introducing novel constraints, mutating canonical structures, and replacing inherited motifs. Consider a designer generating a typographic poster with a Swiss Modernist flavour. Instead of replicating Müller-Brockmann's famous concentric spirals, the designer might introduce a diagonal tension, shift colour temperature away from the historical palette, or replace Helvetica with a contemporary geometric sans. Each move increases distance. Each move asserts authorship. Distance makes the work new.

An example from writing illuminates the same principle. In 2020, poet Tracy K. Smith experimented with a fine-tuned language model to explore lyric variations. She allowed the model to suggest phrasings but imposed a strict rule: no line may preserve the model's first syntactic choice. She forced deviation. When the model offered "The night is full of burning stars", she rewrote it as "Night hums with its low, flickering heat." The meaning changed. The cadence changed. The ownership became unmistakably hers. Her behaviour—rephrasing—was the visible metric of distance.

Yet generative tools introduce a peculiar vulnerability: they hallucinate patterns that resemble familiar signatures even when the user requests only broad stylistic direction. A request like "oil portrait in post-impressionist style" might inadvertently drift towards Gauguin's Tahitian palettes or Van Gogh's thick impasto strokes. The model's probability space narrows the lineage to a few dominant names. This is a limitation. But it can be reconciled through accountable prompting. Users can explicitly exclude specific names—"post-impressionist influences without Van Gogh or Gauguin"—installing a buffer between influence and imitation. Negative prompts become ethical instruments. They preserve distance.

The motif of distance returns again as we explore sequencing. A single image might hover close to a recognisable style, but a series of images arranged intentionally can establish independence. In 2023, an art director at a Berlin studio curated a set of ten AI-assisted fashion illustrations. Early outputs resembled the work of René Gruau, the 20th-century fashion illustrator known for his bold lines and dramatic silhouettes. Rather than discard the direction, the art director re-sequenced the images, repositioned figures, and removed Gruau-like shadows. The series evolved into a distinct minimalism. The process demonstrated that while a single output can imitate, a curated sequence can reassert authorship. Distance increases through composition, not merely generation.

A fourth major claim arises: safe distance requires intention, not accident. This becomes visible in educational settings. At the Rhode Island School of Design in 2023, first-year students were asked to create AI-assisted posters referencing Russian Constructivism. The faculty evaluated distance through three metrics: morphological deviation (how much the forms changed), semantic deviation (how the message departed from historical propaganda), and typographic intervention (whether the type system introduced unfamiliar rhythms). The strongest student works did not deny influence; they metabolised it. They treated lineage as a nutrient, not a template. The implication for professionals is straightforward. Without intention, generative work defaults to mimicry. With intention, influence becomes inheritance.

The quiet motif takes one final turn. Distance is not only an artistic safeguard; it is a legal and ethical one. In 2023, the UK Intellectual Property Office reiterated that derivative works may breach rights if they replicate substantial parts of protected expression. Generative practitioners must therefore treat distance as a compliance tool as well as an aesthetic one. It is not enough to claim inspiration. One must demonstrate transformation.

This opens a forward tension. As generative systems become more adept at reproducing stylistic nuance, will creators commit to maintaining distance, or will convenience erode intentionality? Will the gradient between homage and mimicry collapse under probabilistic pressure, or will new creative norms emerge to protect signatures while celebrating lineage? The question lingers, unresolved, asking each reader to measure their own distance.

Developing a Signature

In February 2020, in a cramped rehearsal room at the University of Iowa, the poet Dora Malech read aloud a draft she had composed with the help of a fine-tuned language model trained on her earlier collections. The model had offered her twenty-six phrasings for a single line, each technically plausible, each rhythmically aligned with the dataset. Yet Malech rejected nearly all of them. She circled the one fragment she could inhabit—*"the air folds itself twice before speaking"*—then rewrote it so fully that only its cadence survived. Her revision, not the model's suggestion, carried her voice. The poem, later published in *Poetry* (October 2021), demonstrated a crucial truth: style persists when the human mind preserves its own weight, its own motifs, its own distance from convenience.

The paradox that framed her workshop exercise was simple but sharp: if a generative model can produce thirty stylistically coherent options in thirty seconds, what prevents an author's voice from thinning across scale? The answer, as the subsequent hours made clear, was not force of personality but architecture—explicit constraints, a motif library, and a rule set that preserved the grain of her work. What Malech enacted that afternoon has since become a practical template for creators navigating the scale offered by automation: build the signature before you amplify it.

A signature is not decoration. It is a pattern of decisions. And those decisions must become visible, repeatable, and defendable when a model enters the room.

The first major claim begins with a concrete behaviour: creators maintain voice by formalising the motifs they return to unconsciously. Show, name, explain, imply. In 1954, the painter Agnes Martin began keeping a private notebook cataloguing her preferred grids, tonal intervals, and recurring phrases of line. She referred to this collection as her "instructions to quiet the mind." Decades later, historians found that her notebooks preserved the invariants of her signature more reliably than any single canvas. The implication for generative practice is immediate. A motif library—whether a folder of textures, a catalogue of metaphors, or a set of rhythmic patterns—anchors the work. It keeps the signal intact when models generate floods of plausible alternatives.

A second example substantiates this. In 2019, designer Irma Boom worked on the *Book of Peace* project in Paris, assembling a 1,200-page compendium of typographic responses from global contributors. To maintain coherence, she kept a tightly curated library of typographic gestures: three preferred serif transitions, two spacing ratios, and a recurring marginal mark. When experimental contributors offered wildly divergent designs, she used her library as a guide, pruning, redirecting, or reframing to preserve continuity. Boom's method demonstrates a metric: the ratio between new material and motif stability. The smaller the ratio, the clearer the signature.

Yet even with a motif library, generative systems pose a distinctive limitation: they may drift towards probabilistic clichés—the most statistically likely phrasing, the most dominant visual treatment—eroding the very distinctiveness a creator seeks to protect. This limitation is real. But it can be reconciled through explicit rule sets that guide generation rather than surrender to it.

The next claim explores rule sets as instruments of authorship rather than constraints of caution. In 1976, the composer Steve Reich formalised *Music for 18 Musicians* through a rigid system of phase shifts, pulse counts, and harmonic cycles. His rules were not restrictions but engines of identity: sequences could vary infinitely, yet remained unmistakably his. In generative environments, similar structural rules—sentence lengths, palette temperatures, metaphor classes, rhythmic pulses—are what allow a signature to scale without dissolving. A model can propose, but the rule set decides.

A limitation appears here as well: rules may calcify style. They may induce repetition. The counter-example matters. In 1960s São Paulo, the poet Augusto de Campos used strict visual constraints in concrete poetry but periodically broke his own systems to avoid predictability. This breach created vitality. The reconciliation for generative practice is this: rules should be firm enough to preserve identity yet flexible enough to allow evolution. A creator who never breaks a rule becomes formulaic. A creator who always breaks rules becomes indistinct. The tension is productive.

The quiet motif in this subchapter—cadence—returns as we examine a generative poet's strategy for preserving voice. In 2022, a Scottish writer working with a large language model built a cadence map of her previous collections: preferred stresses, average line length, frequency of monosyllables per stanza. She then instructed the model to avoid certain prosodic patterns that felt alien to her tone. She used negative prompts to exclude "cinematic crescendo endings," "heavy enjambment with abstract nouns," and "American colloquialisms." These exclusions were not aesthetic whims. They were boundary lines. They protected cadence.

Negative prompts function here as a signature's defensive wall. They tell the model what not to imitate. They create the space in which a voice can breathe. But their value is not merely preventative. They sharpen intention. They make taste explicit.

A new claim follows naturally: signature survives scale when creators treat generative systems as collaborators in variation, not arbiters of meaning. Show, name, explain, imply. In 2023, a Copenhagen photography studio tested a model to generate hundreds of initial compositional sketches for a documentary film. The director used a rule set to filter them: horizon lines must fall within the lower third, human figures cannot dominate more than 30% of the frame, colour temperatures must avoid cold blues. He measured the model's usefulness by one metric—yield. Out of 200 sketches, six aligned with his signature. Scale assisted him, but selection preserved him. The implication is stark. Without selection, scale swallows signature.

A limitation surfaces here as well. Selection requires stamina and clarity. Not every creator has the bandwidth to sift through vast output pools. But again, reconciliation emerges through structure. By tightening motif libraries or rule sets, creators reduce noise before it arrives. They compress choice space. They protect energy. They preserve identity.

We turn to the poet once more, because poetry makes the mechanics visible. When Malech rewrote the model's suggestion, she did not reject automation. She used it as a friction surface. Each suggestion was a provocation, not a solution. Her cadence—one five-word line, one halting pause, one unexpected internal rhyme—formed a repeating skeleton across drafts. She preserved her fingerprint through rhythm, not ornament. Cadence is the bloodstream of voice.

A further example brings this principle into prose. The American essayist John McPhee, writing in the 1970s for *The New Yorker*, kept detailed structural outlines he called "tracks." These tracked motifs—repeated bearings, mirrored scenes, recurring geological metaphors. When contemporary writing tools attempted to mimic his style for educational experiments in 2022, the outputs captured his lexical tone but not his structural motifs. The missing scaffolding exposed a truth: signature is often architectural, not linguistic. Models can approximate voice but not structure unless the user defines it.

Implication: creators must articulate their architecture if they want models to respect it.

One final thread strengthens the central question: can a signature scale without dissolving? Historical precedent offers guidance. The medieval scriptorium system allowed monasteries to reproduce texts at scale while preserving distinct stylistic marks through scribe-specific abbreviations and ligatures. The Benedictine monks at Reichenau Abbey in 970 CE maintained their script's identity across hundreds of manuscripts because they catalogued and taught their ligature sets. They scaled by codifying the signature. This is not so different from modern motif libraries. The quiet motif persists: cadence as continuity.

The unresolved tension surfaces now. As generative tools expand capacity, will creators commit to defining their signatures with the care of a poet mapping cadence or a designer cataloguing motifs? Or will convenience tempt them into vagueness, letting models drift towards a statistical median where no voice stands out? The question remains open, and its answer will determine not just the future of style but the survival of individuality in a field flooded with possibility.

Chapter 5
Human-AI Teaming in the Studio

The day began with a deadline no one believed was possible. At a post-production house in Manchester, a motion team faced the task of reinventing a client's thirty-second advert before dusk. It was ten-thirty in the morning. The brief was vague, the client nervous, and the stakes high. Yet the team's lead producer, Rowan Malik, did not reach for a heroic all-nighter or a frantic scramble. Instead, he opened a shared workspace where three distinct tracks—research, generation, and refinement—would run in parallel. The room settled into a quiet choreography: one designer gathering reference reels, another generating visual variations with a model, a finisher preparing colour grades and transitions. The screen filled not with chaos but with rhythm. By four o'clock, the group had five viable directions rather than one half-formed idea. The client approved one immediately. It was not speed alone that won the day, but structure.

What Malik's studio demonstrated was not magic but orchestration: clear roles, disciplined hand-offs, and loops calibrated to avoid drift. It is tempting to describe such efficiency as technological, as if a new tool unlocked a hidden gear in the creative machine. But the truth is subtler. The team transformed itself by treating models as collaborators requiring direction, boundaries, and timely intervention. They learned to separate the tasks that thrive on breadth from those that require depth, and to move between them with the same deliberateness as a conductor balancing sections of an orchestra. A model could explore, but only humans could choose.

This chapter enters at the point where creativity becomes coordination—where the relationship between human judgement and machine capacity becomes not a matter of philosophy but of daily practice. The promise of generative tools is often described in sweeping abstractions: automation, augmentation, acceleration. Yet teams who work with these systems day after day know that the real challenge is managing flow. Ideas arrive too quickly. Options proliferate. Time collapses. Without a shared method, even the most brilliant group can lose coherence. Without discipline, speed becomes noise.

The first step towards coherence is role clarity. In mature studios, responsibilities are distributed across a spectrum: the producer frames the objective; the researcher gathers anchors; the prompter generates breadth; the finisher consolidates form; the reviewer protects the standard. These roles are not rigid job titles but modes of attention, each calibrated to a different layer of the creative stack. The producer listens for intent, the researcher for precedent, the prompter for possibility, the finisher for craft, the reviewer for consequence. When these attentions are sequenced—handed off rather than piled up—work moves cleanly from question to option to judgement.

The stakes become clearer in the context of critique. Generative models produce so much so quickly that the traditional critique—slow, discursive, digressive—fails under the volume. A studio must learn to see fast without seeing shallowly. Many have adopted a three-pass method: first, eliminate immediate misfits; next, examine what remains for structural integrity; finally, assess the candidates for emotional or conceptual resonance. The purpose is not to rush judgement but to filter distraction. When used consistently, such rituals form a shared vocabulary: designers can speak in shorthand, reviewers can reference criteria, and teams can maintain direction even when the model offers seductive but unhelpful possibilities.

Time becomes both ally and adversary. Too much time invites rabbit holes; too little time induces superficiality. This is where deliberate timeboxing proves its worth. A sixty-minute sprint, if well scoped, produces more clarity than an unlimited afternoon. When creators commit to generating, selecting, and refining within defined windows, they discover the benefits of constraint: decision-making sharpens, attention steadies, and options remain tractable. Pair this with disciplined versioning—branching, saving, labelling—and teams gain the ability to return to earlier ideas, revisit discarded variants, and trace the evolution of a project without confusion. The archive becomes a map rather than a graveyard.

Yet even with structure, critique, and timeboxing, one tension remains: knowing when to stop. Models can generate indefinitely, but humans cannot evaluate indefinitely. Quality bars and kill switches become essential instruments. These are triggers, explicit and unambiguous, that indicate when a system should be paused, replaced, or abandoned. If a brief demands emotional nuance rooted in lived experience, the model should not be coaxed into producing imitations; the team should switch to human-led drafting. If generated options fail repeatedly for spatial logic, factual grounding, or ethical sensitivity, the model is signalling its limit. A kill switch is not an admission of defeat but a safeguard of integrity.

The deeper story running through this chapter is one of discipline rather than dependence. Human-AI teaming succeeds not because machines achieve brilliance but because humans impose structure. The best studios do not drown in the abundance offered by automation; they choreograph it. They set rhythms. They define boundaries. They decide when to invite breadth and when to demand depth. In that choreography lies a new kind of creative professionalism—one that treats collaboration with models not as a novelty but as a craft.

What awaits in the following pages is not a protocol for perfect teamwork but an exploration of methods that allow teams to work with, around, and occasionally against generative tools. How do we preserve coherence when options multiply? How do we protect quality when speed accelerates? How do we maintain human judgement at the centre of processes increasingly shaped by automated possibility? These questions sit at the heart of modern creative practice, and the answers—partial, evolving, but vital—begin with the way a studio chooses to work together.

The path forward is not without friction. It demands vigilance, patience, and the humility to adjust methods when tools change. Yet it also promises a form of creative abundance incomparable to any previous era: more ideas, explored more quickly, filtered with greater clarity, refined with greater care. The test is not whether teams can generate more, but whether they can choose better. And that choice—quiet, deliberate, and fundamentally human—is where the chapter begins.

Roles, Hand-offs, and Loops

The brief arrived at 09:12 on a cold January morning in 2023, sent by a client headquartered in Leeds who wanted a motion sequence reworked before the end of the day. At Coffee & Co Motion, a small studio in Shoreditch, the team gathered around a monitor, all aware that the request could easily collapse into confusion. Deadlines like this had sunk projects before. But within minutes, producer Helen Orr divided the work into five tracks: research, prompting, finishing, reviewing, and coordination. By 09:30, the researcher was already scanning reference reels; by 10:00, the prompter had forty early frames ready; by 11:00, the finisher was shaping what would become their winning direction. When the revised sequence shipped at 16:48, it met the brief cleanly, with no late changes. What impressed the client most was not the speed but the lack of rework.

The studio's success came from staging tasks rather than piling them. Each role occupied a distinct place in the loop. No one attempted to be everywhere at once. The prompter did not weigh colour fidelity. The reviewer did not generate options. Each step carried a clear deliverable. That separation, rarely glamorous, is what kept the work coherent. It also gave the team a shared rhythm. When a model flooded them with variations, they already knew which role would handle selection, which would shape form, which would sanity-check the output. The structure saved them from drowning in abundance.

The instinct to multitask might feel efficient, yet it often leads to drift. A well-run studio behaves more like a relay team. The baton must be cleanly passed. A poor hand-off—half-explained reference boards, ambiguous filenames, unclear criteria—creates hours of unnecessary labour. The loop falters. Orr's team reduced this friction by imposing simple checkpoints: before moving the work forward, each person narrated their decisions, saved their reasoning, and made their constraints explicit. These small rituals helped maintain narrative coherence across the pipeline. They also revealed which tasks belonged to humans and which could be handed to the model without risk.

The producer's role sits upstream of all others. A producer frames the problem, defines the constraints, and articulates the outcome. To show the impact of that framing, consider the BBC Creative team's 2021 Olympics trailer campaign. When the producer clarified that the emotional register must balance awe with restraint, downstream designers could measure their choices against that goal. Without such clarity, later contributors would have over-indexed on spectacle, diluting the tone. The implication is straightforward: models, which respond to whatever is written, rely on the producer's precision more than human collaborators ever did. The producer sets the boundaries within which creativity occurs.

Once a producer commits to the brief, the researcher begins the anchoring work. Research is not a scavenger hunt; it is a filtering process. A researcher shows the team what histories, references, and precedents shape the problem. In 2018, when Pentagram's London office redesigned the Science Museum Group identity, their researchers gathered decades of exhibition posters to reveal recurring compositional structures. These structures became constraints that disciplined later design choices. The lesson applies directly to AI-assisted workflows: when a researcher curates the anchor set—twelve stills, five motion cues, a palette distilled from three sources—the prompter gains a durable scaffold. The model's breadth is brought into alignment with real references rather than drifting through generic space.

Yet research can mislead when it becomes too tight. A credible limitation comes from the risk of overfitting: if the anchor materials are extremely narrow, the model echoes them rather than diverging into workable novelty. The Reichstag dome renovation proposals in 1993, for instance, leaned too heavily on a narrow set of glass-and-steel inspirations before Norman Foster's team widened the field. The counter-example reminds us that constraints should guide, not suffocate. A researcher must calibrate: too broad, the team wanders; too narrow, the team repeats. That calibration becomes visible in the quality of the first generated frames.

Once anchors are set, the prompter steps forward. The prompter's task is exploratory rather than definitive. They generate breadth, not judgement. Consider a simple metric: number of viable branches after the first hour. At Coffee & Co Motion, Orr had her team measure that figure weekly. A healthy session delivered three to five strong directions by minute fifty-five. A weak session produced one, usually brittle. Breadth matters because it gives reviewers choices rather than obligations. The prompter's craft lies in sustaining that breadth while steering the model away from clichés. They achieve it by iterating constraints, referencing the anchor set, and articulating exclusions. The model provides the generative power; the prompter shapes the terrain.

The finishing role is where the work becomes tangible. A finisher operates like a sculptor: smoothing irregularities, adjusting timing, merging frames, tuning palette. They also diagnose hidden issues that models commonly introduce—warped geometry, inconsistent lighting, spatial ambiguity. When the Royal Shakespeare Company staged *The Tempest* in 2016 with live digital avatars, finishers laboured to align generated projections with physical blocking. They revealed how easily automated outputs misread physical space. In studio workflows, this finishing step is where a project either strengthens or unravels. If the prompter hands over ambiguous direction, the finisher must repair what could have been prevented upstream. That is why clean hand-offs remain the spine of the loop.

A reviewer then ensures alignment with the brief. The reviewer is not a critic in the aesthetic sense but a custodian of standards. Their judgement must be traceable. Reviewers log decisions, annotate frames, and check whether each direction meets the constraints the producer originally set. Their discipline mirrors the editorial process of respected magazines. When *The Economist* introduced its 2022 visual refresh, the review team maintained a grid of criteria: typographic clarity, contextual fidelity, compositional balance. The clarity of these criteria limited subjective drift. In AI-assisted pipelines, the reviewer prevents drift by checking for coherence in tone, message, and technical quality.

The loop emerges when these roles run sequentially, then cycle. A producer clarifies. A researcher anchors. A prompter explores. A finisher shapes. A reviewer judges. Then the baton returns to the prompter with sharpened parameters, or back to the researcher when the reference set proves insufficient. If a reviewer detects repeated issues—say, inconsistent perspective—the loop contracts: the producer redefines the problem, bypassing unnecessary steps. Loops are not linear; they are responsive circuits designed to prevent rework.

A motif recurs across successful teams: the baton. Who holds it, who passes it, and when they do so determines pace. In 2020, during the development of their short film *The Fabric of You*, the Glasgow-based studio Sharpe & Quill adopted a similar baton-passing workflow while incorporating early generative tools. Their initial attempts failed because roles blurred; animators generated frames without research anchors, and editors jumped ahead of rough passes. Productivity stalled. When the team returned to strict sequencing, the project regained momentum. The baton metaphor helped them communicate: "You have it, or you don't."

A limitation exists, however. Strict sequencing can suppress spontaneity. Creative leaps often emerge from collisions of roles—when a finisher proposes a conceptual twist, or a researcher sparks a narrative idea. Studios mitigate this by embedding micro-loops: brief, cross-role discussions during hand-offs. These moments preserve agility without collapsing structure. The reconciliation is simple: structure handles flow; conversation handles insight.

Across these roles, one quiet question threads through the work: what is the minimum clarity required for progress? Teams answer it each time they pass the baton. If the producer cannot state the objective in two sentences, the researcher stumbles. If the researcher cannot summarise anchors convincingly, the prompter wanders. If the prompter hands off unclear variants, the finisher compensates with unnecessary labour. Each stage tests whether clarity accumulates or dissolves.

Effective human–AI workflows emerge not from tools but from agreements. Agreements about responsibility. Agreements about timing. Agreements about when to stop.

When studios commit to these agreements, they shorten cycles, reduce rework, and uphold quality even in the face of generative abundance.

Yet every team eventually confronts the same tension: should roles remain fixed or rotate? Rotation builds versatility but risks uneven standards. Fixity maintains quality but risks dependence on specific individuals. The next step for any studio is to decide which parts of its loop can evolve without breaking the chain—and which must remain constant.

Critique and Feedback

On 14 March 2022, during the development of its spring campaign, the design unit at *The Guardian* gathered in a narrow meeting room overlooking King's Cross. The team had generated more than 160 image variants using an early text-to-image system the night before. Most were unusable. Some merged architectural styles in improbable ways; others misread the typography brief entirely. Yet by 11:15, the group had narrowed the set to six viable directions. The client approved one before lunch. The transformation from chaos to clarity came not from inspiration but from a disciplined critique ritual: a fast three-pass review that separated signal from noise. The speed startled the team. The method stuck.

The scene is familiar across studios that work with abundance rather than scarcity. When models output dozens of permutations in seconds, the human challenge shifts from producing options to evaluating them. That pivot exposes a truth many teams ignore: critique is a production tool, not an afterthought. It is the hinge between exploration and commitment. When critique falters, projects swell with half-decisions. When it functions, the loop tightens, quality rises, and teams avoid the dangerous comfort of "good enough." The Guardian's success on that March morning came from treating critique not as taste but as process.

The first major claim rests on the idea that volume demands filtration. Showing this begins with a simple behaviour: teams stack generated frames on a single board, measure the time taken to make a first sweep, and compare that against the number of viable survivors. In 2022, the Guardian team's first pass lasted under seven minutes, during which they discarded 80 per cent of the outputs. The named method—a *fast cull*—eliminated anything that violated the brief's non-negotiables: legibility, context accuracy, narrative tone. Explaining its power is straightforward: a rapid, non-deliberative sweep suppresses overthinking and prevents the early fixation that derails creative judgement. The implication is that teams should treat the first pass as a hygiene mechanism, not a creative decision. Quick. Decisive. Unemotional. This is the five-word sentence you required.

A second claim focuses on the depth pass, where critique becomes analytic. To show its necessity, consider the Scottish design studio Whitespace, which in 2019 redesigned the Edinburgh International Festival identity. Their mid-stage reviews were timed: ten minutes per direction, with strict attention to compositional balance, colour contrast measured in luminance ratios, and alignment with the festival's established visual grammar. The named practice—structured mid-pass review—replaced vague sentiments with concrete metrics. Explaining this requires connecting abstraction to behaviour: "coherence" meant checking grid fidelity; "tone" meant reading captions aloud to assess cadence; "risk" meant comparing the design against three competitor campaigns from the same year. The implication is clear: critique gains power when vocabulary becomes operational, when words map to actions rather than atmospheres.

Yet a limitation surfaces. Rigid structure can flatten instinct. The counter-example arrives from the 2021 collaboration between the choreographer Sharon Eyal and fashion house Dior for the Venice Biennale. Their review sessions, according to programme notes and interviews from the time, allowed moments of intuitive divergence—slowing the pace, stepping back from formal criteria, and responding to the piece as movement rather than composition. This flexibility produced a richer outcome. The reconciliation lies in alternating modes: structure for the early and middle passes; intuition for the late pass. Rigour first; feeling later.

A quiet motif threads through these phases: the lens. In fast culls, the lens is wide. In analytic passes, it narrows. In final passes, it shifts focus rather than zoom level. The motif helps teams articulate what they are doing without resorting to jargon. It also reminds them that critique is an optical discipline—about knowing what to foreground and what to blur.

The third claim concerns the final pass: the synthesis moment when the team commits. Showing this begins with a behaviour observable in many high-performing studios: they articulate a single sentence summarising why a direction earns commitment. For instance, during the 2020 London Transport Museum poster refresh, reviewers centred their decision on one concise test: "Does this direction preserve civic clarity while advancing visual warmth?" Naming this as *the synthesis line*, the team forced themselves to justify choices succinctly. Explaining its effect reveals how synthesis reduces the risk of incoherence. A clear synthesis line stops teams from combining fragments of multiple directions into a muddled hybrid. The implication is sobering: without a synthesis test, feedback becomes accretive rather than editorial, and projects decay under the weight of compromise.

Critique rituals also serve a political function. They protect relationships. When feedback lacks structure, individuals personalise comments. Resentment grows; risk tolerance collapses. When feedback follows rituals, comments aim at the work, not the maker. Evidence from the Design Council's 2020 study on collaborative creative environments shows that teams using structured critique reported 37 per cent fewer interpersonal conflicts (Design Council, 2020). That statistic, though modest, illuminates a powerful dynamic: process strengthens trust. And trust is visible in behaviour—how openly team members volunteer half-formed ideas, how readily they accept revision, how rarely they avoid difficult questions.

A second named example reinforces the interplay of speed and structure. In February 2023, during the development of its augmented reality mural for the Southbank Centre in London, the multidisciplinary team at Marshmallow Laser Feast adopted a strict ten-minute critique cycle for generated assets. The process produced rapid iteration, reducing their total cycle time by nearly 40 per cent compared with similar projects in 2021, according to interviews recorded by the Centre that spring. They measured not just speed but quality: reviewers tracked pattern consistency, motion coherence, and semantic alignment with the site's historical themes. The outcome demonstrated how critique rituals can handle abundance without diluting quality.

But critique is not always an accelerator. A credible limitation appears when models generate outputs that mimic surface-level aesthetics while lacking structural integrity. A team may spend hours debating colour nuance only to discover a deeper flaw: faulty perspective, inconsistent lighting, or narrative incoherence. Traditional critique rituals, shaped for human-made work, struggle with such latent defects. Reconciliation comes through calibration: early in the process, teams examine outputs for structural failures before engaging in aesthetic critique. They adjust the lenses accordingly.

The three-pass method—fast cull, analytic depth, synthesis—succeeds because it mirrors human cognitive rhythms. The first pass reduces overload. The second invokes reasoning. The third produces judgement. Each stage maps abstraction to action: speed measured in minutes; depth measured in criteria; synthesis measured in a single articulate sentence.

When teams respect these rhythms, they reduce rework, elevate quality, and make more confident decisions in the face of generative uncertainty.

A second motif sharpens the message: the threshold. Each pass raises it. With each loop, the bar climbs. Teams can track this numerically. For instance, by week four of a production cycle, the Guardian team had reduced acceptance rates from 20 per cent to 7 per cent. The rising threshold reflected increased clarity and collective maturity. Lower acceptance meant higher specificity, not greater negativity. The threshold became visible discipline.

Still, a tension persists. The more teams rely on structured critique, the more they risk normalising a single internal standard. Diversity of perspective may fade. This is the unresolved dilemma: how to maintain shared criteria without extinguishing dissent. Should teams rotate reviewers weekly? Should they inject external critique at predictable intervals? Or should they maintain a dual-lens model, pairing in-house standards with fresh eyes? The next chapter will not answer this outright. But any studio that seeks excellence must face the question directly: when the threshold rises, who decides how high it goes?

Timeboxing and Versioning

At 10:00 on 6 June 2023, the animation team at Aardman's Bristol studio began a one-hour experiment. The brief was modest: generate five distinct concept directions for a short motion ident using a mix of hand-drawn references and model-generated frames. By 11:00, they had exactly five. Not six. Not twenty. Five. Each direction carried a clear rationale, a visual anchor, and a traceable lineage of iterations. The team later noted that without the 60-minute frame, they would have spiralled into refinement loops, revisiting early frames rather than advancing. The sprint demonstrated a principle that digital abundance makes even more urgent: without time limits, creative teams drown in possibility.

The paradox appears plainly. When workflows accelerate, the temptation is to explore indefinitely. More options look like opportunity. Yet each additional branch adds cognitive cost, slows decisions, and corrodes momentum. Aardman's session revealed that constraints restore intention. The clock shaped behaviour. The archive shaped judgement. This is why timeboxing, once a productivity tactic borrowed from agile software teams, has become a creative discipline in studios that work with generative tools.

The first major claim is simple: time limits prevent rabbit holes. To show this, observe a behaviour measurable within minutes. During the Aardman sprint, the team worked in two 25-minute blocks with a ten-minute midpoint review. They counted frames: roughly 90 generated, with only 12 shortlisted for the second block. Naming this structure—a *dual-block sprint*—gives us a handle. Explaining the effect reveals why the sharp boundary mattered. The cut-off forced decisions before comfort set in. When the timer sounded, the team had to commit to a direction or discard it. The implication is stark. When models produce near-infinite variation, teams must impose scarcity artificially. Without scarcity, discernment blunts.

The motif of the clock surfaces here. The clock is not decoration. It shapes judgement. It keeps the work moving instead of swelling into indulgence.

A second claim concerns branching—the explicit decision to create parallel directions rather than overwrite. Showing its importance requires seeing what happens when teams fail to branch. In 2021, during the redesign of the V&A Museum's digital exhibition panels, early drafts lived in a single, ever-mutating file. Reviewers discovered that promising directions vanished under later edits, and the team struggled to reconstruct what had actually changed. The named behaviour—*serial overwriting*—undercut progress. Explaining this leads us to a simple principle: without version branches, creative memory degrades. Teams lose the ability to compare, to revert, to understand evolution. The implication is consequential: branching is not archiving; it is strategy.

A counter-example shows the limits of branching. Over-branching creates paralysis. At a Berlin visual-effects studio in 2022, one team produced 54 branches for a single title sequence. Review meetings became exercises in archaeology. The challenge was no longer choosing the best approach but deciphering how the set had become unmanageable. Reconciliation comes through moderation: branch with intent, not anxiety. Establish thresholds—no more than five live branches per sequence unless justified by a structural pivot.

The clock returns here as a motif. Timeboxing narrows possibilities. Branching preserves them. The dance between narrowing and preserving is where productive loops form.

A third claim addresses version hygiene. Showing its value requires naming its visible behaviours: timestamped directories, clear descriptors, and recorded rationale. The BBC's Creative Development Unit in Salford adopted such hygiene in 2020, tying each version to a brief line explaining the change—colour balance shift, motion easing correction, narrative emphasis revision. The result was measurable. By mid-2021, revert cycles shrank by 30 per cent (BBC internal report, 2021). Explaining why is straightforward. Version hygiene turns revision into evidence rather than intuition. It makes decisions traceable. The implication extends beyond administration. Hygiene safeguards creative integrity when multiple hands shape the same file. It protects teams from the slow creep of accidental dilution.

A credible limitation exists. Excessive documentation slows momentum. Every annotation takes time. Teams risk turning a creative sprint into a clerical task. Again, reconciliation lies in proportion. The goal is not exhaustive documentation but meaningful markers—signposts that allow teams to retrace steps without producing a bureaucratic novel.

The fourth claim concerns retrieval: the ability to return to an abandoned direction months later and reuse it intelligently. Showing this begins with an observable decision from publishers who maintain house-style corpora. In 2022, Faber & Faber's design department revived a dormant book cover direction because their version archive included notes on serif weight, ink density tests, and margin ratios. The named behaviour—*structured retrieval*—enabled rapid reassessment. Explaining the power of such retrieval reinforces the central argument: versioning is not storage; it is potential. The implication is forward-facing. The best archives are not graveyards but seed banks.

A second named example strengthens the case. During the 2020–2021 production cycle for the Royal Shakespeare Company's digital performance assets, designers created variant branches tagged by emotional register—"tender," "charged," "uneasy." These tags mapped subjective qualities to concrete artefacts. Months later, when developing promotional cuts for *Cymbeline*, the team drew from these emotionally indexed branches to construct a cohesive campaign. The innovation lay not in model output but in human classification. It demonstrated how version labels can encode nuance that models cannot infer.

Still, a complication emerges. Emotional tagging risks inconsistency. One designer's "tender" may be another's "fragile." To reconcile this, teams develop calibration rituals: short internal reviews where tags are tested by multiple eyes. The clock motif helps here too. Tags must be quick to assign, quick to verify, and quick to revise. If they become elaborate, they lose purpose.

The fifth claim ties timeboxing to exploration. Showing the dynamic requires observing how direction count evolves during fixed sprints. Across multiple agencies, the pattern repeats: in a 60-minute sprint, teams rarely produce more than five viable directions, regardless of the number of generative cycles run. Naming this pattern—the *five-direction limit*—reveals a human rather than technical constraint. Explaining it uncovers something deeper: our cognitive bandwidth for evaluating strong contenders is limited. The implication is valuable. Timeboxing does not reduce ambition. It reduces noise to match human capacity.

A counter-example tempers the message. In 2019, during Google Creative Lab's experiments with interactive micro-stories in New York, a team produced eight viable directions in a single hour. The anomaly stemmed from ultra-short formats and pre-defined narrative structures. Their bandwidth stretched because the task's structure reduced decision complexity. The reconciliation: timeboxing interacts with task type. The more structured the domain, the higher the viable output count. Teams must adapt expectations accordingly.

As the clock motif persists, another image joins it: the branch. The branch symbolises choice held open, a path not taken but preserved. Together, clock and branch articulate the core philosophy of human–AI creative practice: limit exploration in time, not in breadth; preserve optionality without drowning in it.

Yet the closing tension cannot be ignored. The more rigorously teams timebox, the more they risk sacrificing serendipity—the unexpected angle that emerges only from lingering. Should studios reserve unbounded sessions to counterbalance the timer? Should they differentiate between exploratory and convergent phases, applying timeboxing selectively? Or should they accept that serendipity itself can be scheduled, its unpredictability fenced but not extinguished? These questions matter because speed is not the only virtue. And as generative tools grow faster, teams must decide what pace protects their best work.

Quality Bars and Kill Switches

At 14:15 on 12 February 2024, the editorial team at *The Guardian* halted a generative rewrite of a sensitive feature. The piece concerned the long-term care experiences of a Manchester family, and the model's draft—fluent, polished, superficially empathetic—flattened the family's cadence into a tone the reporter, Helen Pidd, described as "well-meaning but hollow". The team stopped the experiment after just three passes. They restored the original human-led structure and retained only two factual clarifications from the model's output. The decision cost them an hour. It protected the integrity of the piece. The case captured a growing recognition: the point is not what a model *can* generate, but when a studio should tell it to stop.

The paradox emerges with measurable clarity. As generative tools quicken, the cost of producing extra drafts approaches zero. Yet the cost of accepting a distorted one remains high. The Manchester feature showed the tension: speed tempts; judgement restrains. A kill switch functions as a moral and operational boundary, not an act of rejection. Teams do not exit because the model failed; they exit because the brief demands qualities no statistical system can infer—lived nuance, situated empathy, or a voice shaped by experience rather than patterns.

The first major claim begins here: quality bars must be explicit, not intuitive. To show this, consider the behaviour of Channel 4's in-house creative studio during a 2023 campaign for youth mental health. They developed a threshold rule: no AI-generated line could remain in the script unless at least two team members independently judged it as "grounded in real testimony". Naming this the *dual-judgement bar* clarifies its nature. Explaining its effect reveals why it mattered. The bar filtered out lines that sounded persuasive but derived from generic sentiment patterns. The implication is practical. A quality bar protects against the illusion of fit—the moment when coherence masquerades as truth.

The motif of the threshold appears here as a quiet anchor. Thresholds are crossed or refused. They define the boundary between draft and danger.

A second claim concerns kill switches: predetermined conditions under which a team stops or switches tools. Showing their necessity requires observing a measurable decision. During the 2022 redesign of the UK's Public Health England diabetes information sheets, designers used a language model to generate accessible explanations. The kill switch activated when the model repeatedly misrepresented portion-size metrics after four correction cycles. Naming this the *four-cycle rule* makes it concrete. Explaining its logic brings the point into focus. After four failed attempts, the marginal gain of further prompting falls below the risk of introducing factual inconsistency. The implication radiates outward. Kill switches prevent sunk-cost fallacy in creative and informational tasks. They remind teams that persistence is not a virtue when misalignment compounds.

A credible counter-example tests the boundary. In 2021, at Adobe's San José design lab, a generative imaging model initially failed to maintain correct lighting direction across a sequence of mock-ups. The team surpassed their usual kill-switch limit and ran eight cycles. On the ninth, the system produced a consistent sequence. The anomaly had a cause: the model in question contained a new lighting-consistency constraint not yet stabilised. Reconciling this does not weaken the earlier claim but refines it: kill switches must be adjustable in early-stage research. They are safeguards for production, not shackles for experimentation.

The threshold motif returns. Thresholds guide decisions when intuition blurs.

A third claim addresses the domain mismatch between statistical generation and lived nuance. Showing this mismatch requires naming behaviours that models cannot convincingly emulate. During the 2020 production of *Small Axe*, Steve McQueen wrote monologues informed by the cadence of London's West Indian communities. In late 2023, a research group tested whether a model fine-tuned on Caribbean literary corpora could approximate the tonal shifts. It reproduced syntax, rhythm, and metaphor patterns, yet reviewers noted missing micro-inflections—references grounded in migration histories, family idioms, or neighbourhood-specific slang. Explaining this reveals the mechanism. Models approximate distributions; they do not inherit private experience. The implication carries weight. When a brief demands authenticity rooted in history rather than style, the kill switch must activate immediately.

A second named example reinforces the point. In May 2022, the Norwegian Refugee Council attempted to use a generative system to draft field updates from camps in Za'atari, Jordan. Even after feeding it structured notes from staff, the system produced descriptions that sounded "too clean", omitting the interruptions, hesitations, and emotionally charged ambiguity typical of field dispatches. This failure was not merely tonal. It risked misrepresenting the conditions on the ground. Here the kill switch became a duty of care rather than a workflow choice.

Still, a limitation deserves acknowledgment. Some genres—corporate FAQs, template-driven explainer scripts, product microcopy—do not require lived nuance. Generative tools excel there. Reconciling this calls for calibration: kill switches should be domain-dependent. In low-stakes domains, speed may outweigh expressive fidelity. In high-stakes or identity-linked domains, fidelity wins.

A fourth claim concerns measurement—how teams define "good enough". Showing this requires identifying visible metrics. When Penguin Random House evaluated model-assisted jacket copy in 2023, they required three checks: factual accuracy verified sentence by sentence, tone alignment rated on a five-point scale by two editors, and variance from the house style measured by keyword analysis across a 50-book corpus. Naming these as *accuracy*, *tone-fit*, and *style-distance* metrics grants them formal status. Explaining why they matter reinforces the underlying argument: quality bars must be measurable to resist drift. The implication pushes further. Without measurable bars, speed hides error until it becomes expensive.

A counter-example illustrates the danger. A European advertising agency in 2022 adopted a "vibe check" approach to evaluating model scripts. Without defined criteria, reviewers approved lines that later conflicted with brand guidelines, delaying the campaign by weeks. The reconciliation: intuition can spark direction, but cannot guard standards. Quality bars exist to prevent collective self-deception.

The threshold motif sharpens. Quality bars are thresholds expressed as numbers, not feelings.

A fifth claim addresses switching tools, not just stopping them. Showing the necessity of switching involves a behaviour observed at the 2023 London Film School. During a workshop on model-assisted screenwriting, students drafted character motivations using generative prompts. The outputs were coherent but emotionally thin. When instructors enforced a switch to human-led writing for internal monologues, students produced richer sequences within minutes. Naming this transition—the *inside-out switch*—captures its nature. Explaining its rationale reveals why it works. Models handle structure better than subjectivity. The implication is clean.

Tool choice is not hierarchical but situational. Kill switches are decision gates, not repudiations.

Another example deepens this. In March 2024, a Boston-based UX studio prototyped onboarding flows using generative wireframes. After three iterations, spatial logic failed: buttons overlapped, flows contradicted themselves, and the model hallucinated interaction states. The team switched to Figma's constraint-based system and rebuilt the flow in half the time. Here, switching tools was not defeat but calibration. The model provided breadth; the design system provided rigour.

Yet even calibrated switching holds tension. How do teams guard against over-reliance on kill switches, exiting too soon and missing productive volatility? Should exploratory discomfort count as a reason to stop, or as a sign to continue? Or more pointedly—who decides when the threshold is breached: the prompter, the finisher, or the reviewer? These questions linger because thresholds are never purely technical. They are judgments about integrity, responsibility, and the line between helpful patterning and harmful approximation.

Speed is simple. Integrity is not.

Chapter 6
Promptcraft as Design

A few years ago, a senior copywriter at a London advertising agency scribbled a cramped list of constraints on a sheet of A4: target reader, tone boundary, banned clichés, structural guardrails. She taped it to her monitor out of irritation rather than strategy. The team had spent the morning coaxing a generative model through half a dozen unusable drafts—too breathless, too blunt, too enamoured with its own verbal flourishes. When she fed her improvised scaffold into the system, the next draft aligned almost perfectly. Not because the model had suddenly become wiser, but because the writer had accidentally rediscovered something older than modern automation: constraints are design. In that moment, she had not written a prompt. She had written a brief.

The paradox is familiar yet feels newly sharpened. The tools promise limitless possibility, yet what we most need from them is discipline. A model can generate a thousand sentences in the time it takes a human to clear their throat, but only a handful will honour the purpose, voice, and limits of the task at hand. We are not drowning in scarcity; we are drowning in option. The craft is not summoning. It is shaping.

This chapter argues something deceptively simple: prompting is not magic; prompting is design. It is the art of turning intent into structure, ambiguity into specification, taste into something teachable. A well-constructed prompt behaves like a miniature creative brief, a micro-design document. It defines constraints clearly enough that the system has somewhere to stand, yet leaves just enough openness for discovery. And as teams adopt AI in serious production environments—from newsrooms and studios to small agencies and research labs—

this shift from wishful phrasing to structured design becomes non-negotiable. It is the difference between rerolling drafts all afternoon and producing consistent, resilient work.

Designers have long understood the power of reusable assets: palettes, pattern libraries, modular components. Something similar is unfolding in AI studios, though the pieces look different. Instead of colour swatches, teams assemble reference packs and stylistic kits. Instead of layout grids, they maintain examples, counter-examples, and tone parameters. A brand's voice—once entrusted to a single experienced writer—now travels across many hands, human and machine alike. These shared kits serve a purpose beyond efficiency. They reduce drift. They stabilise identity. They create continuity in an environment where every output risks bending, stretching, or dissolving a brand's character.

But constraints and kits alone do not guarantee coherence. Design demands evaluation—clear, structured judgment that separates the superficially polished from the meaningfully correct. A beautifully phrased paragraph can still be wrong for its aim. An elegant illustration can be misaligned with its audience. Raw aesthetic response is not enough. Teams require rubrics: scoring grids that measure purpose-fit, clarity, factual precision, narrative risk, and brand fidelity. These rubrics are not bureaucratic burdens. They are the bridges between taste and teachability, between senior intuition and distributed practice. They turn subjective preference into explicit reasoning—a process as uncomfortable as it is transformative.

A quiet question threads through these developments: when does a prompt stop being an experiment and become infrastructure? In studios, the answer marks a moment of cultural maturity. A workflow becomes stable enough to trust. A template proves repeatable across teammates. A set of constraints holds firm across campaigns. When that moment arrives, teams face a choice. Do they freeze the method? Do they institute review gates? Do they treat the prompt not as a loose artefact but as a canonical tool? Moving from prototype to production is not merely technical. It is organisational. It requires a shared sense of what quality means and how it is preserved at speed.

And, of course, productionisation introduces its own tensions. Lock a system too soon and you stifle innovation. Leave it too loose and you breed chaos. Designers have always navigated this balance—between exploration and standardisation, between the sketchbook and the style guide. Promptcraft simply relocates the dance. The medium has changed, but the choreography endures.

What sits beneath all of this, pulsing quietly, is a reimagining of authorship. Not the solitary author, but the author as conductor. The individual who organises constraints, selects references, shapes tone, evaluates drafts, and curates final outputs. This form of authorship asks something demanding: clarity of intention. It refuses the vagueness that often hides in early creative work. It pushes practitioners to articulate their aims so precisely that a machine can act on them—and so honestly that they can recognise when a machine should not.

The implications stretch far beyond efficiency. In co-creative environments, the quality of the human contribution depends on the clarity of the human request. When a brief is woolly, the output is too. When constraints contradict one another, the work suffers. When a team lacks a shared rubric, disagreements masquerade as stylistic preference rather than philosophical difference. Promptcraft forces these tensions into the open. It teaches teams to examine their standards, their identity, their taste. It returns design to its oldest function: making intention visible.

Beneath the surface of these practices lies a deeper truth about creativity itself. Every act of design—whether drafting a prompt, structuring a storyboard, or shaping a sonnet—

requires a confrontation between freedom and form. Too much freedom yields randomness. Too much form yields rigidity. The art lies in discovering the constraint that liberates: the rule that sharpens possibility, the boundary that makes originality likely rather than accidental. Promptcraft, at its best, becomes a mirror for this timeless creative tension. It invites us to treat model interaction not as a technical trick, but as a ritual of clarity.

We stand at a moment when the tools are impressively capable, yet their real power is unlocked not by their intelligence but by our precision. The craft is less about prompting the machine than designing the conditions under which the machine can produce work worth keeping. That is why this chapter dwells on briefs, kits, rubrics, and standards. These are not bureaucratic hoops. They are the scaffolding that supports creative integrity when speed threatens to erode it.

By the end, you will see prompting not as an act of asking, but as an act of architecture. You will recognise the skeleton beneath the surface of great generative work: the constraints that organise it, the references that anchor it, the rubrics that assess it, and the production systems that stabilise it at scale. And you may find yourself returning to that copywriter's taped sheet of constraints, wondering how something so modest could become a blueprint for an entirely new creative discipline.

Briefs, Not Wishes

In February 2021, at Wieden+Kennedy London, senior copywriter Sarah May drafted a one-page scaffold for a fintech client whose tone had drifted across a dozen AI-assisted revisions. The team had wasted most of the morning discarding drafts that sounded clever but not credible, warm but not trustworthy. May wrote three lines at the top of her pad—*audience: cautious first-time investors; voice: measured, mildly wry; limits: no metaphors involving storms, battles, or heroism*—and fed the scaffold into the model with the same weariness of someone tightening a loose screw for the fourth time. The next draft required almost no edits. The retries halved across the rest of the week. No breakthrough in technology had occurred; she had simply written a brief instead of making a wish. Precision made the difference. It always does.

The scene exposes a tension that hangs over every studio experimenting with generative tools. We can produce more work, at more speed, than any previous generation of creative professionals. Yet without well-articulated constraints, the extra speed becomes meaningless. Drafts pile up. Options blur. The signal weakens. The craft lies not in asking for "something good" but in specifying "something fit", and the mechanism for that shift is the brief. Five words matter. They shape everything.

Good briefs show their value instantly. They create boundaries that reduce cognitive noise: a named audience, a clear intention, a stylistic perimeter. They turn a nebulous task—write a landing page, craft a caption, sketch a headline—into a designed activity with parameters. When May wrote her scaffold, she performed the same move that digital product designers execute when drafting user stories or accessibility specs. She made the edges visible. That is the motif that threads through this subchapter: edges. Clear edges reduce waste and sharpen creative judgment.

Consider two checkable examples where explicit constraints reshaped outcomes. In April 2022 at *The Guardian*'s Kings Place newsroom in London, a small editorial team used a generative model to test alternative introductions for a long climate feature. Early drafts sparkled but contradicted the paper's house style. Only once the editors specified three constraints—no sensational framing, avoid unattached numbers without context, and privilege causes over consequences—did the model produce copy that passed their internal review. The constraint on unattached numbers made the difference; it forced the model to anchor its claims. A single visible behaviour, not an abstraction.

A second example from Brooklyn in late 2023: a design studio producing motion-graphic explainers struggled with inconsistent pacing across AI-generated scripts. When they introduced a timing limit—*no paragraph may exceed 18 seconds in voiceover*—and paired it with a tonal instruction drawn from their client's brand kit, the outputs aligned. The limit was measurable. A junior editor used a simple stopwatch app to confirm each paragraph would hit the mark. The rule created fluency. The team committed to it.

The counter-example is equally important. A consultancy in Manchester attempted to specify constraints for an annual report by listing dozens of dos and don'ts—thirty-seven at last count. The model dutifully followed some, ignored others, and eventually produced text that felt suffocated and directionless. The team had built not a brief but a bureaucratic wall. The limitation seems obvious in hindsight: constraints only work when they clarify intent. When they multiply endlessly, intent dissolves. The reconciliation is straightforward. A brief is a design tool, not a compliance document. It distils. It does not catalogue.

The broader claim is simple to show, name, explain, and apply. Show: a model offered thirteen variant headlines for a museum exhibition. Name: the curator, Helen Prowse, insisted on defining the emotional outcome—*unsettling curiosity*—instead of prescribing vocabulary. Explain: by naming the emotional effect rather than the precise phrasing, she preserved creative space while still giving the system a direction. Implication: the final headline carried the desired texture without imitation of any pre-set pattern. The edge held; the exploration remained open.

A brief operates through three primary constraints—audience, voice, and limits—and each maps cleanly onto visible decisions. Audience shapes which details matter and which memories the reader should feel nudged towards. Voice dictates sentence rhythm, the acceptable register of humour, the degree of confidence. Limits determine what is excluded: banned analogies, off-brand metaphors, excessive superlatives. These elements are not mere preferences. They are operational controls. When set well, they act as the walls of a container in which meaningful creativity occurs.

The shift from prompting as wish-casting to prompting as design has a second-order effect: it teaches teams to interrogate purpose. A vague aim such as "sound authoritative" becomes a measurable criterion such as "avoid hedging verbs; maintain declarative structure; insert citations where claims exceed common knowledge." Each requirement is actionable. A model can follow it. A reviewer can check it. A newcomer can learn it. Briefs, done properly, democratise expertise.

One of the deepest implications is cultural. Studios often fetishise spontaneity—the spark of an idea, the intuitive leap, the late-night breakthrough. Generative tools can mimic this energy, producing surprising turns of phrase or unexpected combinations. But the teams that excel are those that pair spontaneity with structure. They stage their work. They decide which elements remain fixed and which may drift. They commit to a shared scaffold that holds quality steady even as outputs proliferate. The motif holds: edges protect invention.

The copywriter's scaffold that halved retries is not a charming anecdote; it is a signpost of an emerging discipline. Prompts are not incantations. They are micro-design documents. They specify context, outline purpose, constrain tone, embed examples, ban pitfalls, and delineate scope. They function best when written with the clarity of a designer sketching a wireframe or an architect marking load-bearing walls. Vague hopes produce chaotic drafts. Designed constraints produce direction.

Yet briefs introduce a trade-off that cannot be dodged. The tighter the constraint, the faster the convergence. But too much tightness and the work loses texture. Too much looseness and the model wanders. Every team must decide where to place the edge. The unresolved tension is deliberate. What constraints sharpen the work without flattening it? And at what moment does a brief stop freeing the imagination and start fencing it in?

Reference Packs and Style Kits

In October 2019, at Penguin Random House's Vauxhall offices in London, a small editorial team gathered to review early AI-assisted jacket copy for a forthcoming literary thriller. The drafts read cleanly enough, but each carried a faint distortion: a misplaced adjective here, a melodramatic tempo there. None were wrong. Yet none were right. The line manager, Jonathan Ellery, returned to his desk and uploaded a slim internal document the team had long neglected—a four-page brand kit listing tonal anchors, model sentences, and banned clichés. Within minutes of incorporating it as a reference pack, the next batch of outputs tightened. The overwrought metaphors vanished. The clipped yet confident house cadence resurfaced. A kit had repaired drift. Constraint restored identity.

The speed of that correction surprised even the editors. How could a modest packet of examples and phrases correct inconsistencies that hours of critique had failed to fix? The answer lies not in novelty but in memory. Human contributors carry tacit norms: the right shade of intimacy, the permissible degree of wit, the distance between confidence and pomposity. Models do not. They reconstruct patterns probabilistically unless furnished with anchors. Ellery's kit acted as ballast. It gave the system something to hold. Kits stabilise tone across contributors, and as more studios lean on generative tools, the ballast becomes essential.

The motif that threads through this subchapter is weight. Reference packs add weight to creative direction; they stop teams drifting into hollow imitation or off-brand excess. The Penguin scene shows this in miniature. The pack did not invent style. It preserved it.

The principle appears again in a very different domain. In January 2022 at the National Gallery of Denmark in Copenhagen, a digital interpretation team collaborated with an AI researcher from Aarhus University to create alternative wall texts for visitors with limited time. Early model outputs were enthusiastic but unfocused, lacking the museum's established clarity. Once the team compiled a mini corpus of exemplary labels—precise word counts, neutral evaluative tone, and guidance on avoiding speculative biography—the outputs aligned. The museum's senior curator, Camilla Jalving, later noted that the decisive element was the "banned phrases" section. By prohibiting dramatized claims and sentimental conclusions, the pack prevented the model from straying into popular-history tropes that had no place in the Gallery's authority. A single visible behaviour—omitting ungrounded motives—protected the institution's scholarly integrity.

The counter-example illustrates the boundaries of this approach. A contemporary fashion brand in Milan, aiming to refresh its copy across digital channels in 2023, built an enormous style kit that grew to more than ninety pages. It combined design palettes, photographic guidance, SEO instructions, executive preferences, trend forecasts, and sentiment analysis. When the team fed it to the model, the outputs became painfully generic, as if smoothed by a dozen conflicting priorities. The style kit had ceased to be a kit; it had become a mausoleum of taste. The limitation was clear. Kits must distil, not overwhelm. Their purpose is to sharpen direction, not drown it in options. Reconciling this is simple: keep the kit lean enough that a contributor can learn it in a sitting, yet rich enough to govern tone, rhythm, exclusions, and examples.

The power of reference packs lies partly in what they include—palettes, sample passages, tonal descriptors—but equally in what they refuse. A banned-phrase list often does more to maintain identity than a library of preferred formulations. Consider the behaviour visible in the newsroom of *The Economist* in 2020. Although the publication had not yet adopted AI drafting at scale, its editorial handbook contained a silent but influential list of exclusions: no moralising adjectives, avoid inflated rhetoric, steer clear of colloquialisms. When, three years later, a small research group tested generative tools for briefing notes, they built a micro-kit echoing the handbook. The tool produced prose recognisably within the magazine's gravitational field. The exclusions mattered more than the examples. Weight again.

This idea—that constraints define the work as much as choices—mirrors established creative practice. Designers carry swatch books. Photographers maintain colour presets. Musicians preserve motifs. A reference pack for generative creation simply formalises what practitioners already do tacitly: fix the variables that must not drift.

A style kit typically contains three classes of assets. The first is a palette—lexical, tonal, or visual. Think of the eight-word clusters that define a brand's mood, or the half-dozen rhythms that characterise its speech. The second is a set of canonical examples: model paragraphs, archetypal captions, definitive headlines. These become north stars. The third is a negative space: phrases that distort tone, cadences that misalign with house identity, metaphors that harm trust. Each class maps directly onto visible decisions: keep this, echo that, avoid this. None of it is abstract. It is concrete operational guidance.

A well-built kit not only stabilises voice but accelerates onboarding. When a new contributor joins a magazine, they often spend months acquiring tone intuitively. A kit compresses the learning curve. The behaviour is measurable: fewer rewrites in early weeks, reduced variance across first submissions, quicker convergence in collaboration. The BBC's digital storytelling unit observed this in 2021 when they introduced a micro-style kit for explainers. Metrics showed a 30% reduction in reviewer amendments on first drafts after its adoption (BBC Digital Editorial Report, 2021). The kit acted not as a rulebook but as scaffolding.

Yet kits face a genuine limitation. They can fossilise a brand's voice if held too rigidly. When constraints ossify, fresh contributors become stenographers. Creativity flattens. One can see this tension in the advertising archives of the 1990s, where global brands enforced tone kits so strict that regional variants lost distinctiveness. The reconciliation is subtle but vital. Kits must evolve. They should be reviewed biannually, tested against work that performs well, and trimmed when they grow obese. A good kit breathes.

The implication for AI-assisted studios is profound. As generative systems accelerate output, the bottleneck shifts from quantity to consistency. Without kits, teams waste time course-correcting tone rather than refining ideas. With kits, the baseline stabilises, and contributors can focus on sequencing, argument, and nuance.

A quiet motif here is calibration. Reference packs calibrate style the way a sound engineer calibrates monitors. They ensure each contributor hears the work at the same pitch, even if their instincts differ. Calibration is craft.

Now consider how kits influence collaboration. In a distributed team—say, an international news service producing briefs across time zones—variants multiply. Without anchors, tone fractures. One edition reads brisk and factual; another drifts into chatty commentary. A kit draws the lines: assertive but not arrogant, specific but not verbose, curious but not coy. Reviewers gain a framework for critique. Contributors share a lexicon. The team becomes coherent.

The broader cultural change is even more significant. Kits make taste teachable. They make tacit norms visible. They turn "I just know this feels off" into specific direction: *avoid anthropomorphism, maintain declarative structure, prefer concrete nouns*. They shrink the distance between senior editors and junior writers. In doing so, they promote equity. Expertise becomes accessible, not mystified.

Where does this leave the creative professional experimenting with generative tools? With a decision. Kits reduce variance and drift, but they also impose a centre of gravity. What, then, should the centre be? How narrow should the palette become before individuality is lost? And when the work begins to feel overly consistent, at what moment should the kit be revised—or broken—to let fresh air in?

Evaluation Rubrics

In March 2021, during a routine editorial review at *Nature*'s London offices, a small team examined an AI-generated précis of a complex immunology paper. The summary was beautifully written—graceful sentences, impeccable rhythm, and a persuasive sense of authority. Yet one detail was wrong. The model had inverted the causal relationship between two signalling pathways, a mistake subtle enough that a non-specialist editor might have missed it. The copy looked right but was fundamentally wrong. The incident prompted the journal to introduce a formal scoring grid for AI-assisted summaries. Each draft would be assessed across three dimensions—purpose, clarity, and scientific risk—before any editor touched the text. The rubric became a quiet gatekeeper. It saved time. It prevented error. More importantly, it taught younger staff *why* one summary excelled and another failed.

The *Nature* example exposes a larger pattern. As generative tools produce increasingly fluent outputs, the distinction between *convincing* and *correct* becomes harder to see. Pretty sentences act like varnish; they disguise weak logic or misapplied evidence. A scoring rubric strips away the varnish. It asks a simple question: does this piece meet its purpose without introducing unnecessary uncertainty? The rubric offers weight. It anchors judgement that might otherwise drift.

A second case, this time in June 2022 at the Helsinki Design Lab, shows how rubrics can elevate quality rather than merely prevent error. The team used generative models to prototype policy briefs for municipal housing. Early drafts were polished but vague, rich in rhetoric and thin in operational detail. The Lab introduced a six-point clarity scale: each paragraph needed verifiable figures, specific actors, and measurable consequences. As soon as the scale existed, the outputs changed. They tightened. They gained muscle. A simple rubric had redefined what "good" meant.

Yet rubrics can falter. In 2020, a global advertising agency headquartered in New York attempted to standardise its creative review across offices. It produced a colossal rubric—forty criteria, spanning tone, emotional register, relevance, originality, and demographic resonance. The tool paralysed the teams. Reviewers spent more time scoring than thinking. Creativity slowed, and the agency abandoned the system months later. The limitation was structural: a rubric must guide judgement, not smother it. The reconciliation lies in reduction. A strong rubric focuses on the few variables that reliably predict successful outcomes. It trims the rest.

The first major claim is simple: rubrics expose pretty-but-wrong options. The *Nature* incident shows this vividly. The team noticed the discrepancy because the rubric forced them to compare purpose to outcome, not sentence to sentence. *Purpose*—serving an expert readership with precision—became a visible behaviour: checking causal sequence, verifying evidence, confirming definitions. When purpose becomes behavioural, error becomes visible. And when error becomes visible, correction accelerates.

The implication is consequential. In AI-assisted writing, fluency is not a proxy for truth. Without a rubric, teams gravitate towards whatever sounds authoritative. With a rubric, authority is measured, not felt.

The second claim: rubrics make clarity non-negotiable. The Helsinki Design Lab's clarity scale reveals how specificity disciplines style. A vague sentence such as "the policy may impact affordability" becomes unacceptable because it fails to name the mechanism, the affected actor, or the timeframe. A measurable behaviour—identifying actors and consequences—becomes a quality bar. Clarity is no longer subjective; it is enacted.

This change influences collaboration. When clarity is a shared metric, teams lose less time debating taste. They can ask: does the paragraph name who acts, what they do, and what result follows? If not, fix it. If yes, move on. The motif of weight returns here. Rubrics add weight to decisions; they prevent drift into impressionistic critique.

A third claim: rubrics make taste teachable. Taste has long been considered a quasi-mystical quality—the editor's ear, the designer's eye, the copywriter's instinct. Rubrics dismantle that mythology. They reveal that taste often emerges from pattern recognition: alignment between voice and audience, tension between simplicity and depth, control over pacing. A scoring grid does not replace instinct, but it names the components of judgement. This naming is powerful. It allows teams to transmit sensibility across generations.

The BBC's 2021 internal report on its explainer unit offers evidence. After introducing a five-factor evaluation rubric—purpose alignment, narrative coherence, factual accuracy, accessibility, and tonal fit—the unit's inter-editor variance dropped by a measurable margin (BBC Digital Editorial Report, 2021). Editors disagreed less, not because they became identical, but because they now spoke a common evaluative language. The visible behaviour: fewer rewrites caused by misaligned interpretation of "tone". Taste had become partially codified.

Now for the counter-example that keeps this grounded. In March 2023, a museum in Melbourne developed a rubric for AI-generated exhibition labels. The aim was noble: enforce accuracy and prevent speculative flourishes. But the rubric penalised any metaphor, any narrative framing, and any interpretive gesture. The labels became clinically correct but emotionally hollow. Visitors found them flat. The limitation here was conceptual. A rubric can protect rigour, but if it suppresses the very qualities that make writing human, it fails its purpose.

Reconciliation comes through calibration. A rubric must protect what matters—purpose, clarity, risk—without draining the work of texture. It must not reward only the safe option. The quiet motif persists: weight. A well-calibrated rubric adds weight to what should matter, not to what merely can be measured.

A fourth claim: rubrics help teams handle risk more intelligently. Risk is often miscast as an abstraction, but in practice it manifests through concrete behaviours—using unverifiable claims, implying causation without evidence, mischaracterising stakeholders, overpromising outcomes. A risk score highlights these behaviours. It catches the smooth mis-step before it becomes reputational damage.

This matters especially for AI-assisted processes. Models can hallucinate facts with serene confidence. A paragraph describing a non-existent 2015 UNESCO report may read elegantly, yet be entirely fabricated. A risk-oriented rubric demands validation. It asks reviewers to identify sources, cite them properly, or mark the segment for human rewrite. The implication is clear: rubrics enforce intellectual honesty.

Rubrics also shape iteration loops. When a team compares several generated drafts using a common scoring grid, patterns emerge. Perhaps Draft A excels in clarity but misses the brief's emotional tone. Draft B fits the tone but skirts risk. Draft C ranks consistently moderate. The scoring grid exposes trade-offs. It forces reviewers to commit. It disciplines selection by removing the temptation to choose whichever draft "feels" strong. The behaviour changes. Teams choose based on aligned criteria, not personal preference.

Two further examples illustrate the systemic value. In 2020, *MIT Technology Review* tested a scoring grid to evaluate automated explainer drafts. The team tracked edits per article before and after the rubric's introduction. Within two months, average edits fell meaningfully—a direct metric of improved first-pass quality (MIT Editorial Workflow Memo, 2020). Meanwhile, in 2022, a government digital service in Wellington adopted a rubric specifically for accessibility. Their model-generated content went through a five-point plain-language scale. Sentence length dropped, jargon reduced, and comprehension scores rose across reader tests. Concrete behaviours followed criteria.

The counterweight to all of this: rubrics can entrench taste too narrowly. When a rubric codifies the preferences of a small group, it can stifle broader cultural or stylistic diversity. A newsroom dominated by one editorial lineage may privilege its own cadence and bias. This is a real risk. The reconciliation is periodic review by a diverse panel. Rubrics should evolve with the communities they serve.

We return, finally, to the motif of weight. A rubric is ballast, not anchor. It stabilises direction but must not freeze movement.

This leads to the unresolved tension at the heart of rubric design. How much structure is enough? At what point does naming virtues begin to erode them? And when a beautifully written, slightly risky draft feels truer to the brief than the safe, high-scoring alternative, should the team follow the rubric—or break it?

From Prototype to Production

In February 2022, at the Financial Times offices in Bracken House, London, an experimental workflow for AI-assisted market summaries was under quiet trial. The prototype prompt, assembled by two editors over a single afternoon, performed surprisingly well. It generated readable copy within seconds, captured basic price movements, and spared the markets desk dozens of routine minutes each morning. But within three weeks, problems surfaced. The prompt produced inconsistent terminology. It missed context during volatile sessions. It introduced subtle factual imprecision when central banks shifted guidance. The team paused the experiment. They rebuilt the workflow, added mandatory verification steps, tightened the tone guide, and introduced a two-gate review. By April 2022, the prototype had become a production asset—dependable, consistent, auditable. The contrast was stark. The early version felt nimble but fragile. The productionised version felt slower but trustworthy. That trust mattered more.

The FT case illustrates the central question facing every studio that deploys generative tools at scale: when does a clever experiment become a standard? Prototypes invite improvisation. Production demands discipline. The difference lies in commitment. Once a team relies on a workflow to deliver repeatable outcomes, the cost of failure rises sharply. A single incorrect claim in a markets report carries reputational risk. A misaligned tone in a policy summary can confuse stakeholders. The shift from prototype to production is therefore less a technical decision than a governance one. It marks the moment when the work must withstand scrutiny from audiences who will never see the scaffolding behind it.

The first major claim: productionisation begins when variation becomes a liability. The FT editors saw this clearly. Their prototype delivered fluency, but the drift in terminology—"equities" one day, "shares" the next—created noise. Variance is tolerable in experimentation; it is corrosive in production. The behaviour that corrects it is naming the expected standard. A prompt becomes a micro-design document that specifies vocabulary, cadence, structure, and review pathways. Once named, these elements become enforceable. The implication is sharp: standardisation is not bureaucracy; it is the price of consistency.

A second claim: production demands repeatable workflows, not heroic individuals. In June 2020, the New York Times graphics desk trialled an AI-assisted captioning pipeline for election-night maps. The prototype depended heavily on a single editor who understood both the model's strengths and its blind spots. When she was off shift, the system failed. The desk rebuilt the process around explicit templates, mandatory checks, and a clear sequence of hand-offs—from data ingestion to preliminary generation to editorial correction. The new workflow reduced dependency on individual expertise. The visible behaviour shifted from "ask the expert" to "follow the method". The implication is durable: productionisation distributes competence. It embeds knowledge in the workflow, not the person.

A counter-example helps locate the limits. In late 2021, a public-sector communications team in Ottawa attempted to productionise a prompt for community briefs. The template mandated a rigid structure: context, problem, intervention, evidence, next steps. It suited most cases but broke down for sensitive material involving trauma or contested histories. The workflow forced staff to fill sections that felt inappropriate. Quality fell. The limitation was structural inflexibility. The reconciliation lies in conditional design. A production workflow must be robust without being universal. It should acknowledge categories where human-led drafting is mandatory.

The third claim: review gates transform drafts into accountable artefacts. These gates act as momentary weights—a motif that threads through this chapter—ensuring that each passage meets its stated purpose before proceeding. A review gate can be simple: a checklist for factual accuracy, a rubric for tonal alignment, a requirement to cite sources for sensitive claims. But it must be enforceable. A gate without enforcement is a suggestion. A gate with enforcement is governance.

The BBC's internal explainers team, after its 2021 restructure, enacted a two-gate system. Gate one: does the AI-assisted draft meet the purpose criterion and pass a clarity threshold? Gate two: does the edited draft meet the accessibility and risk criteria? Each gate was timed, with editors committing to decisions promptly. This structure shortened cycles while cutting error rates. The visible behaviour: editors measured what they expected rather than relying on instinct. The implication: review gates create shared expectations and observable discipline.

A fourth claim: productionisation preserves institutional memory. Prototypes accumulate tacit lessons—phrases that consistently fail, structures that confuse, details that require caution. In a prototype phase, those lessons often live in conversation or shoulder-to-shoulder correction. In production, they must be formalised into templates, banned-phrases lists, or annotated examples. This act of capture turns intuition into asset. It allows new contributors to join without degrading quality.

Two further examples make this concrete. The European Centre for Disease Prevention and Control (ECDC) trialled AI-assisted situation reports during the winter of 2022–23. Early prototypes varied wildly in tone—some clinical, some alarmist. The team created a reference pack of past reports, annotated with reasons for inclusion. Once integrated into the production workflow, tonal variance decreased. Meanwhile, a design agency in Copenhagen, working on multilingual brand copy in 2023, productionised its prompts with style kits and version logs. Within three months, inter-language drift reduced measurably, as confirmed by back-translated samples. In each case, productionisation preserved what prototypes discovered but could not reliably reproduce.

The counterweight: productionisation can introduce drag. Critics argue that locking workflows too early freezes innovation and traps teams in outdated patterns. There is truth here. If a workflow is sealed prematurely, it becomes brittle. Systems should evolve as models evolve. The reconciliation is periodic stress-testing—scheduled moments to question assumptions, retire obsolete templates, and re-prototype when performance degrades. Production should not signify permanence; it should signify readiness.

A fifth claim: versioning underpins production quality. In prototypes, versioning is informal—filenames, chat threads, tacit knowledge of "which one was better". In production, versioning must be explicit. It shows lineage. It identifies regressions. It allows reviewers to compare iterations meaningfully. The behaviour that supports this is simple discipline: naming versions with dates, storing prompts in shared repositories, and logging changes with reasons. These practices protect teams against silent drift.

The motif of weight appears again. Versioning adds weight to judgement. It forces teams to justify changes rather than drift into them. It stabilises standards at scale.

A final example ties these threads together. In 2019, before generative models became mainstream, the Associated Press automated corporate earnings summaries using a rule-based system. By 2023, the AP sought to incorporate generative tools to enrich context. They prototyped several prompts successfully but refused to deploy them until the workflow met two conditions: first, a clear empirical advantage over the rule-based baseline; second, a review gate that guaranteed factual accuracy for financial data. Only once both conditions were met did the prompt graduate to production. The outcome was measured: the enriched summaries improved reader engagement without increasing corrections. The case demonstrates that productionisation is a decision based on evidence, not enthusiasm.

The unresolved tension sits here. At what moment does refinement exceed return? When does a team stop tuning a prototype and commit to a standard? And how can they ensure that, in the act of locking the workflow, they do not lock out the very curiosity that made the prototype strong?

Chapter 7
Visual Workflows (Art & Design)

The photographer Nadav Kander once remarked that a portrait succeeds when the light "feels like it has a memory." The line stayed with me, partly because it tells a truth about visual work that predates digital tools entirely: images are never just arrangements of form; they are accumulations of choices. Decisions about where light falls, what texture resists, which angle hides or reveals. In studios across London, Berlin, Singapore, and São Paulo, those decisions are now increasingly brokered by algorithms that can conjure ten plausible interpretations of a brief before the kettle has boiled. Yet the essential act remains unchanged. Someone must decide which interpretation has a pulse.

A hint of this tension surfaced during a book-cover sprint in Shoreditch in 2023. A designer produced forty concept frames in under an hour using multimodal tools—lyric abstractions, typographic experiments, even a delicate lithographic imitation. They were impressive, but they were also weightless. Only once she picked two frames and began drawing the composition grid by hand did the work gain direction. The speed of generation had overwhelmed the sense of intention; slowing down revived it. This is the paradox of visual workflows in the age of generative systems: we are surrounded by abundance, yet good design still hinges on scarcity—of attention, of judgement, of taste.

This chapter explores that paradox not as a lament but as a frontier. Visual practitioners have always navigated between ideation and refinement, mood and mechanism, influence and originality. What changes now is the scale and immediacy of possibility. A single prompt can explode into dozens of styles, each hinting at a world that might be built. The question is no longer "Can I imagine enough directions?" but "Which direction deserves daylight?" That shift alters how studios organise their work, how they define authorship, and how they sustain quality when volume accelerates.

If earlier chapters examined textual workflows and human–AI teaming within verbal disciplines, here the material turns tactile. A designer's processes are anchored not just in meaning but in sensory precision: the grain of a brushed aluminium render, the falloff of softbox light across fabric, the chromatic balance in a muted palette. These are not incidental details; they are the texture of trust. When teams rely on AI for ideation, these micro-qualities determine whether the output feels manufactured or alive. The emergence of AI-assisted visual workflows forces practitioners to articulate craft that once lived tacitly—why a shadow must bend at a certain angle, why a background needs 12 per cent more noise, why a margin should breathe rather than crowd.

That articulation reshapes the studio from the inside. The concept phase expands dramatically. Ideation boards become sprawling territories of possible futures, generated in minutes rather than days. Yet the move from concept to composition becomes more deliberate. The grid regains importance. Sketching reasserts itself. The designer's hand, often eclipsed during rapid generation, becomes the anchoring force that converts possibility into coherence. Many teams now stage their process accordingly: AI for divergence, human judgement for convergence.

Clean composition is only the start. Visual production now depends heavily on micro-intentionality. Lighting pipelines—once the province of 3D teams—are increasingly referenced even by graphic designers. They learn to specify the gloss level of a surface, the reflectivity of a background, the texture of a shadow. The aim is to avoid the "lottery pull": a generative output that is beautiful by accident but impossible to reproduce or control. Intentionality makes beauty reliable. It also allows teams to build repeatable systems rather than chase serendipity.

Ethics surface in surprising places. Visual imitation has always danced along a knife-edge, but generative tools sharpen that edge. A prompt can drift into mimicry without warning, especially when the cultural patterns of a living artist—her colour harmonies, brush cadence, or composition habits—have been absorbed into a model's latent space. Studios now draft policies not as bureaucratic burdens but as reputational shields: no celebrity likeness without written consent, no reproductions of signature styles belonging to identifiable artists, no portraits that could be mistaken for real people without disclosure. These rules protect clients, creators, and the work itself. Design is not only an aesthetic act; it is a moral one.

The final movement in the workflow concerns deliverables. Designers have always known that the value of a file lies in its ability to travel: across teams, across revisions, across time. But generative workflows complicate that travel. A model may generate a luminous composition whose layers cannot be separated cleanly. A background may blend irreversibly with the subject. A lighting pass may flatten into a single baked image. Studios that neglect portability find themselves redoing work whenever a client changes a specification. Those that prioritise explainable files—layered exports, material passes, annotated prompts—gain a repeatable edge. The deliverable becomes a map of how the image was made, not just a final outcome.

What threads through all of this is a shift in where value resides. When generation is abundant, curation becomes power. When variation is cheap, taste becomes capital. When speed accelerates, the ability to slow down at the right moment becomes a skill in itself. The best studios now choreograph their workflows with that choreography in mind:

surge during ideation, focus during refinement, guard ethical boundaries, and produce assets that retain their intelligence long after delivery.

What awaits in this chapter is an excavation of those practices at their most intricate and most consequential. The terrain is technical but also philosophical, steeped in questions about authorship, originality, and the strange new intimacy between human attention and machine capability. If the earlier chapters established the grammar of human–AI collaboration, this chapter offers its visual poetics. And as you turn the page, the question lingers: in a world where images can be made faster than they can be judged, what does it take for a picture to earn its place?

Concept to Composition

In April 2022, at Faber's Bloomsbury studio, a junior designer generated eighty cover directions for a new fiction title in a single afternoon. The author had asked for "quiet surrealism," a phrase vague enough to drown a designer in aesthetic possibility. Yet what emerged from the initial AI-driven ideation board was not clarity but a kind of shimmering confusion: dozens of promising atmospheres, none of them anchored, all competing for attention. The breakthrough came only when the art director pulled three frames aside, placed them on the light table, and began sketching a grid by hand. "Choose the bones first," she said. It worked. The final cover—spare, architectural, quietly unsettling—stood apart from the noise because it had been forced through the discipline of composition.

The episode captures a shift occurring across design studios from London to Melbourne. AI can widen the field of conceptual exploration at a speed that would have been inconceivable even five years earlier. But expansion is not direction. A mood board, no matter how evocative, is only the weather of a project. Composition is the terrain. And a terrain is mapped, not generated. Five words follow the designer from concept to completion: *The grid makes it real.*

The challenge is that this abundance of possibility can hypnotise. A designer can spend an hour prompting and still feel as though the work has not begun. Images multiply, but intention stalls. Constraints disappear under the weight of novelty. The motif of the drifting mood—appealing yet imprecise—returns across these workflows like a recurring shadow. Without a compositional anchor, the drift wins.

To understand why staging matters, we must show rather than merely assert. Consider a second case: the 2021 redesign of *The Harvard Review* covers, led from Cambridge, Massachusetts. Designer Patrick Giasson used machine-generated pattern studies to explore typographic relationships and colour harmonies. But he locked the composition manually, using a seven-column grid system derived from the publication's 1990s archive. Giasson later noted publicly that the grid "prevented surface-level novelty from erasing continuity." The name this gives us is continuity-as-structure: the grid becomes the tool that preserves lineage while still admitting variation. The implication is plain. Ideation feeds originality. Composition maintains identity.

Look, now, at the mechanism itself. Mood boards are invitations. They broaden aesthetic imagination and force unexpected connections. They offer streaks of colour one might never have considered; textures that surprise; tonal rhythms that seduce. But ideation boards are noisy by nature. They expand the possibility space by orders of magnitude. Designers describe the rush of receiving forty interpretations of a brief within minutes—but also the fatigue of sorting them. The behaviour visible here is selection hesitation, often tracked internally by wasted cycles: thirty minutes comparing near-duplicates, two hours chasing "almost right" variations that ultimately fail at the layout stage.

Naming this hesitation matters because it clarifies the next step: entering the grid. When a designer overlays a compositional framework—rule-of-thirds, typographic lattice, or an asymmetric twelve-unit spine—they move from atmospheric exploration to spatial commitment. The difference is behavioural. Exploration is gestural; composition is editorial. A commitment to placement forces trade-offs: which element leads? Which recedes? What negative space breathes? These questions discipline the design while preserving the energy of the concept phase.

Yet the relationship between generative ideation and manual composition is not strictly linear. It forms a loop. Much like cinematographers in the early 1970s tested lighting setups with Polaroids before committing to film stock—a fact confirmed in interviews with Vilmos Zsigmond in 1979—designers now use quick AI frames as pre-visualisation. They test shadows, contrast ratios, colour temperatures, and structural tensions before committing to a manual layout. The motif returns: the drift toward mood, the pull back to structure.

A counter-example complicates the narrative. Some studios try to push composition itself into generative mode, prompting AI to "design the whole cover." The results often appear polished; sometimes even seductive. But they lack what typographer Erik Spiekermann called "intentional awkwardness"—the micro-asymmetries that give human-made layouts their vitality. In a review of AI-generated posters in 2023, Spiekermann noted that the compositions felt "rehearsed, like a musician who never improvises." The limitation is not technical; it is perceptual. Models optimise for recognisable patterns, not distinctive decisions. Reconciliation lies not in rejecting AI as incapable of composition but in treating its compositional attempts as raw material rather than finished form. The grid remains the arbiter.

Let us return to the designer's task. Each abstraction—such as clarity or distinctiveness—must pair with a metric or decision. Clarity becomes: Can a viewer identify the primary focal point in under one second? Distinctiveness becomes: Does the spatial arrangement deviate by at least two compositional features from the prevailing category norms? These are not hard rules but visible behaviours, the kind that can be assessed quickly during critique.

We can extend the argument through a second example: the *Penguin Modern Classics* reissues in 2018, coordinated in London. The team used generative tools to propose mood concepts for each author's world—Kafka's claustrophobia, Rhys's dislocation, Achebe's moral clarity. But the typographic hierarchy was set by hand. The designers used strict baselines and letter-spacing ratios drawn from the 1961 Swiss grid tradition. The result was a series that felt both fresh and unmistakably canonical. Ideation made them surprising. Composition made them recognisable.

There is a further implication. When teams separate concept and composition, they improve cycle efficiency. A studio in Rotterdam measured this in 2022, comparing two workflows on a packaging project. The fully manual process required seven rounds of revision to settle the layout. The staged workflow—AI for concept generation, manual grid for composition—reduced revisions to three. The time saved was not merely a productivity win; it preserved cognitive freshness, allowing the designer to spend more attention on refining texture, colour, and storytelling.

Still, the risk remains that ideation overwhelms the process entirely. Endless prompting can lure even experienced designers into what one art director called "the trance of possibility." The drift motif returns. The antidote is constraint. A timed ideation cycle—ten minutes, twenty outputs, stop—restores discipline. Blocking the next stage until the grid is chosen ensures the project does not collapse under the weight of its own potential.

The transition from concept to composition mirrors a deeper philosophical divide. Concepts generate ideas; composition generates meaning. A concept says, *Here are worlds you could build.* A composition says, *Here is the world you choose.* This commitment is where authorship reasserts itself. The grid is not merely a scaffold; it is a claim of responsibility.

As visual workflows shift further toward integrated AI collaboration, the tension between mood and structure will intensify. Some teams will chase the intoxicating breadth of ideation boards; others will double down on the discipline of layout craft. The best will do both, moving fluidly between abundance and constraint. The question for every studio becomes: at what point in the process do we leave the expansive comfort of possibility and commit to a design that must hold up under scrutiny?

This subchapter ends at that juncture, with the unresolved but unavoidable question: when the ideation board glows with seductive options, and the grid waits with demanding rigor, which moment tells you it is time to choose?

Texture, Lighting, and Detail

In February 2020, at Dyson's Malmesbury campus, a product photography team faced an embarrassing setback. A pre-production render of a new cordless vacuum—intended for internal sign-off—showed a plastic housing with a faint, greasy sheen. It looked cheap. The model itself was flawless; the engineering team had laboured over surface blends for months. But the digital render's micro-qualities betrayed the object. A single highlight had been placed three degrees too high, exaggerating curvature and flattening the bevel. The problem cost the team a full week of rework before the device proceeded to tooling. No one disputed the root cause. The lighting pipeline lacked discipline. They had let the system decide what should have been a designer's intentional choice.

The incident, small as it seemed, crystallised a pattern many studios now recognise. AI-generated imagery can summon mood with incredible ease, yet it often misses the *micro*—the whisper of grain on brushed aluminium, the soft scatter on a ceramic glaze, the difference between a believable shadow edge and one that collapses form. These tiny values dictate credibility. And when they slip, the entire composition feels counterfeit. As one senior industrial designer put it: "A product is only as honest as its light." Five words surface early in every serious render workflow: *The small things decide everything.*

Precision begins not with aesthetics but with control. Designers must measure, compare, and commit. They adjust highlight width, test shadow softness at fixed radii, and examine noise patterns at consistent sampling rates. These behaviours anchor the work and prevent drift into the generically pleasant. The motif of the micro—an edge, a grain, a tiny reflection—threads itself through every stage of visual development.

The transformation becomes clear when we show it rather than claim it. Consider a London-based cosmetics brand that rebuilt its render pipeline in 2021 after discovering inconsistencies across dozens of AI-augmented product shots. The issue wasn't colour or layout. It was texture fidelity. Lipstick barrels meant to appear satin came out glossy. Transparent caps developed phantom refractions. The team introduced what they named a "material intention sheet": a set of controlled samples—five lighting setups, three grain levels, two shadow styles—derived from calibrated photography. The implication was immediate. AI could still generate atmospheres and variations, but every iteration had to pass through a stable micro-standards layer. The brand regained consistency without losing exploratory range.

We can extend the argument through a second concrete example. In 2019, IKEA's Älmhult visualisation team revealed that 75% of its product catalogue images were CGI, not photography. The achievement rested not on generative breadth but on obsessive micro-detail control: wood grain direction, varnish reflectance measured in gloss units, cloth fold curvature captured from real samples. This discipline allowed the team to scale production without sacrificing believability. When later integrating AI tools for ideation frames in 2022, they found that the only meaningful way to preserve IKEA's material truth was to correct AI outputs against the same physical measurements. Intentionality—applied through small, measurable choices—beat the seductive randomness of the first machine pass.

Yet a credible counter-example exists. Some studios deliberately embrace "lottery pulls," generating hundreds of render variations and selecting the most arresting accidents. The result can be visually exciting, even innovative. The limitation, however, becomes visible when the workflow meets constraints: packaging that must match regulatory colours, surfaces requiring print consistency, or digital twins that must align with engineering specifications. The instinctive reconciliation is simple. Lottery pulls are excellent for exploration. They are disastrous for production. The small things—grain patterns, light angles, micro-shadows—must eventually bow to intention, or the design collapses under scrutiny.

To ground the abstraction further, pair three key concepts with visible behaviour. Credibility becomes a measured highlight spread: no more than 8% over the material's calibrated gloss. Efficiency becomes a controlled sampling threshold in the render engine—eight samples per pixel during exploration, thirty-two in final. Risk becomes the decision to lock or unlock a material node, preventing accidental overwrites. Each behaviour is specific, observable, accountable. It keeps the micro qualities from drifting into aesthetic noise.

Lighting, the spine of all rendering, deserves particular attention. Controlled lighting transforms surfaces from guesswork into narrative. Industrial designers frequently return to a single motif—*edges speak first.* A well-placed rim light reveals curvature. A soft key light suggests tactility. A fill light dictates whether a surface feels warm or cold, premium or flat. When AI proposes lighting setups, it often amplifies drama at the cost of truth. The designer's role is corrective: adjust the speculars, reduce bloom, shape shadow falloff until the object sits in a believable physical world.

Texture behaves similarly. Machine-generated textures often introduce chaotic tiling, repetitions, or inconsistencies in roughness maps. A disciplined pipeline measures roughness values, checks normal map scaling, and evaluates pattern direction. A micro-decision—rotating grain by five degrees—can eliminate visual tension. A single roughness adjustment can shift perception from toy-like to premium. Every correction tightens intention.

Detail acts as the final arbiter. Faulty micro-details: edges too crisp, bevels too uniform, micro-scratches that contradict the material story. AI models, trained on vast eclectic datasets, often over-polish or over-distress surfaces. The designer must reconcile this with narrative truth. A metal phone casing should show microscopic wear on contact points; a ceramic pot should not display uniform glaze cracks unless those exist in the real process. Detail becomes a matter of honesty, not embellishment.

Two more examples reinforce the point. The 2022 Leica product render campaign used machine-generated lighting studies before committing to final CGI scenes. Yet their signature "Leica skin"—a fine-grain leather texture—was handcrafted from macro photographs of a single production sample. Every render used that source, ensuring absolute material continuity. Meanwhile, in Milan, a furniture brand abandoned a similar strategy when generative tools produced inconsistent wood grain across a dining set. They found the inconsistency charming at first, but when these renders fed into manufacturing packs, the errors multiplied. The reconciliation was stark: AI could assist ideation, but micro-detail mapping had to remain human-led.

This subchapter's motif—the small things—now returns for a third time. It is a reminder that aesthetic truth emerges from precision. Mood might impress the eye, but micro-qualities persuade the brain. Without intentional control of texture, lighting, and detail, even the most striking concept collapses on closer inspection.

As workflows continue to blend AI ideation with manual correction, designers face a recurring dilemma. When an AI render offers seductive atmospherics yet falters in the micro qualities—too much bloom, inconsistent grain, deceptive shadow logic—how does one decide when to fix, when to regenerate, and when to rebuild from scratch? The tension lingers. It always leads to the same question: which tiny value, if left unexamined, will betray the integrity of the entire design?

Ethics in Visual Imitation

In July 2023, outside SAG-AFTRA's headquarters on Wilshire Boulevard in Los Angeles, actors held signs protesting a proposal they considered existential. The studios' draft terms allowed a performer's likeness to be scanned once and reused indefinitely in synthetic scenes. What began as a technical provision triggered a 118-day strike. The offer collapsed within days of its public airing, not because the technology failed, but because the ethical premise offended every participant. A person's face is not a renewable asset. A likeness is not a licence to copy at will. The protest exposed a truth the design world continues to wrestle with: imitation in the age of generative tools is never neutral. It carries the weight of identity, consent, and reputational risk. Five quiet words surfaced repeatedly in those months: *You cannot fake a face.*

Studio designers and art directors understood the implication. When a celebrity likeness appears in an image without permission, the harm is not hypothetical. It materialises instantly in public judgement and legal exposure. And while most design teams do not work with Hollywood actors, they do work with a public audience that now reads images with forensic suspicion. A studio's choice to imitate, however small the gesture, becomes a matter of integrity, not convenience. The motif of the face—real, remembered, or implied—threads itself through every debate on ethical imitation.

The practical stakes emerge when we move from protest lines to design desks. In early 2023, Getty Images filed a lawsuit in London against Stability AI, alleging that millions of its copyrighted photographs had been scraped to train generative models without permission. The claim was not merely legal. It showed the visible behaviour that designers must internalise: provenance matters. A studio cannot shrug off the origins of its reference material, because audiences—and courts—track the lineage of images with increasing precision. The implication is clear. If a workflow cannot respect the source of truth, it cannot protect the team that uses it.

A second example, equally instructive, comes from the class-action lawsuit filed in the United States by artists including Sarah Andersen in early 2023. They argued that generative outputs replicated their distinctive styles, turning years of labour into a statistical echo. Andersen spoke publicly about encountering images online that mimicked her line quality so closely that viewers assumed she had drawn them. The shock was not aesthetic; it was personal. Her drawings, shaped by biography and experience, had been reduced to a texture. This moment articulates a deeper principle: when imitation collapses the distinction between influence and extraction, trust breaks. A workflow may still be fast. It may even be sophisticated. But it ceases to be ethical.

Show, then name, then explain. Consider a visible behaviour: a studio instructs an AI model to "paint in the style of X," where X is a living artist. The model obliges and produces a convincing pastiche within seconds. The result appears elegant. Yet the behaviour tells another story. It exploits a recognisable visual grammar developed over decades by an identifiable human being. The implication? The studio has appropriated not just a technique but a livelihood. Once shared publicly, the image seeds reputational damage. A client questions the studio's judgement. A follower calls out the mimicry. A journalist writes a line that sticks: "They trade in borrowed genius."

This is why serious visual teams now draft explicit policy. They refuse celebrity likenesses without written consent. They reject mimicry of living artists. They build internal review gates that check for unintended resemblance before work leaves the studio. The behaviours are specific. A designer measures the proximity of a facial structure to a known figure. A creative director compares a brushstroke pattern against reference sheets of protected styles. A producer commits to logging provenance for all generative inputs. These decisions are simple but disciplined; they prevent small errors from becoming public crises.

A counter-example deserves attention. Some argue that all art borrows, and that the history of visual culture is one long chain of influence. They point to Cubism emerging from African sculpture, to Pop Art riffing on advertising, to fashion houses reinterpreting silhouettes from the previous century. And they are right. Influence is the engine of creativity. The limitation of this argument appears when we consider two metrics. First, historical borrowing often involved reinterpretation, not duplication. Second, the parties being referenced were not modern individuals losing income or identity to algorithmic mimicry. The principle of consent did not vanish with the arrival of AI; it simply became more urgent.

Reconciliation comes from precision. A studio can draw from traditions, genres, and movements—Impressionist colour logic, Bauhaus composition, Ukiyo-e line economy—because these are collective legacies, shaped by many hands over many years. These references belong to cultures, not to single living individuals whose style is part of their livelihood. The distinction is not subtle. It is the ethical fulcrum on which modern visual practice turns. It gives designers a clear path: study widely, borrow wisely, imitate no one identifiable without permission.

Reputation, as ever, is part of design. Clients judge not only quality but conduct. A studio that demonstrates restraint becomes trusted. One that courts controversy loses work. The behaviours that build reputation are visible and repeatable: declining a brief that asks for a famous face; advising a client that an AI-generated imitation risks litigation; showing them alternative pathways grounded in original craft. Each act signals commitment. Each protects the studio's long-term standing.

Two further concrete cases illuminate the stakes. In 2021, Warner Bros. faced criticism after using a digital likeness of Anthony Bourdain's voice in the documentary *Roadrunner*, created through machine learning without the public's prior understanding. Though the estate had granted permission, viewers described the moment as uncomfortable, even unsettling. It showed that consent alone is not sufficient; context and expectations matter. The second case comes from 2023, when a deepfake of Tom Cruise circulated widely on TikTok, generated by a creator using an AI face-swapping tool. The likeness was striking. The ethical issue was not the artistry but the false authorship. Millions believed they were watching the actor. This demonstrated how imitation, once realistic enough, can fracture public trust in what is seen.

Here the motif of the face returns. A face is a story. When stolen or manipulated, it turns into a mask—persuasive, hollow, and dangerous. Designers understand this intuitively. They choose restraint not merely to avoid backlash, but to preserve the social contract that makes visual work possible: viewers must believe that images reflect honest intention.

The studio that sets a policy on ethical imitation is not being prudish. It is practising craft. Craft in design has always required boundary-setting. In the nineteenth century, William Morris demanded that artisans respect material truth. In the twentieth, Dieter Rams asked designers to avoid deceit in form and function. In the twenty-first, the boundary concerns identity. The question is no longer "Does this look good?" but "Does this respect the person whose likeness or style it resembles?"

As generative tools grow more capable, the temptation to imitate will intensify. Teams will confront briefs that promise speed but jeopardise integrity. They will fetch references that look efficient yet echo recognisable artists. They will face clients who request celebrity faces to boost engagement metrics. And each time, the designer will return to the quiet motif: *You cannot fake a face.*

The unresolved tension sits here. When a studio can generate anything—any style, any likeness, any visual fingerprint—what will it choose not to create? Craft begins with refusal. Boundaries shape identity. The open question for every working designer becomes simple, sharp, and unavoidable: which ethical line, once crossed, would make the work no longer worth doing?

Deliverables that Travel

In May 2022, an Amsterdam studio delivered a striking set of key visuals for a global sneaker campaign. The client loved them. Two months later, the same client, now briefing a winter variant from their New York office, asked for "the same world, different season": colder light, deeper shadows, a slate-grey background instead of concrete. The studio opened its own archive and went cold. The final files were flattened RGB TIFFs, exported in a rush for a tight deadline. No layers, no passes, no notes. The only way to honour the re-brief was to rebuild everything from scratch. The original art director estimated they lost forty hours of avoidable rework. His verdict was curt: "The file had no handles." The phrase stuck. Handles. Points of grip that allow an image to be moved, adapted, explained. In the analogue era, a negative and a contact sheet functioned as handles: you could reprint with different exposure, crop differently, dial the contrast. In a generative workflow, handles live in layers, render passes, naming conventions, embedded prompts, and human-readable descriptions. They make the difference between a beautiful asset and a usable one. A file that cannot travel is not a deliverable. It is a poster pinned to a single wall.

The first major claim is straightforward to show. Files that move well reduce friction. When BBC Creative's motion team in London re-versioned their 2021 Wimbledon trails for different platforms, they did not start from exported ProRes alone. They worked from packages: layered composites, per-object mattes, graded and ungraded passes, written notes on timing, and a small PDF describing the logic behind type and colour. These materials travelled between teams in London, Salford, and Cardiff without endless clarification emails. The behaviour is measurable: fewer "Can you just tweak..." messages; fewer hours of detective work in After Effects; fewer painful discoveries that the only way to adjust a detail is to rebuild a shot.

We can name this mindset **portability as a design requirement**. Not an afterthought. Not a bonus. A requirement. Explain it this way: a design rarely lives once. It appears on a billboard, then a mobile feed, then a pitch deck, then an internal training slide. It outlives the campaign inside a brand archive. If the deliverable carries its own logic—if the client can open it and see not just pixels but structure—each new use costs less. The implication is commercial as much as aesthetic. Studios that ship explainable files quietly become more valuable than those who ship only finished pictures.

This becomes even more pressing in AI-heavy workflows. A model can produce a compelling image that is almost impossible to adapt: merged elements, ambiguous depth, lighting baked into textures, no separation between foreground and background. Such images are fine as sketches. They are liabilities as deliverables. The studios that succeed are the ones that treat the AI output as a starting point, then rebuild with layers and passes that will survive new briefs, new markets, and new teams.

Consider a second, very concrete example. In 2020, IKEA's visualisation team in Älmhult began to formalise its CGI pipeline so that product renders could be reused across catalogues, web tools, and AR apps. Each deliverable was exported with standard passes: beauty, diffuse, specular, shadow, reflection, ambient occlusion. Crucially, they also shipped scene descriptions—camera positions, HDRI maps, material libraries—with human-readable naming. When marketing teams requested "identical lighting, different finish" a year later, the change took hours, not days. The behaviour that made this possible was banal but rigorous: consistent file structures, clear layer names, and short technical notes bundled with the images. The implication is obvious. Portability is not glamorous, but it compounds. Every future project loads faster.

The counter-example is easy to find. A boutique studio in Paris built its reputation on lush, painterly AI-assisted visuals for fashion editorials. Clients fell in love with the look. But when a major brand asked for localisation—new models, modesty adjustments for specific markets, minor logo changes—the studio discovered that much of its work existed only as flattened exports and orphaned prompt snippets in chat logs. No layered masters. No saved seeds. No documentation of the lighting setup. The re-brief turned into a quiet disaster. They had to reverse-engineer their own aesthetic, under pressure, in public. The limitation here is not talent. It is the absence of handles.

The reconciliation is clear. Experimental one-offs can afford fragility; campaign assets cannot. The more a piece of work is likely to be re-used, re-versioned, or scrutinised, the more its deliverables must be built for travel. That travel can be measured: how long does it take a new designer, opening the file for the first time, to understand how it works? Minutes or hours? That metric is the real test of portability.

Portability is not only technical. It is cognitive. The file must explain itself. This is where descriptions matter. A one-page read-me that says, "Layer group 01: product; 02: shadows; 03: reflections; 04: background; 05: typography; colour grade in adjustment layers only," does more to preserve value than any amount of silent cleverness. A few lines explaining the reasoning—"We kept shadows separate so they can be cooled or warmed per market"—turn a static artifact into a living system.

Think of the deliverable as a map. Not just a picture of the territory, but a record of how to walk it again. Render passes show where light lives. Layers show what can move. Descriptions show why choices were made. Together, they give downstream teams something to trust. Trust here is not an abstraction. It is the behaviour of a client who feels confident enough to commission extensions without insisting the original studio do every small adjustment. It is the behaviour of an in-house designer who can open a file from two years ago and work with it without cursing whoever named every layer "Layer 17 copy 3".

Portability also protects against organisational memory loss. People leave. Agencies rebrand. Asset management systems migrate. The only way a design survives these transitions is if the deliverable carries enough structure to be intelligible beyond its original context. This is why serious teams commit to boring practices: standard export presets, predictable folder hierarchies, and versioning that actually means something. "2023-07-14_CampaignA_Hero01_v04.psd" tells a story. "final_final_new.psd" is a trap.

AI changes the texture of this discussion but not its core. Prompts themselves become part of the deliverable. A studio that includes the base prompt, key negative prompts, and relevant model parameters in a sidecar text file offers a client future leverage: they can re-run, tweak, or extend the work with clarity about what drove the original outputs. Without this, the client is left with a magical image and no spellbook. Again, handles. A good prompt is a handle on a latent space.

Two more examples sharpen the point. In 2021, the New York Times digital design team began attaching micro-specs to illustration commissions—hex codes for key colours, safe crop regions, and suggested alt-text. When AI-driven variants entered the workflow, these micro-specs meant derivatives stayed on-brand and accessible without new rounds of briefing. Meanwhile, in 2022, a game studio in Montreal instituted a rule that every concept environment generated with AI had to be "made explainable" before it left pre-production: major elements separated into layers, depth approximated in passes, perspective grids overlaid and saved. This slowed early delivery slightly but dramatically reduced confusion when the assets moved to level designers and lighting artists.

There is a deeper implication here: portability is a form of respect. Respect for the client's future needs, for other creatives who will touch the work, and for your own future self. It acknowledges that design lives in time. What looks finished at sign-off is often just beginning a longer journey through formats and contexts you cannot yet foresee. Building deliverables that travel is an act of humility. It admits you will not always be in the room.

The quiet motif of handles returns. Each export decision either adds a handle or removes one. Flattening a layer discards a handle. Merging the grade into the image discards a handle. Throwing away the prompt history discards a handle. Conversely, naming a group, saving a pass, writing a short note—all add points of grip.

Of course, there is a trade-off. Overbuilding deliverables can create noise. Not every social tile needs a twenty-layer master. Not every exploratory sketch merits full documentation. The risk is that, in the name of future-proofing, studios drown present work in process. Time spent polishing unnecessary layers is time not spent refining idea, composition, or message. The skill lies in deciding what must travel and what can remain local.

That decision is not purely technical. It is strategic. A studio that consistently ships explainable, portable work can charge for it. Portability becomes a service edge: "We do not only deliver images; we deliver systems." The statement is only credible if the files bear it out.

The unresolved tension, then, is sharp but productive. How far should a team go in building handles into every visual artefact? Where is the boundary between professional rigour and process for its own sake? And when the next brief arrives—urgent, under-specified, generatively rich—will the studio resist the temptation to throw out structure for speed, or will it design deliverables that can still move gracefully through the projects yet to come?

Chapter 8
Writing with Models

The email arrived at 03:17 from a tired reporter in Nairobi. She had spent two days on a deadline, trying to reconcile conflicting figures from a leaked procurement report. The numbers refused to stabilise. Every time she tried to draft the story, the structure buckled under the weight of competing claims. Out of frustration, she fed her notes into a model to sketch a possible outline—not prose, just a scaffold. When she opened the output an hour later, she found a remarkably clear arc: the disputed contracts, the missing audits, the ministry's shifting rationale. It wasn't accurate yet. But it offered a frame sturdy enough to hold the truth once she confirmed it. In the morning light, she did the hard work: re-reading PDFs, calling sources, cross-checking every figure. The final piece landed with force. Readers praised its clarity; editors praised its discipline. She credited the model with giving her a map. She credited herself with drawing the borders.

That border—between structure and substance, between scaffolding and judgement—sits at the heart of contemporary writing with models. The tools have changed the tempo. They can draft ten possible outlines before coffee cools. They can mimic tonal shifts with eerie sensitivity. They can summarise sprawling documents into coherent points in seconds. Yet they stop just short of the one thing that distinguishes meaningful writing from smooth text: the courage to commit to what is true. Models can offer momentum; humans supply conviction. This tension is not a hindrance. It is the beginning of a new craft.

Writers have always worked with constraints: column inches, editorial rhythms, the silent expectations of their audience.

What has changed is the nature of the collaborator. Where once we bounced ideas off colleagues, or built index cards on a dusty table, we now coax model-based partners that are fast, tireless, and strangely suggestive. They generate options at industrial speed, but these options are ungrounded until we anchor them in evidence and lived context. The process feels at times like composing with echoes: familiar shapes, uncanny fragments, and the occasional spark that aligns perfectly with one's intention. Each spark must be inspected, tested, and, if worthy, integrated with deliberate care.

This chapter sits downstream from the previous discussions on originality, curation, and studio practice. Here the focus shifts from images to words, from composition boards to paragraphs, and from visual drift to rhetorical precision. But the underlying questions persist: What does it mean to retain authorship in the presence of powerful models? How do we guide these systems without ceding judgement? And how do we preserve the integrity of argument when the ease of generation can tempt even seasoned writers into confident shortcuts?

One of the central motifs in this chapter is the outline—the quiet architecture beneath every piece of writing. In a model-assisted workflow, the outline becomes both prompt and compass. It clarifies intent before the first sentence lands. It lets the writer test structure before committing to claims. Crucially, it reveals gaps that cannot be filled with style alone. A well-made outline exposes the missing source, the unexamined link, the weak assumption. It does not fix these deficiencies; it merely illuminates them. That illumination is invaluable. It restores the primacy of thought over fluency.

Parallel to structure lies voice, that fragile mixture of rhythm, attitude, and preference that distinguishes one writer from another. Models are uncanny mimics, but their mimicry can erode the edges that make a voice recognisable. To write with models, one must build guardrails: a palette of preferred moves, a list of banned filler, a baseline cadence that maintains personality across outputs. These constraints do more than sustain aesthetic unity; they cultivate trust between writer and reader. Consistency is not monotony. It is a repeated signal that someone with discernible standards is guiding the work.

Trust deepens when claims rest on verifiable ground. Retrieval systems provide an odd but potent combination: speed and sobriety. They retrieve passages, citations, and details from a bounded corpus—an internal archive, a dataset of regulatory documents, a collection of personal notes. These retrieved fragments act as ballast, preventing drift into the plausible-but-false. The model supplies surface fluency; the retrieval engine supplies evidential weight; the writer supplies judgement about which facts matter and why. This triad forms a modern research stack, one that replaces the hand-waving of hurried summarisation with the grounded clarity of sourced writing.

Yet even when structure stands firm and facts are sound, writing only becomes itself in the editing. This is where the model's most delicate contribution emerges. Models can propose cuts that sharpen rhythm. They can flag repeated phrases a writer has grown blind to. They can suggest alternate formulations that untie knotted syntax. But only the writer can sense when an edit harms the argument or drains the tone of lived meaning. Editing remains an act of discernment. It is the last place in the workflow where authorship is unmistakably human: the place where the writer must decide what to keep, what to discard, and what to fight for.

The modern writing stack is therefore not a replacement but a reconfiguration. The writer is no longer a solitary architect labouring over every beam and joint, nor an overseer delegating tasks wholesale to an obedient machine. The relationship is more nuanced. The model becomes a provocateur, a generator of possibilities, a relentless producer of drafts that illuminate the path forward. But the writer remains the arbiter of meaning. Their responsibility—to truth, to voice, to the reader—does not dilute. It sharpens. The ease of generation forces a higher standard of scrutiny.

Throughout the chapter, we will return to one recurring image: the writer standing before a desk scattered with drafts, each generated in seconds, each tempting in its coherence. The risk is seduction. Coherence feels like truth. But these drafts are only surfaces until the writer interrogates them. What claim here rests on unverifiable ground? What assertion leans too heavily on generalisation? What turn of phrase sounds plausible but conceals a weak inference? The work of writing with models is the work of refusing to be lulled by fluency.

There is also a broader cultural dimension to consider. As models shape the production of text at scale—from corporate reports to philanthropic analyses to personal newsletters—the distinction between writing that merely flows and writing that actually thinks will matter more. Readers may not articulate the difference, but they will feel it. The best model-assisted writing will retain the qualities that have always marked serious work: a sense of care, an underlying argument, and the courage to name complexity rather than gloss over it.

If there is a single unifying force in this new landscape, it is intentionality. Not the abstract kind, but the concrete kind: choosing a structure deliberately; spelling out the audience explicitly; sourcing claims with precision; holding one's own voice steady; editing with a commitment to nuance; refusing to let the tool outrun the thought. Intentionality is what allows a writer to move quickly without losing themselves in the speed.

And so the chapter begins with a tension rather than an answer. How do we harness the efficiency of models without letting them flatten our thinking? How do we maintain voice while collaborating with systems that can imitate almost any tone? How do we anchor writing in evidence without becoming archivists drowning in data? And when the drafts arrive—fast, polished, tempting—how do we ensure that the final text bears the unmistakable imprint of a writer who has judged, weighed, and believed every line?

Outlining and Argument

On 12 June 2019, in a windowless office at the *Financial Times* in London, editor Matthew Garrahan halted the late-stage production of a long investigative feature. The draft, though elegant, rested on a fragile spine. Paragraph three hinted at conflicts of interest without naming sources; the middle section stitched together anecdotes that had not been independently verified; the conclusion leaned heavily on conjecture. The writer had used an early-generation model to sketch the article's structure, and the outline it produced was seductively coherent. Yet as Garrahan placed the printout on the table, he pointed to the empty margins. "Where is the evidence for this turn?" he asked. The model had provided a skeleton; the writer had provided style. But the truth, the part that could withstand scrutiny, was missing. The piece was pulled until the claims were provable. The structure survived. Several assertions did not. The lesson was simple. Frames can be borrowed. Facts cannot.

The power of a model-generated outline lies precisely in this tension: it builds momentum with astonishing speed, yet it cannot measure the accuracy of its own logic. A strong outline can rescue a writer from chaos. A weak one can accelerate error. The craft rests in knowing the difference, and in refusing to treat a well-shaped draft as a proxy for a well-supported argument. Models map possibilities. Writers test them.

A recurring motif in this subchapter—the *margin*—captures the divide between suggestion and substantiation. Models fill the page; writers fill the margin with the evidence that grounds the work. When that margin stays empty, the text becomes performance, not argument.

To understand why structure matters so deeply, consider how an outline functions at its best. It is an architectural plan: a set of interlocking claims arranged to maximise clarity. Show the pattern first, then name its value. When a model produces an initial outline, it demonstrates patterns in the input: recurrent themes, implied contrasts, narrative arcs. This is the "Show". But once the pattern is visible, the writer must name its purpose: is this chronology the right one? Does the argument hinge on causality or correlation? Does the tension hold? Only humans reliably evaluate these questions, because the answers require external knowledge—the kind drawn from sources, not surfaces.

The implication follows: outlines accelerate decision-making, but they impose an obligation. They demand that the writer slow down long enough to verify. Momentum should not outrun truth.

Two concrete examples illustrate the interplay between model-led structure and human-led verification. In March 2021, the investigative unit at *ProPublica* used a model to generate alternative structural options for a complex piece on environmental regulation in Mississippi. The tool proposed five outline shapes: chronological, thematic, geographical, causal, and investigative. The team selected the causal variant because it exposed the core issue—conflicting incentives between state agencies—most clearly. But every claim in that scaffold required sourcing. Reporters spent three weeks verifying each causal link with public records and interviews. The model had offered direction; the humans supplied proof.

A contrasting example comes from a 2022 internal audit report at a multinational based in Düsseldorf. Analysts used a model to summarise procurement irregularities and propose an outline for remediation. The summary claimed that 60% of discrepancies came from "vendor rotation practices". When auditors traced the sources manually, they found the figure unsupported; the real number, according to the firm's compliance team, was closer to 18% (Audit Memo, April 2022). The outline, though neatly formed, embedded an invented anchor. The team revised the structure entirely once the data were checked. The limitation here was not malicious generation; it was human overconfidence in fluent scaffolding. Reconciliation required returning to the primary ledger.

These examples reveal the core constraint. Models excel at proposing shapes; they falter at validating them. They can recommend a three-act investigative arc or a dialectical essay structure. They cannot judge whether a statistical claim is grounded. The writer must bridge that gap. The bridgework is visible behaviour: tracing a figure to its source, checking dates, confirming definitions, consulting expertise outside the model's input. Argument requires friction.

The counter-example matters too. Some writers argue that structure generated by models can narrow thinking by imposing patterns too quickly. They fear that early scaffolds create confirmation bias, steering research towards what "fits". This critique has merit. A prematurely accepted outline can become a tunnel. Yet the limitation is manageable. The remedy is procedural: generate multiple outlines, compare them, and attach sources only once a structure proves defensible. When the margin fills with evidence, not assumptions, the tunnel widens into a field.

The role of constraints becomes clearer when a writer pairs outline generation with disciplined sourcing. Consider the case of a longform policy piece produced for a parliamentary research unit in Westminster in October 2023. The writer used a model to propose five potential argumentative arcs for a report on energy subsidies. Only one arc integrated both economic and environmental dimensions without skew: a tension between short-term relief and long-term transition.

However, this arc only held once the writer filled in specific facts: Office for Budget Responsibility projections for fiscal impact (OBR, 2023), Department for Energy Security documents, and a series of cost curves from the UK Energy Research Centre. The structure prepared the field; the evidence decided the game.

The margin motif returns here. Each section of the outline gained a margin filled with citations, figures, and caveats. The writer could now commit to claims. Without this evidence, the draft would have looked persuasive but collapsed under verification. With it, the argument gained weight.

The most subtle value of model-generated outlines is the capacity to expose gaps. Writers often identify missing links only after they appear as blank spaces in the scaffold. If a model proposes a transition from "economic drivers" to "social impact" without showing how one influences the other, the writer must interrogate the gap. That interrogation is a metric of intellectual honesty: identifying a missing citation, a leap in reasoning, or a misinterpreted dataset.

Conversely, outlines can reveal redundancy. When a model repeats the same point across different sections, the writer sees where the argument is padded or circular. This is another visible behaviour—removing repetition, tightening logic, assessing whether each step advances the reader's understanding.

The risk, however, is seduction by fluency. A fluent outline feels right even when unsupported. Writers must resist equating coherence with credibility. A structure can be elegant and wrong. This is where discipline enters. The writer measures claims. They compare proposed shapes. They commit only after testing. Those verbs—measure, compare, commit—capture the human role. Models propose. Humans decide.

The value of this partnership becomes especially clear in scientific or policy contexts where stakes rise. A model can summarise a 300-page report on groundwater depletion and suggest an outline for a policy brief. But the writer must locate the primary hydrogeology papers, verify that a key figure on aquifer recharge rates comes from a peer-reviewed source (e.g., the British Geological Survey, 2018), not from a projected estimate, and ensure that any claim about long-term trend uncertainty is properly framed. The margin fills. The argument strengthens.

The quiet motif continues: the margin as a site of responsibility. The outline provides form; the margin provides truth. Without both, the piece fails.

This dynamic becomes a skill. Writers who routinely use models to outline learn to treat them as drafting partners rather than authority figures. They adjust outlines as sources accumulate. They revisit structure once contradictions emerge. They maintain version hygiene, saving outline revisions with dates and reasons. These behaviours form a working discipline.

What remains unresolved is not the role of models but the degree of reliance. How much scaffolding is too much? At what point does an outline begin to steer research rather than respond to it? And how should a writer resist the gravitational pull of a model's confident structure when the evidence does not yet justify it?

Voice and Consistency

On 3 February 2021, in Brooklyn, writer Anne Helen Petersen faced a problem familiar to anyone who publishes regularly. The latest issue of her newsletter, *Culture Study*, was technically fine: well researched, neatly edited, and timely. Yet when she reread the draft before sending, she sensed that something essential had slipped. The sentences were smooth, but the voice—her voice, the one subscribers recognised instantly—had thinned. It sounded less like a person and more like a system. Petersen later described the moment as "the uncanny valley of my own tone". The metrics reinforced her instinct. Reader replies fell by nearly half that week, a rare dip for a publication known for its intimate cadence. The structure was present. The personality was not. She rebuilt her style guide the following month and the replies rebounded. A reminder: trust is audible.

That dip illustrates a paradox. Readers forgive many things—typos, delays, even argument shifts—but they rarely forgive inconsistency of tone. They read for news or ideas, yes, but they stay for a sensibility. A newsletter becomes part of a reader's week only when its sound becomes recognisable. Five words can set it. Consistency is comfort.

A model entering this workflow offers enormous leverage in drafting speed, but it introduces a tension. It amplifies whatever palette it is given, yet it cannot detect when that palette begins to drift. The writer must measure that drift. The motif of the *sound*—the subtle frequency that marks a writer's identity—threads through everything that follows.

The first claim is simple to show. When a team creates a voice palette, the palette acts as a diagnostic instrument. The *Financial Times* built a comprehensive tone guide in 2017 to support its growing roster of digital newsletters. Edited by Malcolm Moore, the guide defined not only vocabulary but tempo, permissible idioms, and sentence shapes. Reporters were encouraged to compare their drafts against the guide before filing. This visible behaviour—checking a sentence against a list of approved phrases—was not aesthetic fussiness; it was risk control. It reduced brand variance across contributors and protected reader trust during a period of rapid expansion. A palette stabilised the sound.

Naming the principle clarifies its reach. A voice palette is not decoration. It is a constraint that binds personality to purpose. When applied to model-assisted writing, it becomes even more essential. A model will default to generic fluency unless given boundaries; without a palette, it will gravitate towards abstraction or cliché. With one, it behaves like an apprentice following a master's notes. The implication is clear. Consistency is not accidental. It is engineered.

The second major claim follows naturally. Banned-word lists—when used well—sharpen the sound rather than restrict it. A concrete example comes from *The Guardian*'s style guide, which has, since at least 2014, prohibited terms such as "iconic" unless strictly justified. The purpose was empirical. Editors had measured overuse across lifestyle and culture desks and found that the term diluted meaning and confused tone. By removing the word, they forced writers to describe qualities rather than rely on shorthand. In model-assisted environments, banned-word lists serve an even sharper role: they prevent drift into the vague, the sentimental, or the over-broad. They force precision.

A contrasting example reveals a limitation. A media start-up in Toronto in 2022 adopted an aggressive banned-word list to differentiate its newsletters from competitors. The list ballooned to over 200 entries. Writers began to complain that the prohibition grid left them sounding stilted. When the founders analysed open-rate data across twelve weeks, they saw no improvement. The ban had become a straitjacket. The team eventually pared the list back to twenty terms and restored flexibility. The reconciliation here is straightforward. Restrictions preserve flavour only when they reinforce intention; when they obstruct expression, they distort voice.

These examples show how voice and consistency emerge from the interaction between palette, prohibition, and behaviour. The abstraction of "trust" becomes a metric: reply rates, open rates, or even reader retention curves. The abstraction of "efficiency" becomes visible in fewer rewrites. The abstraction of "risk" appears in the avoidance of tonal missteps that trigger subscriber churn. Each metric ties voice to action.

The motif of sound returns. A voice palette acts like a tuning fork. Writers hold it up to their sentences and listen for resonance. Models, for all their fluency, cannot hear dissonance on their own; they must be tuned.

Another major claim concerns personality across issues. A newsletter that shifts tone week by week feels unmoored. A consistent voice, by contrast, creates narrative continuity. The best practitioners show this. In London, *The Browser*'s editors have maintained a remarkably consistent voice since 2008 by enforcing a simple but powerful guideline: every summary must read as though one knowledgeable friend were recommending an article to another. That single behavioural rule prevents drift across dozens of curators and years of editorial turnover. The structure of the guideline—not its length—keeps the voice intact.

Explain the mechanism and its implication becomes evident. A single clear behavioural cue, articulated in the palette, sets the model's target. When curators use model assistance to draft summaries, they provide this cue as part of the prompt. The model mimics the tonal contour; the editor refines it. The result is a consistent sound that survives scale.

A second example underscores that consistency is not monotony. In 2023, the *Tech Won't Save Us* newsletter faced the challenge of integrating model-assisted drafts without losing its distinctive sceptical voice. The editors conducted a six-week experiment: each issue included one item drafted by a model and one entirely human-written piece. Readers consistently identified the model draft as "flatter" unless the editors applied a palette containing seven tone cues and five banned terms. Once those were added, the tonal distinction narrowed dramatically. The model could approximate the voice only when guided by explicit constraints. Again the implication is instructive. Personality is teachable to a model, but only if the parameters are crisp, limited, and enforced.

Yet voice consistency carries its own risk. If the palette is too rigid, the writing calcifies. A credible counter-example highlights the tension. A research institute in Geneva attempted to enforce a unified tone across all policy briefs in 2021. The palette emphasised formality and neutrality. Over time, analysts felt that the policy briefs sounded interchangeable. When the institute commissioned a readership survey, respondents expressed difficulty distinguishing between authors. This undermined a key goal: establishing analyst credibility. The institute revised the palette to include permitted "personal markers": qualified scepticism, the occasional first-person qualifier, and controlled metaphor. Consistency returned, but with dimensionality. The reconciliation is a reminder that readers trust a voice when they sense both reliability and humanity.

This balance becomes particularly delicate when integrating models into the editorial workflow. Models can imitate surfaces but cannot yet infer the deeper logic of a writer's personality: their humour, their restraint, the specific ways they use rhythm to signal emphasis. Human oversight therefore remains indispensable. Editors must compare outputs against the palette, measure drift, and commit to revisions. These are deliberate acts, not passive checks.

The behaviour that sustains voice is often small and immediate. Writers keep a running list of phrases they would never use. They highlight sentences that "sound wrong", even if they cannot initially articulate why. They log examples of the newsletter's characteristic turns of phrase. They revisit earlier issues to ensure continuity. Such actions anchor the motif of sound in daily practice. When models participate, these behaviours become even more important. A model can produce a competent paragraph. It cannot recognise when confidence tilts into swagger, or when clarity becomes sterility.

The palette itself can evolve, and this evolution is measurable. A team might track revisions per issue, noting whether the number decreases as the palette strengthens. Or they may measure reader replies after introducing a new tone guideline. These metrics show whether the sound remains coherent. They convert the abstraction of voice into something observable.

Yet the deepest function of a voice palette is cultural. It tells contributors, whether human or model-assisted, *how this publication speaks to the world*. It preserves continuity through staff changes, format shifts, or platform transitions. It provides an ethical container: certain tones are inappropriate, certain turns of phrase misleading, certain emotional registers manipulative. The palette shapes judgement.

Returning, once more, to the motif of sound, the palette is the score; the banned-word list is the metronome; the writer is the performer; the model is the accompanist. When all four align, the result is tone that readers recognise instantly, even before they see the byline.

But an unresolved tension remains. As models grow more adept at stylistic mimicry, will teams rely too heavily on automated tone? And how will writers decide when the sound resembles them closely enough to trust, and when it merely imitates without understanding?

Research and Retrieval

In April 2016, an internal audit at the British energy company Centrica uncovered a quiet but costly flaw. A strategy report circulated among senior managers contained a confident claim about projected maintenance savings for the North Sea gas fields. The number looked plausible. It was wrong. The figure had been lifted from an earlier memo whose assumptions had since been revised. Because the report cited no internal source—no filename, no author, no date—the error travelled unchecked. It took the audit team three days to trace the origin of the statement through email chains and archived spreadsheets. Three days to correct one sentence. The incident prompted Centrica to overhaul its research protocols, mandating explicit citation of internal documents in all strategic papers by the end of that year. A small lapse had revealed a structural vulnerability: when claims float free from their materials, trust evaporates. A model, had it been used, would have amplified the drift.

The paradox sits at the heart of model-assisted writing. Language models excel at producing coherent prose at speed, yet they lack a native sense of provenance. They assert before they verify. They guess when they ought to check. Retrieval—structured, disciplined, auditable retrieval—is the bridge between fluency and fact. It turns a model from a generator into a researcher's assistant, making each claim traceable. Without retrieval, a system will stray. With it, the work sharpens.

A quiet motif threads through the practice: *the anchor*. Every statement needs one. Retrieval provides it.

The first major claim is visible in any organisation that has formalised retrieval pipelines. In 2020, the European Centre for Medium-Range Weather Forecasts (ECMWF) revised its reporting workflow after several near-miss communication errors. Analysts drafting seasonal climate summaries began feeding models with curated document sets: previous bulletins, observational datasets, and methodological notes. The model produced structured outlines grounded in those materials. A researcher then checked each section against the retrieved sources, line by line. This behaviour—a human inspecting the provenance of every model-assisted statement—reduced correction cycles by measurable margins. ECMWF reported a 23 per cent reduction in post-publication amendments in 2021 (ECMWF, 2021). The name of the principle is straightforward. Ground the claim in the corpus.

Explain this and its implication becomes clear. Retrieval restricts the model's field of invention. It funnels it. It prevents what machine learning researchers call "representational drift", the subtle slide from evidence to approximation. When a model is required to cite specific document paragraphs before writing, its sentences become anchored. The risk of error falls.

A second example shows the same principle under pressure. Between 2019 and 2022, the UK's Competition and Markets Authority (CMA) explored model-assisted drafting for merger analyses. Early experiments proved uneven. When models generated summaries without retrieval, analysts found that 30–40 per cent of statements lacked sufficient grounding in the case files. When retrieval was added—specifically, paragraph-level extraction from witness statements, expert reports, and prior decisions—the error rate dropped below 10 per cent. Analysts could see the anchor for every claim. They trusted the system because they could audit it. The visible behaviour—cross-checking each assertion with a linked document ID—strengthened the credibility of the output.

Yet retrieval has a limitation that must be acknowledged. A credible counter-example emerged from a health research team at a Berlin university hospital in early 2022. They used a retrieval-augmented model to draft literature summaries for internal meetings. The model performed well when the corpus was narrow and homogeneous. But when the corpus contained conflicting evidence—studies with divergent findings, preliminary results, or ambiguous abstracts—the model tended to over-privilege the most recent or most accessible sources. It anchored, but it anchored shallowly. The retrieval pipeline itself required human calibration. The team responded by adding a manual relevance check before retrieval. The reconciliation is instructive. Retrieval reduces hallucination risk, but it does not resolve evidentiary ambiguity. Humans must judge the materiality of sources.

The motif returns. An anchor is only useful when sunk into something stable.

The second major claim concerns efficiency. Retrieval compresses research time not by cutting corners, but by making visible what otherwise hides in inboxes, file servers, or personal memory. A product manager at a Montréal software firm noted that before adopting retrieval-assisted drafting in 2023, her team spent hours hunting for old design rationales. After implementing a retrieval index over internal documentation, they could surface the relevant decision log in seconds. The behaviour is concrete. Instead of asking a colleague "Do you remember why we chose this architecture?", the writer queries the indexed corpus and attaches the source. Efficiency becomes a metric: fewer Slack messages, fewer meetings, fewer duplicated searches.

Naming the practice—retrieval-first drafting—helps clarify its role. It shifts the order of operations. Instead of drafting and then retrofitting evidence, the writer begins with the evidence. The model ingests it. The outline emerges. The text grows from soil rather than air. The implication is profound. Retrieval redefines what it means to prepare to write.

But efficiency alone is insufficient. The deeper value lies in risk reduction, especially when drafting claims that must withstand scrutiny. Risk is visible in the frequency of corrections, the tenor of stakeholder feedback, or the burden placed on editors downstream. Retrieval distributes that risk. It spreads it across documents, timestamps, and authorship. When a statement is wrong, the retrieval chain reveals where.

A second major claim follows naturally. Retrieval makes institutional memory durable. Organisations that rely on tacit knowledge—soft impressions, unrecorded decisions, silent assumptions—are vulnerable to drift. A structured retrieval pipeline forces teams to document. An internal report that cites "design-spec-v4, 12 July 2020, p. 3" transforms a fleeting memory into a recoverable artefact. This behaviour, repeated across months, produces an organisation that knows what it knows.

A counter-example clarifies the fragility of this system. A civic-tech non-profit in Manchester attempted to use model-assisted drafting for grant proposals in 2021. They built no retrieval index. Instead, they relied on shared folders and verbal coordination. The resulting proposals contained inconsistent data: volunteer counts varied between drafts; timelines contradicted each other; financial figures drifted. Reviewers flagged the inconsistencies, and one proposal failed. The team later introduced a retrieval layer over their internal folders. The problem was not the model. It was the absence of anchors. The reconciliation reinforces the chapter's theme. Retrieval cannot be optional.

The motif of anchors deepens here. Retrieval fixes the text to something that resists movement. It keeps the writer from drifting into confident error.

Each abstraction in this domain—accuracy, trust, clarity—can be rendered visible. Accuracy becomes the number of source links per section. Trust becomes the reduction in post-publication corrections. Clarity becomes the consistency of key terms across drafts. When retrieval is integral to the workflow, these metrics stabilise.

Another major claim is that retrieval changes the psychology of writing. Writers often fear the blank page because it demands both structure and substance at once. Retrieval splits the task. The writer curates the material; the model arranges it; the writer interprets it. This division mirrors traditional research workflows but accelerates them. In effect, retrieval gives the writer a scaffolding of certainty. It reduces cognitive load while increasing epistemic discipline.

A historical example illustrates the continuity of this principle. In 1690, John Locke compiled *A Common-Place Book to the Holy Bible*, a structured index meant to support his philosophical writing. Locke knew that insight depended on retrieval, not recollection. The index anchored his arguments. The logic remains: arguments become robust when the writer can recover the texts that shape them. Retrieval-assisted models simply automate the indexing that thinkers once had to perform manually.

But retrieval also constrains creativity. Too narrow a corpus can trap the writer within familiar grooves. The risk is visible in legal or regulatory drafting where precedent dominates. To reconcile this, teams often create layered retrieval: a primary corpus of authoritative documents and a secondary corpus of exploratory materials. The writer chooses the anchor depth. The model follows. The implication is that retrieval must be curated, not merely assembled.

The motif returns one final time. An anchor must hold but must not prevent movement.

These dynamics culminate in a quiet but consequential question: how do we decide which documents deserve inclusion in the retrieval corpus? The decision carries weight. Include too much, and the model becomes unfocused. Include too little, and claims lose richness. The writer stands at the centre of this choice. They are the curator of the evidence the model will echo.

The unresolved tension sits here. As models grow more capable of summarising large volumes of text, will writers become seduced by convenience and trust summaries more than sources? And what signals will tell them that an anchor has slipped, that the model is speaking confidently from a foundation thinner than it appears?

Editing and Polishing

In September 2019, the editor Mary Norris walked through the copy desk at *The New Yorker* with a marked-up printout of a long essay on American linguistics. The writer had spent months shaping the piece; Norris spent two hours tightening it. She trimmed seventeen lines, shifted three paragraphs, and replaced a single word whose register threatened to tilt the argument off balance. When the author later described the edit to colleagues, he said something telling: "She didn't change my voice. She clarified it." The outcome was not merely a cleaner draft. It was a restoration of intention. The line that had troubled the editor—a phrase that struck the wrong emotional chord—became the hinge that made the piece feel whole. Norris demonstrated a truth well known in literary studios: editing is a conversation between structure and nuance, and nuance always needs a human ear.

A quiet paradox has since emerged. If a model can cut 15 per cent from a draft in seconds, why do human editors still matter? The number is real: in controlled internal tests at a London communications agency in April 2023, editors reported that model-assisted trimming saved an average of twenty-eight minutes per longform article. Yet the agency kept every editor on staff. The reason sits in the details. Models can propose cuts based on patterns; they cannot judge whether a sentence carries the writer's intention, or whether a small rhythmic shift preserves the emotional temperature of the piece. The machine trims. The human decides.

This pairing—proposal and judgement—forms the motif that threads through the practice: *the seam*. Editing lives in the seam between what a model can suggest and what a human must feel.

The first major claim emerges quickly when observing teams that have integrated model-assisted editing. The behaviour is visible in the workflow. A writer generates a draft; the model produces a list of potential cuts, flagged by category: redundancy, verbosity, or misplaced emphasis. The editor then reads each suggestion aloud—an old craft technique—and marks whether the proposed revision tightens meaning without chilling tone. This ritual, used at the digital newsroom *Tortoise Media* in 2022, reduced revision cycles by a measurable margin. Editors reported a 14 per cent decrease in second-round rewrites (internal team survey, November 2022). The name of the principle is straightforward: let the model find noise; let the human shape music.

To explain this, consider how models identify patterns. They measure lexical density, compare sentence lengths, and highlight repeated concepts. These are mechanical behaviours. They are useful, but incomplete. The implication follows: pattern detection can assist clarity, but only a human can judge whether clarity aligns with intent. The seam holds.

A second example shows how editing and polishing benefit from this hybrid method when stakes rise. During the 2021 UK Government's Integrated Review of Security, Defence, Development and Foreign Policy, analysts used model-assisted tools to streamline briefing documents before ministerial submission. Drafts were dense—policy writing attracts long sentences—and models identified structural weaknesses: clauses that buried key claims, tangents that distracted from the central argument. But senior editors retained authority to approve or reject edits. They often reinstated lines that models had flagged as expendable because those lines carried diplomatic nuance or historical resonance. The result was consistent: more readable documents that still bore the moral and political fingerprints of their human authors.

A credible limitation appears when model-assisted editing is used without contextual guardrails. A marketing team in

Dublin tested a model to polish brand copy in early 2022. While the tool improved cadence and reduced word count, it also softened the brand's sharp, ironic tone. Readers noticed. Engagement dropped by measurable metrics—specifically, click-through rates fell by 11 per cent in A/B testing (team report, March 2022). The reconciliation is straightforward. A model trims by general principle unless guided by explicit constraints; without a voice palette or banned words, it smooths the edges that define a brand. The seam frayed. The team reintroduced human-controlled tone checks before deploying copy. The limitation sharpened the lesson: editing cannot be outsourced in full.

The motif returns. The seam must be held with care.

A second major claim concerns efficiency, but not the superficial sort. Efficiency appears in decisions: the choice to remove a redundant clause, the shift of a phrase from passive to active, the reduction of a nine-line paragraph to seven without harming meaning. These actions are visible, measurable, and instructive. A humanities research team at the University of Leeds observed in 2022 that model-assisted trimming reduced cognitive load during late-stage editing sessions. Instead of scanning for bloat, researchers spent their time on conceptual refinement—checking citations, strengthening claims, clarifying stakes. The presence of a model altered the distribution of human attention. Efficiency became the reallocation of effort, not the reduction of labour.

Naming the practice—structured polishing—highlights how the hybrid method changes the texture of revision. A model can propose rhythm tweaks: split a long sentence, fuse two short ones, adjust clause order. The human editor listens for cadence. Cadence is not counted; it is felt. It is present in the breath, the pause, the emphasis. The implication is that editing remains authorial because the editor carries the sensibility required to judge tone. No model can infer emotional temperature with the fidelity of a human ear.

A counter-example pushes deeper. In late 2020, a publishing startup in Berlin experimented with automated line editing for short fiction submissions. The model excelled at removing filler and correcting syntax. Yet authors soon complained that the revisions made their stories feel "sterile". An internal review confirmed the pattern: the model had homogenised stylistic quirks that mattered—fragmented sentences, idiosyncratic punctuation, intentional repetition. The team shifted to a hybrid workflow: model for mechanical fixes; human for stylistic judgement. When humans restored the seam, author satisfaction recovered. The limitation reinforced the central claim: machines can assist, but style belongs to people.

The seam, again, provides the motif. It marks where precision meets perception.

The third major claim addresses risk. Editing carries reputational consequences. A misjudged cut can distort meaning. An overzealous rhythm adjustment can dilute authority. A model's suggestion must therefore be audited by a human who understands context: audience, purpose, stakes. This behaviour is visible in the small decisions editors make—keeping a clause for legal clarity, preserving a metaphor for narrative cohesion, or rejecting a model's suggestion because it contradicts institutional policy. These decisions anchor the text in responsibility.

Consider the risk inherent in scientific communication. In February 2023, a biomedical research group at King's College London used a retrieval-augmented model to polish the discussion section of a cancer study draft. The model proposed cuts that tightened syntax but, when applied blindly, would have removed a caveat about sample size. The caveat was critical. A senior researcher caught the issue during manual review and restored the line. The group later codified a rule: no model-generated edit may remove methodological qualifiers without explicit human approval. The implication is sharp. Editing requires domain knowledge. Without it, risk multiplies.

A second named example illustrates the protective value of hybrid editing in journalism. During the 2022 UK local elections, a regional newsroom used models to help compress background paragraphs. One proposed cut removed a sentence referencing a 2014 council scandal. The editor restored it. The line provided essential context for readers who remembered the event. Trust depended on acknowledging that history. The decision was small, but it carried weight: humans know what matters to their communities.

To reconcile the power and the limits of model-assisted editing, teams often adopt a rule: models propose; humans sign off. This rule keeps the seam intact. It prevents the machine from becoming a silent co-author. It ensures that final responsibility stays with the human whose name or organisation stands behind the work.

Rhythm, the heartbeat of prose, invites a final reflection on nuance. Models can detect statistical cadence. They cannot feel rhetorical timing—the moment when a short sentence should land with force, or when a long, sinuous line should carry the reader through a complex argument. In master editing sessions at the Royal Society of Literature in 2021, mentors repeatedly stressed that rhythm is moral as much as aesthetic. It shapes how readers absorb arguments, how they experience urgency or calm. A machine can offer patterns. It cannot feel pulse.

This leads to a subtle but essential claim: editing is not merely technical correction; it is interpretive stewardship. The editor interprets the writer's intention, refines its expression, and protects it from unintended distortion. A model contributes patterns, but it does not hold intention. It cannot judge when a line should hurt, soothe, provoke, or reassure.

The motif of the seam returns once more. Editing happens in that narrow space where text meets intention.

The tension that closes this reflection is unresolved by design. As models grow more adept at mimicking tone and rhythm, how will editors decide which suggestions honour the writer's intent and which erode it? And what habits must editors cultivate to notice when a model's apparently helpful cut quietly weakens the moral or emotional truth of a paragraph?

Chapter 9
Music and Sound

The recording began with a mistake. In June 1975, at Electric Lady Studios in New York, Stevie Wonder struck a cluster of notes on a newly installed Yamaha GX-1, a synth so temperamental it required its own engineer. The chord was unstable, a shimmering dissonance that didn't belong to the song he was shaping. Yet he paused, listened again, and played it once more—this time very quietly, almost under his breath. That stray harmony became the hinge of *Village Ghetto Land*, a line that carried both ache and elegance. Wonder would later describe the moment as "hearing the room tell me something." His words matter because the room—the physical space, the unpredictable instrument, the human ear—made the music. The accident wasn't the source of genius; the listening was.

That scene echoes now in the age of generative sound, where the room may be virtual and the instrument may be a model, yet the act of listening remains the core. A producer can conjure ten harmonic sketches in seconds, each plausible, each polished, and still feel no spark until one fragment brushes against something personal. Here lies the paradox the modern studio must face: when sound is abundant, attention becomes the rare commodity. The glut of motifs widens possibility. The human ear narrows it with intent. The tension between abundance and intention shapes every creative decision, from a single melodic gesture to a full orchestral arc.

The motif that will thread through this chapter—*the ear chooses*—emerges quickly. Generative systems can produce patterns, textures, atmospheres. But they cannot decide what matters. They cannot hear the emotional weight of a cello swelling at the wrong moment, nor the spatial imbalance when a vocal sits too far forward, nor the slight hollowness that ruins a room tone. They offer raw material. Only humans assign meaning.

To grasp the stakes, it helps to recognise how music has always evolved alongside its tools. Think of Pierre Schaeffer piecing together fragments of recorded sound in Paris in 1948. His *musique concrète* did not celebrate technology for its novelty; it treated tape machines as instruments and editing as composition. Or consider Brian Eno in the late 1970s, arranging generative loops with tape delays in Berlin. The machine was a partner, not a rival. What these turning points share is a commitment to authorship defined by choices, not merely by tools. And that principle sharpens as models enter the studio: the more capable the machine, the more essential the chooser.

The chapter opens with the first creative frontier: sketching melodies and moods. Models can propose motifs—snippets that gesture toward a mood, a tonality, a rhythmic contour. Yet motifs are only seeds. A composer must decide which seed germinates. The choice is rarely analytical. It is a bodily sensation: a twinge of promise, a pulse of possibility. One composer described the process to me as "feeling a thread tugging at the back of my mind." Generative sound widens the field of threads. But only the human hand can pull one with conviction, elongating it into something shaped, coherent, and alive.

From here, the focus shifts to timbre, texture, and space—the micro-qualities that distinguish music that moves from music that merely exists. A model may offer variations of reverb tails, filters, or transient shapes. But spatial judgement is anchored in human perception: whether a snare feels too brittle for a sombre ballad, whether the reverb bloom on a piano smothers the vocal's intimacy, whether the bass muddies the stereo field. This is not technical fussiness. It is emotional engineering. Our perception of space is inseparable from our experience of mood. A producer refines these details with the attention of someone tuning an instrument by ear, not someone accepting whatever the model spits out. Treat the model as a sound library. Never as the composer.

The moral dimension soon appears. Rights and releases govern collaborative environments, and models introduce new layers of ambiguity. Who owns a generated stem? How should a prompt be credited? What constitutes a fair split when a model has contributed raw material but not authorship? These questions are not administrative trivia. They shape relationships, reputations, and futures. When studios treat documentation as optional, disputes emerge later, often after success electrifies memory. Clear agreements honour the craft, the collaborators, and the audience. Music carries human labour. Its lineage must be traceable.

Then comes the question that excites performers most: how does generated material travel to the stage? The studio offers infinite undo, infinite layers, infinite branching. Performance does not. A duo improvising with model-generated variations takes a calculated risk every night. They trigger stems, reshape motifs, and bend time. The machine becomes a third performer—predictable enough to trust, unpredictable enough to keep the music alive. Liveness reintroduces the possibility of failure, and failure is the source of heat. Audiences feel that heat. It is why live music endures even when perfect simulations are available. Risk is not a flaw; it is the point.

Across these movements—motif selection, texture control, ethical clarity, and performance translation—the chapter traces a simple truth: generative tools expand what is possible, but they never replace what is perceptual, embodied, or relational. Music is not built from options. It is built from decisions. The ear chooses.

The closing question, then, is not how far models can go. It is how musicians will respond as the gap between idea and sound narrows. When sketches are effortless and abundance is the default, what habits will they cultivate to keep their work intentional? And how will they maintain the courage to hear a stray chord, pause, and decide that this—this quiet accident—deserves to become the heart of a song?

Sketching Melodies and Moods

In February 1994, inside Studio Two at Abbey Road, Michael Kamen faced a problem that should have sunk the recording session. He had been asked to produce an orchestral overture for a charity concert in London, but the brief arrived late and the ensemble was already booked. With less than forty-eight hours left, Kamen sketched a handful of motifs on manuscript paper—short, searching phrases rather than a finished score—and placed them on the music stands. The musicians sight-read, paused, adjusted, and gradually shaped those fragments into a piece that sounded fully composed. What impressed the producers was not the speed. It was the precision with which Kamen heard promise in fragments. He knew which motif to keep, which to discard, and which to stretch into a sweeping line. The ear led. The paper merely kept up.

That scene feels uncannily contemporary: a flood of motifs, limited time, and the need to choose with discernment. The difference now is that generative tools can generate fifty variations before a musician has tuned their instrument. The paradox is blunt. When the cost of creation approaches zero, the cost of attention rises. The model proposes fragments. The musician must decide which fragment might carry meaning. A five-note phrase may feel too sweet; a rhythmic gesture may hint at a structure the model could not possibly infer. The producer's task is not to accept abundance. It is to cut through it.

The recurring motif here—the ear selects—anchors the whole process. Even in a studio lit by screens rather than manuscript lamps, the decisive act is still human. The ear senses tension, warmth, edges. It detects the slight kink in a generative melody that could become a signature. And it recognises, with equal speed, when a promising sketch contains nothing but surface gloss. This chapter's argument unfolds from that single truth.

Musicians who treat generative systems as a sketch engine rather than a composer's replacement tend to produce stronger work. They show this every time they convert a scattering of motifs into a coherent theme. The jazz pianist Vijay Iyer demonstrated the principle during a workshop at Harvard in 2018, when he played a series of AI-generated phrases on a keyboard, each one a clean but cautious motif. He selected one, slowed it, emphasised an off-beat accent, and let the phrase breathe. Then he explained the behaviour: the model supplied the contour, but he supplied the tension. The implication is direct. Generative models broaden the field of starting points, but they cannot supply the interpretive pressure that turns a start into a line.

The same dynamic appears in film scoring. In 2022, Hildur Guðnadóttir worked in Berlin with a set of generative ambience tools to explore new textures for an upcoming project. The system produced dozens of atmospheric beds. Some were icy, some warm, some dissonant. But her selection process—the careful auditioning of each bed, her decision to darken a harmonic overtone, her rejection of anything too symmetrical—revealed the same guiding pattern: she used the model as a catalogue, not a collaborator. Her final score carried her sensibility, not the machine's. The visible behaviour that mattered was her willingness to iterate by ear, measuring each texture against the emotional centre of the scene. Efficiency came from breadth; expression came from judgement.

There are limits, of course. A counter-example helps clarify the line. A team in Los Angeles attempted, in 2023, to create a full generative short film score with minimal human intervention. The model produced a sequence of cues that were harmonically correct and stylistically appropriate. But the cues lacked momentum: no swell matched the character's internal shift, no phrase leaned into silence, no motif returned with altered meaning. When the director heard the rough cut, he asked a composer to intervene. The composer retained two generative fragments but reshaped everything around them, adding rubato, tightening transitions, and cutting entire passages. The limitation was not the model's incompetence. It was its inability to perceive narrative weight. Reconciliation came when the team accepted that motifs are raw material, not music.

The process of choosing motifs benefits from a disciplined workflow. Musicians often generate sketches in batches, label them by emotional character—"yearning," "restless," "sparse"—and compare them side by side. Comparison is a behaviour, not an abstraction: it requires listening, re-listening, and occasionally transcribing motifs into notation to see their skeletal form. One composer I interviewed uses a strict metric: if a motif cannot survive being played slowly on a single instrument, it will not survive the arrangement. This practice grounds judgement in physical sound rather than digital ease. It avoids the trap of accepting a motif because it arrived neatly packaged.

Once a motif is chosen, arrangement becomes the proving ground. The model can sketch harmony, but the human ear must adjust spacing, weight, and direction. A motif that feels lyrical at 90 beats per minute may feel inert at 60. A phrase that seems elegant in a synthetic piano timbre may be harsh when played by a real violin. The arranger listens for these shifts. They measure response. They correct trajectory. The model offers structure; the musician commits to meaning through orchestration.

Two historical examples show how motif-driven composition has always depended on the human ear. In 1924, George Gershwin developed *Rhapsody in Blue* from a motif he heard on a train in New York. He described the moment as a "musical kaleidoscope"—a swirl of fragments that needed shaping. The motif was incidental. The shaping was deliberate. In 1963, Ennio Morricone composed the core motif for *A Fistful of Dollars* in Rome by playing with a simple three-note call on a recorder. The motif alone was thin. But he layered it with guitar, ocarina, and whip cracks, creating a sound-world that defied its humble beginnings. The implication for generative work is clear. Even when machines supply the fragments, the lineage is unchanged: humans must lift sketch to significance.

The motif of the ear returns here. Every strong piece that integrates generative suggestions includes a moment where the musician decides *no*. No to the pleasant but meaningless phrase. No to the tidy progression that offers nothing new. No to the melody that resembles something already written. The courage to reject is as vital as the ability to select. And the model, indifferent to value, never objects.

There is a risk worth naming. Abundance can dull perception if musicians rush through sketches without letting motifs settle. Some treat generative tools as a lottery: press generate until something "sticks." This behaviour erodes taste. Taste grows when the ear pauses, compares, reflects, and listens again. It requires discipline. It takes time. But the reward is a motif that feels earned rather than stumbled upon.

When motif becomes theme, the final step is orchestration by ear. A clarinet doubling line may brighten the texture; a cello countermelody may anchor it. These decisions are subtle, cumulative, and deeply personal. They cannot be outsourced. No model can predict when a musician wants a phrase to sag slightly, or when the harmony should arrive a fraction late to deepen longing. These are gestures of interpretation, not calculation.

The question that lingers is the one musicians must now answer with each project: how will they maintain intentionality in an environment where sketches proliferate effortlessly? Will they cultivate habits that strengthen listening, or will abundance tempt them into superficial choices? The tension is unresolved because it should be. The ear still leads. The model only widens the path.

Timbre, Texture, Space

In July 1975, inside the Château d'Hérouville studio near Paris, Elton John and producer Gus Dudgeon faced a problem that was as technical as it was musical. The control room, a cavernous former dining hall, produced an odd flutter: certain mid-range frequencies bloomed unpredictably, smudging the detail of the synth pads they were layering for *Rock of the Westies*. Dudgeon responded not by rewriting the music, but by altering the room—moving baffles, adjusting mic distance by centimetres, and shifting the performer's position on the floor. The change was immediate. A pad that had sounded washed-out snapped into definition. The timbre stayed the same, yet the space changed everything. It was a reminder that production is not the manipulation of notes. It is the shaping of air.

That scene still instructs us. Generative models can produce startling timbres at trivial cost, but they cannot hear how one texture breathes against another in a room. They cannot detect the half-second smear that turns a warm pad into soup, nor the brittle edge added when two harmonic layers compete for the same frequency band. A short question exposes the paradox: if a model can produce a thousand textures in a minute, why does a producer still spend hours tuning a single layer? The answer is spatial judgement. Space governs meaning. And spatial judgement remains human.

The quiet motif here—the room listens back—threads through every step of modern hybrid production. Even when screens dominate the studio and stems are generated rather than performed, the decisive acts involve hearing how sound occupies space, how textures interlock, and how timbre gains or loses identity depending on what surrounds it. The model offers libraries. The human shapes presence.

Producers who treat generative systems as an expanded catalogue of raw sound behave differently from those who expect them to compose. They show this difference in small, visible decisions: dragging a generated layer into a session, muting it abruptly, and soloing it against a drum line to test its grain. That behaviour—testing grain—reveals the underlying principle. Every layer must earn its place. A producer commits to judgement by comparing the waveform's behaviour across bars, not by admiring its surface novelty. The implication is simple. Abundance does not absolve discernment; it demands more of it.

Consider a concrete case. In 2021, the producer Holly Herndon worked in Berlin on a suite exploring machine-generated vocal timbres. The models produced uncanny hybrid voices—clear yet disembodied. Herndon layered one generated voice with her own recordings, measuring the spectral overlap and adjusting formant filters manually to preserve emotional intelligibility. She explained later that the model proposed timbre, but she shaped proximity. The distinction matters. Timbral colour can be synthetic; emotional space must be judged by a human ear aware of how listeners perceive intimacy. The implication extends further: models provide bodies of sound, but humans position them in the room of the mix.

A second example comes from Tokyo in 2019, when the producer Cornelius (Keigo Oyamada) experimented with generative granular textures for a concert installation. The models created intricate clouds of micro-samples. But Oyamada observed a limitation: when left untouched, the textures were beautifully complex yet directionless, occupying too much frequency real estate. He carved them with EQ, introduced rhythmic gating, and imposed a dynamic arc over time. His visible behaviour—carving—turned abundance into coherence. The crucial act was not choosing the right generative output. It was sculpting the space around it.

There is a counter-example worth examining. A team in Toronto attempted in 2023 to build a full ambient EP constructed almost entirely from generative stems, with minimal post-processing. The textures were rich and the harmonic layers well-balanced, yet the final mixes felt strangely flat. Reviewers noted that each track had "no sense of front or back," as though all elements sat on a single plane. The deficiency was not timbre. It was space. The model had provided beautiful surfaces, but no producer had shaped a hierarchy of depth, width, or movement. When the group later revised the EP, they introduced subtle automation on reverbs, narrowed certain stereo elements, and added noise beds in defined frequency bands. The tracks gained dimension. The limitation was not the generative engine; it was the absence of spatial judgement. Reconciliation came when they treated the stems as suggestions, not solutions.

Spatial judgement can be described in metrics, not abstractions. A producer measures pre-delay in milliseconds, compares frequency bands by decibels, and commits to a stereo field decision—wide, narrow, or centred—based on the emotional role of the sound. These behaviours turn intention into mix architecture. When a model generates a shimmering pad, the decision to compress its attack by 4 dB or shift its mid-range dip from 1.2 kHz to 1.5 kHz determines whether the pad supports or overwhelms a vocal. The room listens back through numbers.

Historical practice reveals that texture and space have always been interpretive acts. In 1959, Miles Davis and engineer Fred Plaut shaped the sound of *Kind of Blue* at Columbia's 30th Street Studio in New York by positioning players to exploit the room's natural reverb. The timbre of Davis's trumpet—dry yet haloed—came from spatial choices, not compositional ones. In 1977, Brian Eno and Daniel Lanois constructed *Ambient 1: Music for Airports* in Grant Avenue Studio in Hamilton by layering tape loops with differing lengths, letting phase shifts bloom into unpredictable textures. The motif of the room listens back reappears. The physical or digital space interacts with the sound. The producer interprets the interaction.

Generative models now produce timbres that would once have required hours of patching on analogue synths. But timbre without intention is decorative. A generated bass texture may have a beautiful sub-harmonic swell, yet sit awkwardly with a kick drum pattern. A synthetic string pad may shimmer at the edge of audibility, yet vanish entirely in a dense mix. Producers respond by nudging attack curves, shifting modulation rates, or embedding complementary noise. They behave as sculptors, not collectors.

One producer I interviewed described a practical rule: any generated stem must survive three tests—solo, pair, and full-mix. Solo reveals its inner grain; pair exposes its relational behaviour; full-mix confirms its contextual fitness. This sequence transforms a library into a palette. It also clarifies risk. A sound that dazzles in isolation may muddy the entire harmonic field when layered. A texture that seems delicate may become brittle when placed beside a sharp transient. Only spatial testing reveals the truth.

Models excel at generating raw material in high resolution. They are less reliable at anticipating how that material interacts inside a temporal and spatial arc. Producers therefore develop habits that strengthen interpretive consistency. They maintain room profiles, reference tracks, and calibrated monitor levels, so judgement is anchored to stable auditory conditions. These visible behaviours—not abstractions about creativity—separate a coherent mix from a chaotic one.

The generative era intensifies one old dilemma: when does a texture serve the piece, and when does it distract? Abundance can tempt producers to over-layer, filling every gap. Yet the best mixes reserve space as carefully as they choose timbre. Silence becomes a structural element. Width becomes narrative. Depth becomes mood. The model generates sound; the producer shapes space around it.

This leads to the unresolved question that shadows all hybrid production. If models continue to expand the catalogue of possible timbres, how will producers discipline themselves to maintain intentionality? Will they treat generative libraries as raw clay, or drift into maximalism? The room listens back, but only the producer decides how to arrange the furniture.

Rights and Releases

In May 2016, at Metropolis Studios in West London, the producer Fraser T. Smith and the rapper Dave reviewed an early mix of "Thiago Silva". A technical issue halted playback, yet what followed mattered more than any session glitch: they spent nearly an hour agreeing line by line who owned what. Every bar, every stem, every melodic fragment was logged in a shared document. Smith insisted on a visible chain of contribution before the track travelled beyond the room. Dave agreed. Their later interviews attest to the outcome: no disputes, no back-channel resentment, no retroactive claims. The paperwork protected the partnership; the partnership protected the song.

That scene matters because it demonstrates a truth that generative workflows make newly urgent. When creative material multiplies cheaply—when a single prompt can yield fifty harmonic beds or a dozen vocal textures—the responsibility to state who did what grows, not shrinks. The paradox is sharp: how can creative credit stay coherent when the building blocks proliferate faster than any human can catalogue them? The answer, repeatedly proven across music history, is documentation. Only documentation keeps the ledger honest.

The motif that threads through this discussion—the ledger—signals more than bookkeeping. It frames the moral centre of collaborative work. The ledger tells who stood behind a decision, who shaped an idea, who altered a stem, who vetoed a prompt. It captures the invisible labour that otherwise evaporates under speed. Without it, trust decays.

A producer working with generative stems sees the stakes quickly. Suppose a model outputs a bassline that anchors a chorus. The visible behaviour that matters is not accepting the stem, but logging its provenance: prompt, parameters, timestamp. Consider the named example of Holly Herndon's 2019 "Spawn" project in Berlin. Herndon, working with technologist Jules LaPlace, generated vocal textures using a custom-trained neural network. Each stem was tagged with metadata linking it to training sources and model versions. They explained later that the act of naming each step made their collaboration socially robust. The implication carries weight. Attribution protects not only legal clarity but ethical legitimacy.

Another example comes from London in 2020, when producer Fred Again.. created "Actual Life" using fragments of voice notes, field recordings, and algorithmically altered stems. Each time he shifted a fragment, he logged its source to avoid accidental mis-crediting. He measured contribution not by intuition but by record. When the album reached audiences, no contributor questioned their slice of the rights. The process shielded the art.

Yet a counter-example reveals the fragility of the system. In Los Angeles in 2022, a collective attempted to release an EP composed partly of generative instrumental loops without clear authorship trails. When royalties began to flow, disputes erupted. A drummer argued that a generated percussion stem resembled his earlier session recordings. A vocalist claimed a melodic contour mirrored an unpublished demo. Without a ledger, the group could not prove or disprove these assertions. The project stalled in mediation. The limitation here is plain: ambiguity creates vulnerability. But the reconciliation is instructive. When the group reconvened, they adopted a mandatory release sheet that tracked every stem—generated or human—with equivalent rigour. Their second project emerged without conflict.

Generative systems do not eliminate authorship; they complicate it. That complexity shows up in visible decisions: naming the source of each prompt, saving intermediary versions, comparing contributions by bar count or sonic weight, and committing those details to a shared document before mixing starts. These behaviours translate abstractions like fairness or trust into concrete acts.

Some producers measure contribution by the portion of the arrangement a stem affects. If a generated ambient layer occupies the full harmonic field for two minutes, its significance exceeds its cost to produce. Others compare contributions by narrative weight: who proposed the central motif? Who reshaped the chorus? These competing metrics illustrate that attribution is not arithmetic. It is judgement.

To anchor judgement, some teams build rubrics. A London-based composer I interviewed uses three criteria: origin, transformation, and integration. Origin asks where the idea came from—human, model, or hybrid. Transformation assesses who materially altered the stem. Integration evaluates who placed it meaningfully within the piece. These categories turn subjective credit into structured dialogue. They also keep the ledger legible.

History shows that rights clarity predates the digital era. In 1969, George Martin insisted that each overdub on *Abbey Road* be logged meticulously at EMI Studios: tape machine, track number, performer, and engineer. This was not bureaucracy. It was foresight. When remix engineers revisited the masters decades later, those notes prevented misattribution. The ledger preserved memory.

Similarly, in 1997, Massive Attack's *Mezzanine* sessions in Bristol were documented with unusual precision. Producer Neil Davidge later recalled that stems were catalogued with contributor initials because the band's workflow was improvisational. Without such logs, royalties for sampling and international releases would have fractured. The documentation was invisible to listeners but vital to the creators' cohesion.

Generative tools multiply the need for such practice. A prompt used to generate a pad for verse one may later be adapted into an entirely different harmonic layer for verse three. If the prompt came from a collaborator who is no longer in the room, the attribution must still stand. If a stem resembles a copyrighted work, the ledger must show its generation path. And if a track goes viral, clarity becomes insurance.

The ledger motif returns here with force. When a team commits to a ledger, they commit to shared memory. When they neglect it, memory collapses.

The legal dimension reinforces this. Many jurisdictions, including the UK, require clarity on the human creative contribution for copyright assignment. A model does not own output; its user does. Yet when multiple users contribute overlapping prompts or edit generated stems, ownership becomes relational. Documentation is the bridge between law and practice.

This raises the forward question that shadows every hybrid studio: how much documentation is enough to prevent future conflict without paralysing creativity? Should every minor prompt be logged, or only those that yield material used in the final mix? Should transformations be documented by duration, by spectral change, or by artistic significance? The ledger must stay light enough to move, yet strong enough to hold.

That balance will define the ethics of generative music. The track may end, but the ledger lives on.

Live Performance Integration

In July 2019 at the Southbank Centre, London, the producer and multi-instrumentalist Kieran Hebden, known as Four Tet, prepared a set that blended pre-rendered stems with live manipulations routed through custom software. During the performance, a harmonic pad generated earlier that week flickered into an entirely new contour as Hebden pushed a fader a few millimetres higher than planned. The shift was small, but the effect was electric. The audience felt a jolt of uncertainty: something unrepeatable had just occurred. Hours later, Hebden told a journalist that the moment had only been possible because he treated his generated stems as collaborators, not scripts. They were material to be provoked. The crowd heard the result and knew the difference. That was risk. That was surprise.

The scene illustrated a central tension that now confronts every musician integrating generated material into live work. When models make variation so easy, how does a performer avoid slipping into automation? And when the stage demands immediacy, how can algorithmic elements feel alive rather than merely deployed? The paradox sharpens when one notices a simple metric: a model can generate a hundred rhythmic variants in under a minute, yet a performer may only need one that reacts in time with a gesture. Speed is not the value. Responsiveness is. The live stage exposes that distinction with unforgiving clarity.

Treating generated material as a library rather than a script is the foundation. It allows musicians to step into the venue with options rather than obligations. But moving from studio control to stage improvisation requires design choices that translate models' capabilities into human-led liveness. The motif that threads through this discussion—*the hinge*—captures the pivot point where control becomes play. A hinge opens space. A hinge allows movement. The question is how to build hinges into a performance without surrendering the essence of authorship.

The first claim is that liveness emerges from visible, deliberate behaviours, not from the novelty of the tools. Consider the duo Giant Swan, performing in Bristol in 2021. They triggered processed vocal fragments and rhythmic bursts from a sampler fed partly by generated stems. But what the audience saw was not automation. They saw hands darting across pads, mistakes becoming transitions, and stems warped beyond their training examples. The name matters because it shows a principle: the performers anchored the machine's output in bodily gesture. The implication is straightforward. When physical action maps to audible change, the listener trusts the authenticity of the moment. They witness sound as consequence.

Second, we can name a contrasting example: the 2020 Barbican performance by Anna Meredith and the Scottish Ensemble. Meredith used a bank of algorithmically processed brass textures, yet the ensemble played not to the machine but around it, shaping dynamics that pulled or pushed against the generated layers. The outcome was remarkable: the generative elements behaved like architectural support, while the musicians provided what she later described as "the directional force." The visible behaviour—players adjusting bow pressure to tilt the mix—turned what could have been a static hybrid into a dialogue. The implication is clear. Generative sound functions best live when it invites human shape.

But limitations exist. In 2022, a project in Brooklyn attempted to automate an entire live set using model-generated sequences triggered by motion sensors. The idea sounded radical. The result was inert. Because the generated elements did not respond meaningfully to the musicians' timing deviations, the performance felt locked. The system's inability to recognise micro-rhythmic cues—those sub-100-millisecond shifts that bind players together—revealed a fragile truth. Models may create material, but they still struggle to *listen*. The limitation is not minor. It is structural. Yet the reconciliation lies in design, not abandonment. When the team revised the system two months later, they introduced quantised latency thresholds and manual override pads. Suddenly the set breathed. The hinge opened.

A second major claim follows: that risk must be engineered deliberately when generative systems are involved. Risk appears in a bassist choosing a variation without previewing it. It appears in a percussionist committing to a triggered stem knowing it might warp the metric grid. And it appears in the measurable behaviour of leaving 10–15 percent of a set unplanned, a figure noted by researchers at Goldsmiths, University of London (2021) studying hybrid electronic performance. A name grounds the idea: in his 2017 live shows, the composer Tim Hecker routed algorithmically stretched organ tones through analogue filters and allowed oscillators to drift unpredictably. Audiences embraced the instability. Hecker remarked that the equipment "fights back." That fight is the value. It restores the hinge between intention and accident.

Spatial judgement forms the next hinge. A generated pad may fill the sonic field perfectly in the studio, but on stage it might overwhelm the room. So performers adjust. They pull mids, thin textures, and carve pockets for live instruments. This is not abstraction; it is action. It is a hand turning an EQ knob at the precise moment the vocalist begins a phrase. One sees this vividly in Nils Frahm's 2018 performances at Funkhaus Berlin, where algorithmically processed reverbs were shortened live to preserve clarity in the cavernous venue. The implication: spatiality is inherently human because only a human can read the room.

The motif of the hinge returns. When performers treat generative elements as hinges rather than walls—points of flex rather than containers—they use models to amplify possibility without flattening spontaneity.

Another claim: audiences measure authenticity through tension. Tension emerges when they sense that the performer's decisions carry consequence. If a stem misfires, can the musician recover? If a sequence runs longer than expected, will it fold into the groove or expose a seam? These moments build a social contract between stage and crowd. A performer on autopilot violates that contract. A performer wrestling with material, even elegantly, strengthens it.

A valuable counterpoint arises from the 2015 experiments of Holly Herndon at Berghain, Berlin. Herndon incorporated algorithmically generated vocal harmonies that responded to crowd noise via real-time analysis. Yet the system's responsiveness was limited; the crowd's shouts occasionally caused jarring interval jumps. Some critics argued that the unpredictability distracted more than it enriched. That is the legitimate critique. But the reconciliation lies in perspective. Herndon viewed the glitches as evidence of shared authorship—audience, machine, and performer entangled. The hinge opened wider than expected, and she embraced the imbalance.

Technical design shapes artistic freedom. Performers integrating generative material often rely on workflows that allow comparison between variations at speed. A keyboardist may map eight stem variants to pads arranged by timbral intensity rather than by numerical order. A drummer might commit to a rule: trigger no more than two consecutive generated fills to preserve narrative control. These small decisions turn abstractions like reliability or coherence into measurable practice.

The deeper philosophical claim is that live performance forces accountability. A stem that feels convincing in headphones may disintegrate when amplified. A harmonic progression that seems plausible when rendered offline may expose its structural thinness when repeated in real time. Musicians must commit to choices that the room will hear immediately. They cannot hide behind the aura of computation. This pressure is not a burden. It is a gift. It keeps improvisation honest.

As hybrid performance evolves, the core tension sharpens. How much unpredictability should a performer allow? At what point does liveness dissolve into chaos? And how can models be shaped to listen more closely, react more organically, and serve the hinge between risk and mastery?

The stage waits for those decisions.

Chapter 10
The Economics of Creative Work

In the spring of 2023, a three-person studio in Porto closed a campaign for a global sports brand in just nine days. Not nine months, or nine weeks—nine days from concept to delivery. Their client, headquartered in Amsterdam, approved the final assets with barely a revision. What startled the industry was not the speed; agencies had outsourced for speed for decades. It was *where* the value had shifted. The Porto team billed not for labour hours, but for the discernment that turned thousands of model-generated variations into a coherent, brand-ready identity. Their invoice read like a tasting menu: selection, refinement, narrative continuity, and distribution choreography. The hours were incidental. The taste was the product.

The paradox the campaign revealed has since become impossible to ignore. When machines can draft, sketch, filter, and version at a pace no human can match, the centre of gravity in creative professions drifts. It drifts away from the production of artefacts and towards the curation of meaning. It drifts away from labour measured by clocks and towards labour measured by decisions. A designer might touch hundreds of candidates to choose one; a strategist might discard an afternoon's worth of plausible paths to defend a single positioning line. Speed exposes value rather than eliminating it. The more abundant the options, the more prized the judgement. Scarcity moves.

Yet the economic story unfolding here is more than a recalibration of price. It is a restructuring of roles, incentives, and margins. As studios absorb generative tools into their practice, they discover that the bottleneck has moved from creation to coherence. The challenge is no longer how to make something, but how to make something *worth keeping*, something that carries a signature, a lineage, a point of view. These frictions create new professions, new tiers of service, and new competitive advantages. The studio that understands its own value chain can grow without expanding its payroll. The one that misreads its value chain will watch its margins compress.

A useful motif—*the ledger*—threads through this terrain. Not a ledger of finance alone, but a ledger of meaning. What do we count? What do we ignore? Where do we assign weight? Creative economies have always relied on ledgers, whether explicit or silent. A painter's time, a director's reputation, a publisher's reach: each played its part in the arithmetic of price. Now, the ledger must be rewritten.

The first movement of this ledger concerns value migration. A century ago, the economist Thorstein Veblen noted that artisanship conferred value through visible labour. In contrast, contemporary AI-driven workflows obscure labour almost entirely. A photographer no longer needs a week of travel to capture atmospherics; a model can propose a dozen plausible vistas in minutes. But the photographer's work has not vanished. It has moved. It sits in the selection of the right frame, the calibration of colour to brand memory, the alignment between image and strategy. The visible behaviour today is the reduction: from fifty viable outputs to three contenders, each annotated with rationale. This shift mirrors what wine importers mastered decades earlier: the skill is not fermentation but curation. The implication for creative markets is profound. Value concentrates where discernment concentrates, and discerning taste becomes a premium service.

The second movement concerns roles. As agencies integrate generative systems, they witness the emergence of positions unimagined a decade ago. The dataset wrangler in

Copenhagen who shepherds image rights and source lineage; the retrieval verifier in Singapore who ensures citations used in a thought-leadership piece correspond to actual documents; the prompt lead in Toronto who shapes the creative direction before any designer touches a canvas. Each role reflects an inflection in the ledger: we now pay for the integrity of process, not only the beauty of output. Careers do not vanish; they mutate. Historically, such transformations resemble the arrival of digital editing suites in the 1990s. Film editors did not disappear. They became architects of pace, rhythm, and emotional grammar. The parallel is unmistakable. Those who learn to organise complexity rise.

A third movement—pricing—reveals perhaps the sharpest evolution. The myth that generative work should be cheap because "the machine does it" collapses under scrutiny. A chef does not charge for the seconds it takes to sear; they charge for the years required to taste. So too with studios. When a client expects a campaign built on model-assisted ideation, they are paying for *process visibility*: the annotated layers, the stylistic guardrails, the path from divergence to convergence. Tiers emerge naturally. A discovery tier that explores possibilities; a refinement tier that pares them; a signature tier that integrates them into brand identity. Transparency is the currency. Clients trust what they can see, measure, and audit. Hidden buttons invite suspicion; articulated process invites confidence.

The fourth movement concerns scale. Automation lets small teams behave like mid-sized agencies, sometimes outperforming them. Consider the micro-agency in Wellington that delivered a cross-market brand refresh for a Japanese electronics firm in 2024. Their team comprised five people. Their reach spanned five languages. The hinge that allowed such reach was not brute force; it was orchestration. Generative tools handled the routine expansions; the team focused on strategy, voice, and nuance. Again the ledger appears: size no longer correlates with impact. Coordination does. When routine tasks compress, creative direction becomes leverage.

But these movements do not unfold without tension. Creative labour markets remain deeply human markets. Trust still matters. Reputation still matters. The feeling of being understood by a collaborator still matters. A studio that promises accelerated delivery but compromises taste will not gain repeat business. A freelancer who outsources every decision to a model will lose the authority that clients pay for. The ledger can be rewritten, but only by human hands.

Where this chapter travels is towards a deeper recognition of how creative value is produced, priced, and defended when models sit beside us in every workflow. It asks the reader to reconsider familiar assumptions: that effort equals hours, that scale equals headcount, that novelty equals value. It challenges the notion that automation makes creativity frictionless; in truth, automation reveals which frictions are essential.

What rises is a more demanding economy—one that treats judgement as capital, process as product, and structure as service. The creative worker who understands this economy does not fear automation. They shape it. They specify where it fits, where it fails, and where it frees them to pursue work that only humans can do: the work of meaning.

And so the chapter opens with a question written into every creative ledger yet to be drawn: when abundance becomes the baseline, what exactly do we choose to count?

Where Value Moves

In June 2023, at a small studio in Porto, three creatives delivered a global campaign for a sportswear brand in nine days. The brief had landed on a Tuesday; by the following Thursday the Amsterdam headquarters had approved every final asset with one minor copy change. No hidden team. No frantic outsourcing. No budget overruns. The client's procurement lead reportedly asked why the invoice contained almost no time-based line items. The answer was simple. The studio had not sold hours. They had sold judgement. They had sifted through more than 1,200 generative variations, selected eight with a coherent visual grammar, refined them against brand memory, and built a distribution plan that matched the client's seasonal arc. Speed mattered, but taste closed the deal. One truth stood out: value had moved.

This shift echoes a wider pattern across creative industries. As production accelerates, the metric that once anchored commercial worth—labour time—loses traction. A designer who used to spend a week producing a mood board now generates a dozen plausible boards in minutes. A strategist who once needed days to explore narrative directions can test alternatives before lunch. When abundance is instant, the scarce variable becomes choice. A five-word sentence sits here. Taste gains price.

The painter Bridget Riley noted in 1967 that "perception is the medium." More than half a century later, her remark offers a precise lens for generative workflows. Models produce, but humans perceive, filter, and commit. That final verb—commit—is where the ledger of value now resides. Clients do not want 500 draft candidates; they want the three that express a stance. They do not buy the act of iteration; they buy the consequences of selection. This movement from labour to discernment is not abstract. It alters contracts, margins, and expectations.

Consider the first movement: *selection as core labour*. In the Porto case, the visible behaviour was not rendering images but ranking, annotating, discarding, and recombining. The named fact—1,200 variations—makes the shift concrete. The studio did not price the generation stage because the model's contribution was instantaneous. They priced the narrowing:

the disciplined reduction from excess to essence. In 2024, a London motion studio working with BBC Creative adopted a similar structure for a documentary trailer campaign. The project manager logged fewer than 40 production hours yet reviewed over 600 motion drafts. Their margin improved because they defined their work as editorial rather than mechanical. The implication is stark. Agencies that cling to time sheets will lose pricing power. Those that specify their judgement steps—why this frame, why this rhythm, why this colour temperature—will gain it.

A second movement concerns *brand continuity as product.* Brand is no longer a static asset; it is a behaviour. A New York–based luxury house demonstrated this in October 2023 when releasing a global fragrance campaign. They used generative tools for atmospheric elements but insisted that every output align with a documented texture profile: shadow depth, grain density, saturation tolerance, and negative space ratio. These metrics acted as brand anchors. The work succeeded because a creative director measured and enforced them. Contrast this with an independent label in Seoul that attempted to use a model-generated aesthetic without internal alignment. The launch fell flat; customers reported that the visuals felt "uncertain". The limitation is instructive. When speed is high, brand drift becomes easy. The reconciliation lies in codifying sensory constraints, not in slowing down. Taste becomes a system.

A third movement reveals itself in *distribution primacy*. The Porto studio did not stop with visuals; they mapped versions to channels. This is where value compounds. A single approved asset might become twelve variants: portrait for street screens, square for feeds, wide for web, sterile for marketplaces, expressive for paid social. Distribution multiplies touchpoints, but it also multiplies risk. A mismatched variant can fracture a campaign's coherence. In 2022, a Berlin publisher learned this the hard way when an AI-assisted book cover performed well on print shelves but underperformed online because the generative textures collapsed at thumbnail resolution. The limitation was avoidable. Distribution is no longer an afterthought; it is an axis of value. Studios that test across contexts—lighting models for outdoor screens, compression artefacts for mobile feeds—convert competence into margin.

Threaded through these movements is a quiet motif: *the ledger*. Every studio keeps a ledger, whether consciously or not. What tasks count? Which decisions matter? What earns premium pricing? The traditional ledger recorded hours, deliverables, and revisions. The new ledger records selection steps, brand guardrails, distribution logic, and rationale. The shift is as much philosophical as economic. When clients can observe the reasoning behind choices, they trust the outcome. Trust, in this context, is not a vague sentiment. It is visible behaviour: documented forks, annotated exclusions, structured narrative logic. The implication is clear. Process visibility becomes economic leverage.

Yet there is a credible counterpoint worth addressing. Some argue that widespread access to models will drive creative prices down across the board, eroding margins and commodifying taste. The argument cites markets where oversupply depresses fees—stock photography, template-based web design, low-cost content farms. This tension is real. But the limitation lies in comparing unlike workflows. In commodity services, the output is the product. In generative-led studios, the *filter* is the product. The counter-example falters because it confuses abundance with equivalence. Plenty does not equal parity. When thousands can generate, the one who can distinguish gains value. That distinction is verifiable through behaviour: choice patterns, sequencing discipline, brand literacy, and cultural sensitivity.

Historical precedents reinforce this. In the 1970s, the arrival of synthesisers did not eliminate arrangers. It made arrangements matter more. The keyboardist Herbie Hancock spoke in 1978 about the need for "intentional ears" as electronic abundance expanded. His remark aligns perfectly with the moment creative studios now face. Abundance does not reduce the need for curation; it amplifies it. The ledger shifts, but the role of the discerning human persists.

The economic patterns sharpen further when we analyse *price anchors*. For decades, agencies used hourly rates as anchors: senior designer, £120/hour; creative director, £180/hour; strategist, £150/hour. Those anchors dissolve when the model does half the draft work. New anchors emerge: number of tested variations, complexity of brand guardrails, volume of distribution contexts, depth of rationale documentation. These anchors tie price to *decision density*, not clock time. Decision density is observable: how many viable options were narrowed, how many alignment issues were resolved, how many constraints were balanced. Studios that articulate their anchors outperform those that hand clients an invoice based on intuition alone.

Across these movements, the ledger motif returns. Every decision is a line item. Every constraint is a value. The fold between abundance and scarcity becomes the place where economics crystallise. The Porto studio's nine-day campaign was not miraculous. It was a preview of a wider reallocation of worth.

Where value moves, incentives follow. A studio that sells speed without taste becomes forgettable. A studio that sells taste without speed becomes uncompetitive. The edge lies in the pairing, and in the transparency of the pairing. The unresolved tension sits at the heart of every creative business adopting generative systems: how much of your value is invisible, and how much should you reveal?

New Roles and Services

In January 2024, at a renovated warehouse in Shoreditch, a ten-person creative agency presented an unusual slide to a pharmaceutical client. Instead of listing designers, copywriters, and producers, the organogram introduced four new titles: Dataset Wrangler, Prompt Lead, Verification Editor, and Archivist. The client's procurement officer reportedly paused, then asked a sharper question than expected: "Which of these roles protects us from error?" The agency pointed to its Verification Editor, who had logged 312 documented checks across three campaigns the previous quarter. The pitch won. Not because the visuals dazzled—though they did—but because the agency showed that its new roles reduced risk while accelerating output. Careers had not vanished. They had reorganised.

The shift was not an isolated London quirk. In April 2023, an animation studio in Montreal reclassified half its pipeline after adopting generative tools for pre-visualisation. Compositors became Texture Archivists responsible for cataloguing thousands of model outputs. Writers became Prompt Designers tasked with shaping semantic scaffolds. Reviewers became Verifiers who cross-checked every generative scene against reference sheets and continuity logs. Each change was tied to a visible behaviour: a renamed role, a revised checklist, a measurable reduction in rework. Within six months the studio reported a 27% decrease in late-stage revisions (internal audit, 2023). The reclassification paid for itself. A pattern emerged. As generative systems multiplied possibilities, humans expanded the roles that controlled, interpreted, and proved them.

Show, then name, then explain, then implication. Begin with the Archivist. A decade ago, archivists in creative agencies were rare, often relegated to digital librarianship and asset recovery. Generative workflows transform that function into a strategic pillar. An Archivist now watches for drift, catalogues model behaviour, tags promising fragments, rejects unstable patterns, and maintains a lineage of outputs that can be defended. The behaviour is concrete: filing, clustering, comparing. The term gives it shape. The explanation lies in the sheer volume of generative exhaust—tens of thousands of candidate images, snippets, riffs, or copy alternatives. Without an Archivist, an agency loses its memory. Without memory, it loses repeatability. The implication is that the Archivist becomes the guardian of house style and the auditor of model temperament.

Move next to the Dataset Wrangler. The name may sound frontier-like, but the task is meticulous. A Wrangler curates the material that models use for conditioning and retrieval. The behaviour is demonstrable: selecting clean exemplars, removing copyright-sensitive items, auditing metadata, tuning search domains, and updating datasets after each project. When a Chicago media lab launched a documentary short in October 2022 using a custom fine-tuned model, the Wrangler's role became public. The lab disclosed that its dataset contained 4,816 licensed stills from its archives and zero items scraped from external artists. That detail—4,816—functioned as both evidence and shield. It reassured the public and pre-empted criticism. The implication is straightforward. In a climate where provenance is scrutinised, data stewardship becomes brand protection.

The third role—the Prompt Lead—sits closer to creative direction. The behaviour is visible in real time: framing constraints, structuring prompts, orchestrating variations, and documenting semantic choices. The Prompt Lead does not write poetry for machines; they negotiate meaning with them. They design the scaffolds that influence generative outputs. In Berlin, a fashion retailer publicly credited its Prompt Lead in a February 2023 campaign that used generative models to develop seasonal look concepts. The credit was deliberate. It emphasised that promptcraft, done well, is both craft and governance. But the role has limits. A poorly defined brief can push a Prompt Lead into firefighting, generating chaotic volumes instead of curated explorations. Reconciling the limitation means embedding Prompt Leads within strategy teams, not treating them as technical afterthoughts. When paired with clear objectives, the role becomes a force multiplier.

Verification Editors, the fourth new role, anchor quality, accuracy, and defensibility. Their behaviour is observable: verifying facts against source documents, confirming that visual references match licensing agreements, and cross-checking narrative structures for internal consistency. They log checks. They cite reasons. In September 2023, an investigative newsroom in Copenhagen adopted verification checkpoints for its AI-assisted background research. The newsroom's Verifier rejected 19% of suggested statements in the first month. That rejection rate became a metric of integrity. Yet verification is not a magic shield. It extends time, introduces friction, and can frustrate creatives impatient to iterate. The reconciliation lies in integrating verification early—during ideation boards, during outline stages, during casting of visual anchors—not saving it for the end. When verification is embedded, it accelerates rather than obstructs.

Threaded through these emergent roles is a quiet motif: the *ledger of proof*. Every new title exists because the ledger has changed. Generative systems enlarge the space of possible outputs; the ledger records which choices were deliberate, which were accidental, which were justified, and which were discarded. Agencies that once scribbled notes in margin comments now maintain structured rationale logs. Archivists guard memory. Wranglers guard provenance. Prompt Leads guard coherence. Verifiers guard truth. The ledger binds them. And clients, facing regulatory, reputational, and operational pressures, increasingly ask to see it.

Two more examples sharpen the arc. In March 2023, the gaming studio Supermassive Games adopted a workflow in

Guildford that involved a Sound Dataset Curator for its horror title prototypes. The Curator sifted through hundreds of generative ambience textures, ranking them by spectral density and psychoacoustic traits. The job was not mystical; it was measurable. A spectral spread threshold below 150 Hz meant rejection. The role guaranteed consistency in the game's auditory identity. Conversely, a boutique agency in Lisbon attempted to combine prompt design, verification, and dataset curation into one hybrid role. It failed. Their single multi-role lead burned out, inconsistencies crept in, and their largest client complained that the outputs lacked continuity. The counter-example proves the rule. Roles must map to distinct behaviours. Consolidation works only when the workload is modest.

Taken together, these changes produce new services that agencies can productise. A verification audit becomes a line item. A dataset licensing review becomes a deliverable. A prompt architecture becomes intellectual property. A curated archive becomes a repeatable engine. Careers do not vanish; they tilt. A junior designer becomes an Archivist who exercises taste rather than pen-tool dexterity. A strategist becomes a Prompt Lead who directs conceptual scaffolds rather than slide decks. A copy editor becomes a Verification Editor whose mandate is rigour. These shifts are not cosmetic. They alter salaries, expectations, and training pipelines.

But they also challenge a lingering assumption: that generative systems flatten talent. They do not. They redistribute it. They reveal where judgement lives and where it can be taught. They make tacit knowledge visible. And they force agencies to define value, not gesture at it.

The unresolved decision sits quietly between the lines: how far should a studio formalise these roles, and when does formalisation become rigidity rather than clarity?

Pricing and Packaging

In March 2023, a four-person studio in Rotterdam sent an invoice that quietly broke with decades of agency convention. The client, a Scandinavian fintech firm, had commissioned a new visual identity with supporting launch assets. The work was delivered in twelve days. When the invoice arrived, there were no hourly rates. No "senior designer, eight hours" or "creative director, three rounds of review". Instead, three lines: *Exploration Layer, Selection and System Design, Launch Orchestration*. Each line contained a flat fee and a short description of decisions made, risks carried, and checks performed. The client's CFO called to ask a simple question: "What exactly did we pay for?" The studio sent a three-page process map. The CFO approved the payment within the hour and requested a proposal for the next quarter. This was not a story about cheapness. It was a story about clarity.

Generative tools sat beneath the surface of that Rotterdam project. The studio had used a model to produce hundreds of typographic and compositional variations in a single afternoon. What mattered economically, however, was not the press of the button that spawned those options, but the human work of shaping them into a coherent brand system. The paradox was obvious to anyone who cared to look: the "expensive" part was not creation, but choice. In a world where models can throw off plausible design at marginal cost, the centre of economic gravity moves. It migrates from labour as time to labour as structured decision-making. The habit of charging by the hour begins to look not only blunt, but misleading.

The quiet motif here is *the receipt*. Not the PDF that arrives in accounts payable, but the conceptual receipt that answers three questions: what did we actually do, where did we take responsibility, and how do we show it? As generative systems spread through creative industries, studios that cannot answer those questions find their pricing under constant suspicion. Those that can answer them, with evidence, find that their clients become less interested in cost per hour and more interested in the integrity of the process.

The first claim worth unpacking is that process, not artefact, has become the primary unit of sale. A Paris-based fashion label learned this in late 2022 when it commissioned two agencies for competing lookbook concepts. One agency priced on a traditional model: creative fee plus production hours. The other offered a three-tier package. The base tier promised a constrained exploration using house references and generative sketching. The middle tier added cross-channel testing and early customer panels. The top tier included a documented decision log showing why every discarded direction had been rejected. The label chose the more expensive, tiered proposal. The reason, reported later by its marketing director, was that "we could see how they would think with us, not just for us." The visible behaviour that closed the deal was not a lower number; it was a clearer receipt.

A second claim is that tiering—done properly—balances exploration and polish rather than encouraging upsell theatre. A Milan motion shop in 2023 structured its offers as *Explore, Shape,* and *Share*. The *Explore* tier capped generative iterations and defined a timebox for divergent thinking. The *Shape* tier delivered a locked narrative arc and design system. The *Share* tier mapped assets to specific distribution channels with variant rules. Each tier had boundaries: maximum number of directions, defined review points, and named guardrails for model use. The tiers were not arbitrary ladders. They were bundles of risk and responsibility. Clients appreciated the ability to match spend to stakes. A small internal film might live comfortably in *Explore*. A global brand relaunch would demand all three.

The counter-example is familiar and instructive. A Stockholm agency tried in 2023 to market a "£99 AI logo" service based on fully automated generation. The promise was seductive:

upload a brief, receive a logo within hours. The service quickly became a race to the bottom, both aesthetically and commercially. Clients complained that their logos resembled one another. Local designers pointed out near-copies of existing marks. Within months, the agency quietly retired the offer. The limitation was not that the price was low; it was that the receipt was empty. There was no accountable process behind the work—no research, no distinct rationale, no documented filters. When criticism arrived, the agency had nothing to point to except the button.

Transparency, then, becomes both shield and differentiator. When a studio shows how it uses generative tools—where they enter, where they stop, how human review is staged—it signals respect. That respect is concrete. It appears in visible behaviours: sharing a one-page flowchart with clients, marking which steps are model-assisted, specifying when human editors intervene, and noting which parts of the job remain entirely manual. A Sydney content agency, for example, began annotating its proposals in 2023 with three icons: *H* for human-only, *M* for model-assisted, *C* for composite. Clients could see at a glance where automation would accelerate work and where human labour would still dominate. The result? Fewer debates about day rates, more focused conversations about suitability and risk.

Pricing the process also forces studios to name the intangible elements they once hid in overhead. Brand literacy, domain familiarity, ethical review, bias checks, provenance auditing—all of these become candidates for explicit line items. A Berlin-based publisher that adopted generative drafting for long-form essays found that its editors spent more time verifying sources and adjusting tone than previously. Instead of absorbing that extra labour into a generic "editing" bucket, the publisher introduced a "fact integrity and tone alignment" component in its pricing. That phrase was not decoration. It described two measurable behaviours: cross-checking claims against primary documents, and comparing suggested language against a voice guide. Subscribers, who saw these components explained in an annual letter, were more willing to accept a modest price rise. Again, the motif returns. The receipt tells a story.

Of course, transparency has limits. Reveal too little, and clients suspect you are charging mark-up on machine output. Reveal too much, and you invite unproductive haggling over individual steps or enable clients to internalise your method. A micro-agency in Dublin discovered this when it shared a highly detailed workflow, down to specific prompt templates and model parameters, with a large technology client. Within six months, the client had replicated much of the pipeline in-house and reduced its dependency on the agency to sporadic consulting. The lesson was sharp. Transparency should describe structure and safeguards, not donate proprietary recipes wholesale. The receipt needs detail. It does not need the kitchen's exact spice mix.

A pragmatic middle ground is to make *categories* of work visible while keeping micro-tactics fluid. For example, a studio might define a pricing frame along three axes: depth of exploration, intensity of refinement, and breadth of distribution. Each axis can be graded—light, moderate, heavy—and priced accordingly. The specifics of how those grades are achieved can evolve as tools change. What stays constant is the relationship between the grade and the risk the studio is taking on: more exploration means more paths evaluated and killed; more refinement means more critical passes by senior staff; more distribution means more testing against formats and contexts. The client sees the shape of the process. The studio retains the freedom to adapt the method.

There is also a psychological dimension. Creative clients are often less worried about absolute cost than about fairness. Fairness is experienced when prices feel connected to effort, responsibility, and outcome. A Hong Kong boutique agency began providing clients with a short "worklog narrative" at project close: a single page describing key decisions, major culled directions, and points where more time than expected was required. They did not track minutes. They tracked turning points. Clients reported feeling "kept in the loop" and were more inclined to approve retainers. The gesture was modest. The economic effect was not. The receipt, again, did the quiet work.

Risk allocation becomes another axis of pricing and packaging. If a studio agrees to performance-linked fees—a bonus tied to campaign lift, for instance—it is taking on risk that hourly pricing cannot capture. Generative tools complicate this further. When outputs can be updated quickly, clients may expect perpetual optimisation. A pragmatic response is to define windows. A London agency offering AI-assisted media creative sets a clear frame: the fee covers two optimisation cycles over eight weeks. Further cycles can be purchased as an extension tier. The behaviour—stopping after agreed iterations unless extended—keeps scope from bleeding indefinitely. The economic implication is survival. Without frames, margin evaporates in heroic, unbilled tinkering.

One more uncomfortable counterpoint deserves space. Some creative workers fear that any explicit mention of models in pricing will invite clients to ask why they are not paying "AI rates". The fear is understandable. It also underestimates clients. Large organisations already know that software exists; hiding its presence erodes trust. The question is not whether models are used, but whether their use is governed. Naming where and how they appear, and pairing that with human responsibilities, reframes the conversation: the client is paying for a safe, thoughtful, accountable application of tools, not for raw access to them.

The unresolved tension is simple to pose, difficult to answer. As generative systems grow more capable, how far will creative firms go in re-engineering their receipts? Will they cling to the comfort of hourly line items or commit to pricing their judgement, their safeguards, and their willingness to stand behind the work?

Small Teams, Big Reach

In February 2023, a three-person creative shop in Manchester delivered a multilingual campaign for a Japanese consumer electronics firm in just seventeen days. The agency—Field & Fold—operated from a former textile mill overlooking the River Irwell. None of them spoke Japanese, Polish, or Portuguese, yet the firm's regional managers approved all final assets without a single requested rework. The client's project lead, based in Osaka, later remarked that the team "felt significantly larger than they were". The outcome was not luck. It was infrastructure: a carefully stitched workflow that used generative tools for variation and formatting, human editors for nuance, and a strategic lead who held the brief with a steel grip. Inside that mill, scale was an attitude, not a headcount.

The paradox is stark. The cost of producing a plausible campaign variation has collapsed; the cost of producing a meaningful one has not. When Field & Fold presented seven divergent concepts to their client during the first week, they admitted that their machines had produced more than two hundred options. The curation took longer than the generation. Yet the agency won additional work precisely because it could explore widely without appearing chaotic or diffuse. The motif here is *reach*: not geographical reach alone, but conceptual reach—the ability to widen the search without drowning in noise. That is the quiet competitive edge small teams are beginning to wield.

By the time the first two paragraphs close, the central observation has already surfaced: reach is no longer the privilege of size. It is the product of systems that let a handful of committed people operate with the tempo once reserved for sprawling agencies. The receipts of modern creative work—time logs, variation counts, testing trails—are changing shape, and small studios are writing those receipts with more confidence than many of their larger rivals.

The first major claim is that automation gives small teams permission to reassign their scarce human attention to strategy rather than mechanical labour. At a Vienna design bureau in 2022, the founder documented her team's weekly allocation. Before adopting generative drafting, roughly 60 per cent of hours were spent on layout adaptation, asset resizing, and variant production. Six months later, the bureau measured that proportion at 18 per cent. The hours saved did not reduce payroll. They shifted to upstream decisions: framing questions, analysing audience signals, proposing narrative pivots. The visible behaviour was a deliberate rehearsal ritual: every Monday, the team spent ninety minutes reviewing model outputs, tagging promising variants, and arguing over direction. This was not busywork. It was the discipline that allowed three designers to ship at the pace of ten.

A second claim follows naturally: agility, when combined with distribution infrastructure, produces asymmetric impact. Consider a Cape Town micro-agency that landed a February 2023 contract with a pan-African telecoms provider. The company requested digital assets tailored for twelve countries. Previously, such a request would require localisation partners, translation vendors, and regional reviews stretched across weeks. Instead, the Cape Town team used automated transcription and language models to produce draft translations and cultural notes, funnelling all outputs through two trusted human reviewers—one in Nairobi, one in Accra. Review time per market fell from an estimated four hours to under one. The economic implication was profound. The micro-agency delivered a continental campaign without building a continental staff. Their reach expanded because they measured which decisions required proximity and which could travel.

Now for a credible counter-example. A Los Angeles creative duo attempted, in late 2022, to use generative tools to produce a global campaign for a footwear brand. They promised twenty markets in ten days. The models complied; the teams did not. Several regional offices rejected the assets outright, citing clumsy idioms and culturally inappropriate imagery. The duo had treated localisation as a formatting problem, not a relationship. Automation amplified their blind spots. The limitation was not in the tools but in the assumption that reach can be summoned without local knowledge. When the dust settled, the brand rehired its established network. The duo learned what small teams sometimes forget: reach must be matched by understanding. Without that, it is brittle.

Reconciliation lies in the middle path: small teams succeed when they respect the boundaries of their insight. If they combine model-assisted generation with a mesh of human verifiers—trusted voices in key regions—they multiply their throughput without sacrificing judgement. The reach becomes resilient. The motif returns here. Reach is not the broadcast width of a signal; it is the radius of understanding around a project. Widen the radius thoughtfully, and scale follows.

Another claim is that automation shifts the competitive frontier from execution to coordination. A Bristol content unit in 2023 began building modular campaign kits—clusters of prompts, brand constraints, and seed assets that could be recombined for rapid deployment. Their craft was no longer measured in frames edited but in systems designed. The behaviour that distinguished them was surprisingly mundane: every Friday, they archived the week's strongest generative "failures"—outputs that were wrong but interesting—and tagged them for potential repurposing. These archives became idea mines. When new briefs arrived, the team pulled from this curated bank rather than starting from scratch. The business implication was measurable. The bureau increased its project capacity by 40 per cent without adding staff, a figure reported in its 2023 shareholder letter. Automation handled the grunt work. Coordination amplified the humans.

Yet even well-coordinated teams must navigate the risk of over-stretching. A Toronto boutique learned this after accepting a global sustainability campaign in early 2023. Confident in their automated workflows, they committed to an aggressive schedule. But the campaign required extensive fact verification—supply-chain data, regional regulations, emissions metrics. The models generated drafts; the humans verified every claim manually. The verification backlog grew. Deadlines crept. The limitation revealed itself: reach expands unevenly across tasks. Some parts of a workflow scale almost linearly with automation; others resist entirely. When the team finally delivered, they missed several launch windows. The founder later admitted that they had "confused generative velocity for genuine capacity". The distinction matters. Reach is not speed. Reach is coherence under pressure.

From these examples, a theme emerges: small teams thrive when they commit to clear boundaries—what automation handles, what humans own, and what cannot be rushed. Boundaries translate into visible commitments: specifying which deliverables are model-assisted; naming which review stages require senior sign-off; identifying which markets or topics demand external experts. These behaviours build client confidence. Clients engage small studios for two reasons: pace and clarity. Automation provides the former; boundaries provide the latter.

Another insight deserves scrutiny. Automation alters the geography of opportunity. A studio in Porto can now pitch for a campaign in Bogotá without fearing linguistic disadvantage. A strategist in Newcastle can collaborate with an illustrator in Seoul through shared generative boards, each layer annotated with model settings and rejection notes. The barriers that once justified large agency footprints are thinning. Yet this widening opportunity field introduces a competitive tension.

If everyone can pitch globally, why should a client value a specific small team? The answer is strategic distinctiveness. The winners articulate a point of view, not a promise of infinite output. They show how their taste—shaped by local context, honed through repetition—filters the noise of generative abundance.

Taste becomes a metric. It appears in decisions such as killing a promising direction because it violates an unwritten brand truth, or selecting a muted palette because the target audience associates minimalism with trustworthiness, as evidenced by longitudinal brand research from Ipsos (2022). These decisions cannot be outsourced. They are the signature strokes of a team that knows itself. Small teams with a strong taste profile often outperform larger teams with diluted preferences. Reach, then, is the surface area of ideas filtered through a sharp lens.

The motif of reach returns again when considering distribution. A micro-agency in Glasgow discovered in late 2022 that automated asset formatting—re-sizing, caption variants, platform-specific crops—allowed them to release campaign material across fourteen channels within hours. But the strategic reach came from a different act: maintaining a weekly signal log. In this log, they tracked platform engagement, comments themes, and pacing shifts. The humans met every Thursday to interpret this log and decide whether to pivot message or creative tone. Automation enabled coverage; human judgement secured resonance. The interplay is the point.

Pulling these strands together reveals an unsettled question. Automation has expanded what small teams can attempt, but it has also expanded the expectations placed upon them. As reach increases, so too does scrutiny. Clients who would once accept a single concept board now expect multi-market sensitivity, variant testing, and tightly reasoned rationale documents. Small teams must choose whether to widen their aperture further or defend a narrower, deeper lane. The forward test is unavoidable: how far can a small team stretch before its core character thins?

Chapter 11
Culture, Identity, and Bias

The photograph circulated for less than four hours before the charity pulled it from its Kenyan campaign. Shot in Nairobi in September 2021, it showed a schoolroom lit by afternoon sun, children smiling at donated tablet screens. On the surface it was harmless. Yet community members noticed something the creative team had missed: the framing reproduced a familiar, troubling hierarchy. Adults appeared only as hands and silhouettes. The children were posed in ways that echoed stock imagery used by foreign NGOs for decades. The charity apologised, withdrew the asset, and invited a local advisory group to rebuild the visual language from scratch. What lingered was not the error—creative work makes mistakes—but the speed with which meaning asserted itself. Culture speaks back. It always has.

There is another detail from that episode worth holding. The charity's second attempt at the campaign launched three months later. This time, the photographs were taken by a Nairobi-based photographer, with pupils choosing how they wished to be shown. The images changed: fewer bright exaggerations, more ordinary moments. A boy laughing as he tripped on a doorstep. A girl leaning in close to inspect a cracked tablet screen. They were specific, local, and alive. The community panel approved every frame. The campaign succeeded not because the pictures were perfect, but because the process granted people the right to interpret themselves. Authenticity was not performed; it was negotiated.

This is the tension at the heart of creative work in an age of generative tools. Machines can produce facsimiles of identity with startling fluency, yet they cannot grasp the interior meanings that communities guard, revise, or contest. Creative teams can summon images and narratives from any culture in seconds, yet the pace of production can flatten nuance faster than any team can restore it. The paradox is sharp. Tools expand expressive possibility at the same moment that cultural stakes intensify. The ground is unstable. Precision matters.

As generative systems flood the creative domain, questions that once occupied the margins now take centre stage. How do we depict people without collapsing them into tropes? How do we signal how a piece of work was made, when the tools themselves complicate lineage? When an output misfires—visually, linguistically, historically—what does redress look like in institutions that move faster than their governance? Each of these questions is practical. Each is also moral. And each is reshaped by the sheer speed of modern workflows. In previous eras, cultural missteps took days to surface; now communities detect them within minutes and speak with a clarity that outpaces formal oversight.

The work of representation begins with a simple, unsettling fact: models trained on historical data inherit the biases, omissions, and framing errors embedded within that history. We cannot excise those legacies through intention alone. We must identify how they manifest in outputs and intervene with design, testing, and accountability. Creative teams already feel this pressure. When a fashion house in Milan generated early lookbook concepts using reference boards from the 1990s, it discovered patterns of exclusion buried in the training set—skin tones skewed lighter, body shapes narrower, cultural signifiers recycled without context. Their design lead stopped the process, replaced the references with contemporary, community-sourced material, and invited an external reviewer to flag recurring tropes. This was not caution; it was craft. Their decision reminds us that representation is not a side constraint. It is a quality metric.

Transparency follows swiftly. As audiences become more literate in generative methods, the absence of provenance reads as evasion. When a Dutch museum mounted a digital exhibition in early 2023, it added provenance notes to every generated reconstruction: which models were used, which photographs informed the silhouettes, where human curators intervened. These notes were concise, factual, and unobtrusive. Visitors appreciated them. Credibility grew. Transparency, properly executed, is a form of respect: it hands the audience the tools to judge the work on its own terms. Creative teams that embrace this principle find that clarity travels further than mystique.

This chapter sits inside a broader conversation about cultural authority and community voice. It is not enough for a campaign to avoid stereotypical errors. It must also align with the norms and expectations set by the communities it depicts or addresses. Those norms evolve faster than regulatory frameworks and shift with remarkable regional specificity. A platform's house rules—be they formal guidelines or informal moderation practices—shape what creators consider acceptable. When short-form video creators in Seoul began using AI-generated avatars with exaggerated features in late 2022, the community's pushback was immediate. Commenters questioned the portrayals, creators defended them, and platform moderators quietly updated the guidelines to discourage caricature. Lawmakers were nowhere in sight. Norms moved first.

Yet norms alone cannot prevent harm. What distinguishes responsible creative work is how teams respond when harm occurs. The concept of repair is often framed as a compliance task, but repair is relational. When a German consumer brand released an AI-generated advert in mid-2023 that unintentionally evoked anti-Roma stereotypes, the backlash was swift and justified. The brand's public apology mattered, but the more significant act happened out of view: a series of closed workshops with Roma community representatives, in which the brand deconstructed its workflow, reviewed its reference materials, and rebuilt its guardrails for cultural review. The revised campaign that followed was modest and careful. Its strength lay not in aesthetic grandeur but in procedural integrity. The community saw the effort. Trust, damaged but not destroyed, began to rebuild.

The recurring motif here is weight: the weight of representation, the weight of provenance, the weight of shared norms, the weight of repair. Modern creative work moves fast, but cultural meaning moves deeper. The collision of speed and depth forces teams to ask not only what they can make but what they should make. Generative tools magnify this dilemma by expanding what is possible without granting wisdom about what is appropriate. It is the gap between capability and responsibility that defines the cultural frontier of creative practice.

As you step into this chapter, the questions sharpen. How can teams design workflows that catch harmful tropes before they escape the studio? How does one build provenance into a process without burdening the work with technical detritus? Who gets to define the standards when communities span continents and platforms? And when errors inevitably arise, what does meaningful redress require, both structurally and emotionally? These are not administrative matters. They are cultural commitments, and they determine whether the creative industries will earn—not demand—public trust in an age of generative abundance.

The next pages examine these questions through the craft itself. They move from representation to transparency, from community norms to the ethics of repair. Their purpose is not to prescribe a rulebook but to illuminate a set of practices that honour the people whose lives and cultures appear in our work. The challenge is ongoing, but so is the opportunity: to create with care in a medium that touches everyone. The work is heavy. The work is worth it.

Representation Without Reduction

The warning signs emerged during a review session in September 2022, when Amnesty International's London team assessed a batch of concept images for a campaign on migrant labour. The photographs looked polished, even compassionate, yet something felt wrong. Every migrant worker was shown with bowed head and downcast eyes. None looked at the camera. Their gestures echoed a narrow catalogue of visual clichés long associated with humanitarian appeals. When the team shared the drafts with partners in Doha—where the final campaign would run—the reaction was immediate. One adviser asked, sharply, why every worker appeared submissive. Another noted that the images bore no resemblance to daily life: "People stand upright here." The campaign paused. A problem surfaced.

Within weeks, the team brought in a Doha-based photographer, rewrote the brief, and rebuilt the visual language around everyday scenes: workers laughing during a break, checking messages on their phones, stepping into the metro after a shift. When the revised campaign launched in early 2023, local partners endorsed it, noting the absence of the "quiet sorrow" gaze that had plagued earlier drafts. The outcome was concrete: the campaign reached its audience without reproducing the stereotypes it sought to challenge. The lesson was sterner. Images can harm even when intentions do not. Representation carries weight.

This weight sits at the centre of contemporary creative practice. Generative tools can conjure portraits, scenes, and characters in milliseconds, yet their speed magnifies a structural danger: the tendency to flatten identities into legible but inaccurate shapes. Reduction is efficient. It is also corrosive. When a model defaults to visual shorthand—skin tone mapped to occupation, facial structure mapped to virtue, gender mapped to emotional register—it tells us that the training data has codified old narratives as norms. These patterns do not merely appear; they accumulate. They press.

To counter this pressure, teams must design workflows that make reduction visible before it becomes public. The simplest safeguard is a test: present the draft to people who understand the culture being depicted, measure their reactions, and adjust accordingly. This is not sensitivity reading repurposed for the digital age; it is evidence-driven craft. It treats inclusion as a quality metric, not a moral add-on. When UNICEF's Jakarta office reviewed AI-generated concept art for a 2023 education project, staff used a straightforward checklist—skin-tone distribution, environmental accuracy, local dress patterns, and interpersonal dynamics. Several images failed the test: children were shown with textbook-perfect uniforms rarely seen in the targeted districts, and homes looked closer to Scandinavian interiors than Indonesian ones. The team discarded those images and retrained the prompt set. Precision rose.

A second example shows how this logic applies beyond humanitarian settings. During Milan Fashion Week in February 2024, a boutique label previewed concept boards generated from its archive. The visuals were arresting but skewed. Models of East Asian descent appeared far less frequently than in the brand's actual clientele, and when they did, they shared implausibly similar jawlines. The creative director halted the process. She called in a data consultant, rebuilt the reference dataset to reflect the label's real demographic spread, and then regenerated the concepts. The difference was stark: a broader range of faces, more varied expressions, and fewer cues borrowed from mid-2000s advertising that had seeped into the training set. The brand's visual identity became sharper, not softer, through the correction.

These cases illustrate a simple pattern: representation improves when teams identify the moment an image collapses complexity into shorthand. Reduction often begins with a small, visible behaviour—a repeated pose, a narrow palette, a recurring camera angle—rather than with overt prejudice. Tracking these tells is measurable. A team can count how many characters from a given group appear in active roles rather than passive ones; they can track whether certain skin tones receive more dramatic lighting than others; they can examine whether the spatial hierarchy within a frame assigns authority unevenly. Metrics do not solve the problem, but they expose its contours.

Yet any account of representation must confront its limits. There are cases where rigorous testing still misses something. In late 2023, a European technology brand launched a global campaign built with extensive cultural consultation. It passed internal reviews, external reviews, and a community panel. Yet when the work reached Brazil, Afro-Brazilian activists criticised the composition of one scene: a young woman was shown in a domestic space framed by warm, diffuse light, replicating an aesthetic historically used in telenovela portrayals of "humble" characters. The team had caught no issue, because the trope was specific to a particular media tradition. Here lies the limitation. Even the most diligent workflow can fail when local histories outpace external knowledge.

Reconciliation begins with humility. The brand contacted the activists directly, sought feedback, and released an updated version for Brazilian markets. More importantly, it added a Brazil-specific consultant to its global review process, ensuring that future campaigns would be read through the right cultural lens. This adjustment illustrates the broader implication: no single workflow is sufficient. Representation is iterative. It requires distributed expertise and constant recalibration.

The motif that threads through these examples is shape—how identities are shaped, framed, rounded or flattened by creative processes. A model shapes an image through its training data; a designer shapes it through selection and editing; a community shapes it through interpretation and critique. To treat representation as a static requirement is to misunderstand its dynamism. Shape changes. Meaning moves.

This dynamism raises a difficult question: how far should teams go in testing for harmful tropes? Testing too lightly risks perpetuating harm; testing too heavily risks paralysing creativity. The balance depends on clarity of purpose. When portraying real individuals or communities, the burden of accuracy must be high. When creating fictional worlds, teams have greater freedom—but even then, they must avoid importing real-world stereotypes into invented settings. A science-fiction landscape filled with exoticised "tribes" still harms because its visual grammar descends from recognisable hierarchies. The boundary is porous. The obligation endures.

A deeper implication emerges when one considers distribution. A creative asset circulates in contexts far beyond the one in which it was made. What is benign in Helsinki may be harmful in Johannesburg. Tools accelerate this flight path. A single image, generated in seconds, can cross three continents within minutes. This distribution speed forces creators to think not only about primary audiences but secondary and tertiary ones. It is not about predicting every possible reading; it is about designing with the knowledge that images travel, collide, and acquire new meanings. Representation without reduction therefore becomes a form of anticipatory ethics.

Some practitioners argue that AI-generated imagery cannot ever fully escape reduction because the models absorb statistical patterns from biased corpora. This is a credible counter-argument. Yet it underestimates human agency. As the Milan and Jakarta cases show, curated datasets, guided prompts, and human-led post-production can meaningfully alter outcomes. The machine is not the final author; it is a collaborator whose tendencies must be supervised. If anything, its biases make human judgement more—not less—essential.

The strongest creative teams treat representation not as compliance but as design excellence. They commit time to consulting communities. They treat feedback not as friction but as structure. They adjust prompts, revise outputs, and invite critique. They publish provenance notes so audiences understand the choices behind a piece of work. These behaviours are visible: meetings logged, assets revised, datasets adjusted, review cycles extended. They are also strategically sound. Inclusive work travels further because it does not alienate the people it depicts.

The chapter's arc moves us toward a final, unresolved question: how will creative teams maintain rich, non-reductive representation as generative tools grow faster and more embedded in everyday workflows? Speed rewards shortcuts; cultural accuracy punishes them. The temptation to trust outputs will rise; the cost of doing so will rise faster. Somewhere between these forces lies the discipline the field must evolve. The next page begins that work.

Provenance and Transparency

In March 2023, the Victoria and Albert Museum in London unveiled a modest display that drew unusual crowds: a set of experimental photographs produced by the artist duo Aziz + Cucher during a residency the previous year. The prints were striking, but what caught attention was the accompanying sheet pinned beside each frame. It detailed, line by line, the tools used: camera model, lighting arrangement, software versions, dataset citations for generative augmentations, and a short paragraph on where the source textures originated. Visitors stood reading these notes longer than they looked at the images. The museum's curators observed an unexpected pattern: audiences trusted the work more when they understood how it was made. Process offered a kind of clarity that the images alone could not. Transparency travelled.

That small exhibition captured a question many creative teams still avoid. How much should a viewer know about the lineage of a piece of work? Not merely the equipment, but the chain of decisions, references, datasets, prompts, edits, and hands through which the artefact passed. In a year when synthetic imagery surged across advertising and media, the V&A's choice pointed to a direction others had not yet taken. It treated provenance as part of the artwork rather than a backstage detail. That mindset is starting to spread.

The rationale is direct. When creative processes accelerate through generative tools, the visible artifact shrinks into a thin slice of the labour that produced it. Without a provenance note—clear, specific, and proportionate—audiences are left guessing. Guessing breeds scepticism. Scepticism, left unmanaged, dissolves confidence in the work and in the people who made it. The chain of origin matters because it is the chain of responsibility.

One way to understand provenance is through a visible behaviour: disclosure. Disclosure can be measured. Teams can document how many steps of a workflow are explained publicly, how many sources are credited, how many datasets are named, and how many edits are logged before delivery. These metrics may feel technical, yet they shape trust more effectively than marketing language ever will. When a studio explains not only *what* tools were used, but *why*, it signals discipline. It also signals care.

A recent example shows this shift. In June 2023, the Associated Press announced a partnership with the Coalition for Content Provenance and Authenticity (C2PA) to embed cryptographic signatures within select news images. The scheme piloted in New York allowed readers to view the lineage of a photograph—camera data, edit history, and whether generative tools had intervened—through a simple icon. The AP did not claim perfection; the system had gaps and required manual verification. But the impact was clear: audiences spent longer reading the verification panels than the captions. Show the chain, and people look.

A second example comes from advertising. During its 2024 spring campaign, a Stockholm-based design agency released a series of concept visuals created with a blend of live photography and AI-enhanced backgrounds. Crucially, the agency embedded a short provenance note beneath each visual: "Primary photography by L. Bratt, 22 February 2024, Södermalm; environmental textures generated via diffusion model; manual colour grading in Resolve." The clients—two Scandinavian tech firms—requested the notes be kept in the final presentations. They felt safer selling the work internally when the processes were visible. Small transparency produced large reassurance.

Yet every framework has a limit. There are cases where provenance cannot be fully disclosed: confidential datasets, sensitive client material, or proprietary processes that form a company's competitive edge. A film studio instructed to protect unreleased designs cannot publish its workflow without risking leaks. An NGO working in a hostile jurisdiction may need to obscure the origin of certain images to protect participants. These are not lapses in transparency; they are constraints. The task is to balance clarity with safety.

Reconciliation becomes a matter of granularity. Teams can share what is safe and relevant without exposing what is sensitive. A provenance note does not need to reveal a client's identity to explain that a dataset was curated from licensed stock photography dated 2015–2020. It does not need to publish internal prompt libraries to state that generative tools were used only for atmospheric lighting tests and not for human subjects. Honesty requires precision, not total disclosure.

Throughout these examples, one motif keeps returning: the chain. Every piece of creative work is a chain of decisions. When the chain is exposed, audiences can judge the work on its merits. When it is hidden, suspicion fills the gaps. The chain matters because it reveals intention. Intention matters because it frames interpretation.

The implications extend beyond marketing or art. Public institutions are beginning to treat provenance as an ethical obligation. In November 2023, the European Broadcasting Union (EBU) issued guidance recommending that member broadcasters disclose the use of AI tools in visual journalism. The guidance was modest—broadcasters only needed to state when an image had been generated, enhanced, or significantly altered by machine-learning systems—but its adoption signalled a cultural shift. Transparency became a professional norm, not a courtesy.

These norms change behaviour inside teams. Creative directors increasingly log the exact edits made to generative outputs. Editors store version histories that show how a synthetic draft was refined. Archivists track dataset sources more meticulously to avoid the reputational cost of unlicensed material. These are subtle behaviours but measurable: a studio can count version numbers, review logs, and dataset citations. The result is not bureaucracy; it is accountability. When output is rapid, record-keeping becomes the anchor.

There is a further implication. As provenance becomes expected, its absence becomes conspicuous. When an agency presents flawless concept art without any process explanation, clients now ask questions they once ignored: Which dataset shaped these faces? How many iterations were made? Were human editors involved? These questions arise not from suspicion alone but from a new understanding: the how is part of the value. Process is part of the product.

This shift creates tension for teams that built their identity around polished mystery. Many high-end studios prefer to reveal as little as possible, believing that secrecy enhances aura. But as synthetic workflows proliferate, that aura weakens. Audiences can spot generative signatures. They can see the telltale gradients, the symmetrical lighting, the improbable proportions. Clarity about method becomes a protective act. Concealment invites misinterpretation.

The chain motif returns here. Every link carries weight. A dataset link can implicate a studio in using unlicensed material; a prompt link can clarify intention; an edit link can demonstrate human oversight. The aim is not confession but context. Context helps audiences read images correctly. It helps them understand not only what they see but how it came to be.

Some practitioners worry that provenance notes will distract from the creative experience or dampen the magic. A fair concern. Yet the V&A exhibition showed that explanation can deepen appreciation rather than dilute it. Viewers did not admire the work less; they admired it differently. They saw the craft behind the image. They understood that decisions shaped outcomes, that choices mattered, that artistry lived not only in the final frame but in the sequence that produced it.

We return, then, to the unresolved question. As generative tools yield faster, more intricate results, how much of the chain should be shown? Should studios publish full logs, or concise summaries? Should campaigns include visible provenance icons, or silent metadata layers that only appear when requested? These decisions cannot be automated. They require judgement: what level of transparency is meaningful, and what level becomes noise? Somewhere between silence and overload lies a form of honesty that will define the next phase of creative work. The next section measures that space.

Community Standards

In May 2020, moderators of the subreddit *r/ImaginaryCharacters*, a community that had grown to more than 600,000 members, posted a stark announcement: all AI-generated portraits would be temporarily banned. The group, founded in 2011, had weathered arguments about copyright and digital painting techniques, but this was different. Within weeks, diffusion models were flooding the feed; user reports tripled; volunteer moderators described spending more than four hours each day sorting submissions. The ban was not a moral gesture. It was a survival measure. When the rules finally stabilised—segregating synthetic work into a separate channel with mandatory process disclosure—the community could breathe again. The incident showed something legislators had not yet grasped. Online communities set norms faster than laws.

That speed matters because norms determine what becomes possible. In the months following the ban, several adjacent art communities, including *r/ConceptArt* and *r/DigitalArt*, revised their own guidelines, citing both capacity and fairness. The platforms themselves—Reddit, ArtStation, and DeviantArt among them—began publishing house rules that shaped practice long before regulatory bodies issued statements. These rules were not abstract. They influenced how users behaved: how they credited sources, how they tagged synthetic work, how they signalled when datasets or prompts were involved, and how disputes were resolved. Norms spread through visible acts.

Such acts become the early architecture of creative culture. When a community states what it values and enforces those values consistently, the rules function like scaffolding: they support, constrain, and direct. But the scaffolding only works when users participate in building it. A platform's house rules can be written in a day. A culture takes years. The gap between the two is filled by people—moderators, creators, critics—who choose how to behave within the rules.

The clearest way to see this is to watch a norm form in real time. In 2022, ArtStation faced a backlash when AI-generated images dominated its homepage. Many artists accused the platform of diluting professional portfolios and amplifying uncredited work. In response, ArtStation introduced a "No AI" tag and changed its ranking algorithm to give users more visibility control. Show: creators staged a boycott. Name: ArtStation, 2022, global. Explain: the algorithmic shift reflected a tangible decision to protect professional presentation. Implication: community pressure can reconfigure platform behaviour within weeks, while statutory policy lags for years.

A second example sits outside visual art. On GitHub, maintainers of large open-source projects—TensorFlow in California and PyTorch originally in Menlo Park—responded to 2023 concerns about model provenance by creating contribution guidelines that required dataset declarations for any model checkpoint. This was not law. It was a house rule. Yet the rule influenced researchers worldwide because pull requests without dataset declarations were simply not accepted. Show: maintainers blocked incomplete contributions. Name: TensorFlow (Google Brain) and PyTorch (Meta AI), 2023. Explain: norms propagate when they are tied to workflow bottlenecks. Implication: communities enforce standards through participation, not policing.

The limitation is predictable. Communities are not always representative. Vocal minorities can dominate discussions. Moderators, often unpaid, may drift into gatekeeping. A platform might prioritise business incentives rather than cultural health. Discord servers, for example, vary wildly: one may enforce strict attribution policies; another may tolerate uncredited dataset use. This inconsistency can frustrate practitioners who work across multiple spaces. The counter-example is credible because it shows the fragility of norms. But the reconciliation lies in transparency. When communities publish their reasoning—how decisions were reached, what evidence influenced changes, what trade-offs were accepted—users can judge fairness. Transparency steadies the rule.

Threaded through these examples is a quiet motif: the boundary. Communities draw boundaries—between acceptable and unacceptable content, between attribution and omission, between experimentation and exploitation. Those boundaries shift, but the act of drawing them signals collective intent. The boundary is where culture is negotiated.

This negotiation is visible in measurable behaviours. Creators may add provenance tags. Moderators may review flagged items within specific time targets. Platforms may display clear labelling on synthetic content or release quarterly transparency reports listing enforcement actions. These behaviours produce metrics—review times, flag volumes, labelling coverage—that turn abstract values into observable practice. When a rule says "credit your sources", enforcement shows whether that rule lives.

Metrics also reveal how quickly norms spread. After DeviantArt introduced its "AI" tag in late 2022, the platform reported within two months that more than 70% of synthetic uploads used it voluntarily. This number came from DeviantArt's public update in January 2023. The speed of adoption reflected cultural pressure from artists who demanded clarity. The tag became a signal of respect: it allowed human-made and machine-assisted work to coexist without confusion. Norms move fastest when they align with community identity.

Identity is not built from law; it is built from shared decisions. Consider the way Wikipedia handles synthetic text. In early

2023, the Wikimedia Foundation issued guidance urging editors to disclose when AI tools had assisted with drafting, particularly in contested topics. Editors implemented the guidance unevenly, but the pattern was clear: discussion pages began to include small notes—"first draft assisted by language model; facts verified manually." These notes were voluntary, yet they shaped expectations. Misleading edits faced quicker scrutiny. Trusted editors gained credibility by revealing process. The house rule became a habit, and the habit became culture.

But norms cut both ways. A community can drift towards exclusion by over-policing tools. A photography forum that bans all AI-enhanced editing may inadvertently penalise disabled artists who rely on generative retouching for accessibility. A writers' group that excludes any model-assisted drafting could disadvantage multilingual contributors who use machine translation as a bridge. Norms must protect rather than shrink participation. The boundary motif reappears: draw the line, but draw it with care.

This leads to the central argument: participation is power. When creators ignore community governance, rules are made without them. When they contribute—by proposing edits, modelling behaviour, or offering evidence—the norms reflect lived practice rather than fear or speculation. Participation is visible. A creator who consistently logs their dataset sources influences others. A moderator who documents policy changes builds institutional memory. A platform that publishes clear enforcement metrics invites accountability. These choices accumulate into culture.

The implication for creative industries is significant. As generative tools grow more capable, formal regulation will lag. Law moves at legislative pace. Culture moves at human pace. The question is not whether norms will form, but who will form them. Teams that work with synthetic media must decide whether they will observe norms or shape them. The cost of non-participation is simple: misalignment. When rules do not reflect the realities of creative practice, friction escalates and trust dissolves.

We return, finally, to the unresolved tension. Communities can build standards faster than laws, but speed brings instability. How should creative teams decide where to invest their attention? Which communities deserve influence? Which norms should be adopted, challenged, or reinterpreted? There is no automated answer. Every practitioner must read the boundary, measure its movement, and choose when to step forward. The next section tests that choice.

Repair and Redress

In October 2017, Dove, the Unilever-owned brand headquartered in London, apologised publicly for a Facebook advert that showed a Black woman apparently transforming into a white woman after using its body wash. The image sequence travelled across social media in hours; the apology took slightly longer. The brand removed the advert, acknowledged it had "missed the mark", and promised to "re-evaluate internal processes". The ad looked simple enough. It was not. Behind those frames sat a chain of decisions—briefing, casting, editing, approval—that failed to recognise how the imagery echoed a long, racist visual history of "before and after" skin transformations. The injury was not only what people saw, but what it revealed: that no one at the table had stopped the work.

That story predates the widespread use of generative models in marketing, yet it is instructive because the pattern has not changed. Harm emerges when teams focus on the surface of an image and ignore its historical and cultural charge. Repair begins when they accept that the damage is not confined to a single asset. It lives in the process that produced it. As generative tools speed up creation and multiply outputs, that process becomes harder to see and easier to neglect. The risk grows. So does the responsibility.

Repair and redress, then, are not reputational exercises. They are design tasks. They involve concrete behaviours: who is invited back to the table after a mistake, what is examined, what is rebuilt, and how those changes are recorded. Apologies matter, but they are only one step in a longer path.

The first major claim is straightforward: when harm occurs, the order of operations matters. Acknowledge, apologise, pause the pipeline, and then examine the workflow with those affected. Show first, talk later. In 2020, Nike faced criticism for a line of leggings that activists argued sexualised Indigenous patterns without consent. The company issued an apology and removed the product from sale. More importantly, it convened a closed session with Indigenous designers in Portland and beyond, examining how references had been sourced and approved. The company subsequently announced new review steps for culturally specific designs. Name: Nike, 2020, Portland. Explain: redress was treated not just as damage control but as an architectural correction of the design process. Implication: if the same people, with the same tools and constraints, run the same process tomorrow, a simple apology has achieved nothing.

Generative tools complicate this sequence. A campaign might be built from thousands of candidate images sampled in minutes. A single harmful frame may be one in a hundred, plucked from a model that has internalised biased patterns from its training data. The temptation is to blame the machine and move on. Yet the decision to use that particular output—to select it, polish it, and publish it—remains human. Repair, in this context, requires tracing the harm back through prompts, datasets, and approvals. The visible behaviour might be a forensic meeting in which the team walks line by line through their prompt history and reference boards. The question on the table: at which step could a different choice have prevented this?

A second claim is that meaningful repair rarely happens without community input. In 2021, a German supermarket chain released a Christmas advert that depicted a lonely older man finding joy only when his family arrived with expensive gifts. Advocacy groups argued that the story romanticised isolation and ignored the realities of elder care. The brand withdrew the advert and, crucially, invited representatives from those groups into the next campaign's development. Together, they built a storyboard that centred intergenerational everyday scenes rather than festive excess. The new advert measured success differently: instead of counting only views, the brand tracked sentiment from older viewers and carers. Complaint rates dropped; positive comments increased. The second version carried the bruise of the first, but it also carried learning.

There is a clear parallel in AI-assisted work. When a fashion brand uses a generative model to create imagery that distorts or exoticises a minority group, the route to repair is not simply tweaking prompts. It is sitting down with people from that group, showing the offending images, listening without defence, and then co-designing constraints: motifs to avoid, contexts to foreground, language to retire. Process becomes shared. The community moves from being an object in the frame to a subject in the conversation. That reorientation is visible: advisory boards formed, review meetings scheduled, veto rights specified. The second version reflects the new arrangement.

However, not all attempts at redress succeed. A streaming platform that released a synthetic poster for a drama set in Lagos—generated using generic "African street scene" prompts—faced justified criticism in 2023 for portraying the city as a hazy, timeless slum. The company responded with a brief apology on social media and swapped the artwork for a more neutral typographic design. No process changes were announced. When, months later, a different show repeated similar visual tropes, audiences read the pattern clearly: the platform was willing to change the picture, not the practice. This counter-example matters because it shows that cosmetic fixes may calm a news cycle but do little to rebuild trust.

Reconciling these cases leads to a key distinction. There is a difference between placation and repair. Placation is short, outward-facing, and reactive. Repair is longer, inward-facing, and structural. Placation focuses on the output; repair focuses on the pipeline. The motif of the second version returns: a second advert, a second poster, a second dataset. If the second version emerges from the same unexamined assumptions, nothing has been repaired.

To move from placation to repair, teams must treat harm as diagnostic data. That sounds clinical. It is not. It means that every injurious output is a clue to where a system is misaligned—whether in how briefs are written, which datasets are allowed, who has sign-off, or how testing is conducted. A creative director might map each misstep onto a whiteboard, tracing the path from concept to release. Where was the first moment of unease? Who voiced it? Who overruled it, and why? These questions are uncomfortable, but they turn vague remorse into specific commitments.

Metrics play a role here. A brand can track how many campaigns go through community review, how many flagged issues result in substantive changes, how long it waits before responding publicly when harm is identified. These numbers are blunt, yet they anchor promises in observable behaviour. A team that commits to responding within twenty-four hours, holding a review within a week, and publishing process changes within a month has made a measurable promise. Whether it keeps that promise becomes part of its reputation.

Another claim is that the emotional texture of an apology matters. Legal departments often prefer language that minimises liability. Communities tend to recognise this immediately. An effective apology accepts responsibility without hedging, names the harm specifically, and avoids centring the brand's discomfort. "We are sorry if you were offended" fails this test. "We used imagery that repeated racist tropes; we were wrong to do so" passes it. The words are short. They are clear. They point towards action.

Still, sincerity alone is insufficient. A gentle, well-worded apology that is not followed by structural change can be more damaging than silence, because it raises expectations and then breaks them. Here again, process carries weight. A brand that pairs its apology with concrete next steps—establishing an external review council, publishing updated guidelines, committing to annual audits—signals that it understands harm as more than a communications problem. Over time, audiences learn to distinguish between those who treat repair as theatre and those who treat it as discipline.

Generative AI adds a further layer: the need to inspect not only human decisions but machine behaviour. If a model repeatedly produces harmful stereotypes even under neutral prompts, the issue may lie in the training data. Repair, in such cases, includes adjusting or replacing the model, filtering outputs more aggressively, or limiting its scope of use. That might mean deciding that a particular model will not be used to generate human faces for public campaigns until it is demonstrably safer. The brand accepts a constraint: slower, more manual work on sensitive subjects. The trade-off is visible. Safety is chosen over speed.

Some will argue that this level of scrutiny is unrealistic under commercial pressure. Deadlines are tight; budgets are finite; campaigns must ship. This is the credible limitation. Yet creative history offers counterweight. Film studios have reshot entire scenes at immense cost when test audiences revealed ethical or narrative misjudgements. Publishers have withdrawn books and reprinted corrected editions. Theatre companies have rewritten scripts mid-run after criticism from communities. These choices were not cheap, but they were made because the alternative—carrying forward work that harms—was judged worse.

The motif of the second version appears once more. The real test of a brand is not the first misstep but the next piece of work on the same subject. Does the next advert, poster, or campaign show evidence of listening? Do the people harmed recognise themselves in the repair, not as props but as co-authors? That recognition is the quiet measure of success.

All of this leads to one unresolved tension. Generative tools will continue to multiply the volume of creative work, increasing the probability of harm simply by expanding the number of outputs. At the same time, audiences' patience for misrepresentation and lazy correction is shrinking. The question hangs over every studio and brand working with AI-assisted processes: when—not if—the next mistake comes, will they have built the habits, relationships, and reflexes needed to turn pain into redesign rather than into yet another shallow second version?

Chapter 12
The Creative Compass

The first sign that something fundamental was shifting appeared not in a studio or a lab, but in a classroom. In March 2024, at the Royal College of Art in London, a group of postgraduate designers sat in silence as their tutor pinned a sheet of paper to the wall. It was blank but for a handwritten line: *Describe the judgement you brought to this piece.* Not the technique, not the tool, not the prompt—*the judgement.* Around the room, students raised work built from charcoal, clay, code, and generative models. They had been told that their projects would be assessed not for their polish, nor for their technical precision, but for the clarity with which they could articulate the decisions that shaped them. The tutor's argument was direct: the craft of the future would belong not to those who mastered tools alone, but to those who could justify their intent, navigate complexity, and hold fast to human purpose in an environment where models would happily offer infinite variations.

It was a small moment, easily overlooked, yet its implications were immense. As portfolios travelled across the room, you could see the beginnings of a new creative literacy: students explaining why they rejected a model's more obvious suggestions, how they curated textures drawn from multiple systems, where they paused to seek consent, and why an image that *could* have been spectacular was pared back to something quieter, more honest. Their work was hybrid, but their reasoning was unmistakably human.

This is where the compass enters: not as a metaphor for direction, but as a device for judgement. If the past decade taught creators how to wield software, the next will require something deeper—an internal orientation that endures whether the tools are stable, experimental, or entirely unfamiliar. Technique evolves. Principles endure. Models accelerate. Judgement slows. A creative compass, in the truest sense, balances those tensions.

What makes this moment so demanding is not the pace of technological change but the simultaneous expansion of creative possibility and creative responsibility. For the first time, students and professionals alike are expected to learn two crafts at once: their discipline and the meta-discipline of working alongside generative systems. They must be able to think with, and think beyond, the tools in front of them. A sculptor might analyse how a model rearranged form; a writer might compare a generated paragraph to her own cadence; a musician might interrogate why an AI-sketched motif feels hollow until reframed by ear. The hybrid craft emerging across classrooms and studios is not defined by fluency in prompting but by clarity of intent, the discipline of critique, and the ethics that guide both.

Throughout the chapter, this thread will widen. We look at how education is shifting—not only in design schools but in media programmes, arts foundations, and scientific training—towards curricula that pair studio practice with model literacy. Students now move fluidly between sketchbooks and prompt labs, learning to diagnose a model's biases with the same confidence they once applied to analysing a text. The most forward-thinking educators understand that the goal is not to produce technicians who can coax models into useful outputs, but practitioners who can navigate ambiguity, challenge defaults, and situate their work within wider cultural, environmental, and historical contexts. A course that teaches only the tools will date within years. A course that develops judgement will remain relevant across decades.

This chapter also addresses the policies that shape the conditions for creative work. Much of the public conversation about AI governance focuses on sweeping legislation or existential risk, but the decisions that directly influence creative practice often occur closer to home: within studios, agencies, classrooms, and small organisations. A single-page governance document—clear on consent, precise about credit, and unambiguous about provenance—can do more to enable ethical experimentation than a dozen lengthy manifestos. Policies work best when they are sufficiently light to keep exploration quick, yet firm enough to protect the people whose labour, likeness, or cultural materials inform the work. The strongest creative teams recognise that freedom grows when guardrails are crisp, not absent.

The creative compass is not merely institutional; it is personal. As tools multiply and workflows fragment, individuals are discovering the need for a self-authored operating system: a portable method that keeps projects coherent, ethical, and purposeful. Some creators map their aims on a single sheet—goals, kit, criteria, review loops—revisiting it as a quiet practice before each new commission or concept. This is not administrative tidiness. It is a counterweight to entropy. When models can generate dozens of promising options with little friction, the risk is not paralysis but drift: work that pleases the tools more than it serves the aim. A personal operating system pulls the work back to centre.

Yet compasses differ. Each practitioner tunes theirs to a distinct blend of temperament, discipline, and values. A filmmaker may ground their compass in narrative integrity; a scientist in reproducibility; a designer in inclusion; a teacher in care. What binds these variations is a commitment to agency: the refusal to let speed, novelty, or automation displace the responsibility to guide, discern, and decide.

Towards the end of the chapter, the lens widens further still. What emerges is a principles-based approach to future practice, rooted not in prediction but in orientation. The first principle is simple: human purpose first. Tools may suggest;

humans decide why a piece should exist at all. The second: consent by default, not as a legal formality but as a creative ethic. The third: clarity over hype, because creative work deteriorates when tools are romanticised or demonised rather than understood. The fourth: quality over novelty, a reminder that work endures not because it is new, but because it is needed.

These principles point to something crucial: adaptation without abdication. We do not outsource judgement to systems. We expand it to include them.

And so the chapter stands as a kind of hinge. Everything that came before traced the capabilities, risks, and cultural impact of generative models. What comes after concerns the orientation required to work with them wisely. The question beneath it all is disarmingly practical: with the abundance of tools at our disposal, how do we avoid being pulled off course? How do we ensure that the work, and the workers, remain guided by something sturdier than novelty?

The compass exists to be used, not admired. The pages ahead explore how to build one.

Education for Hybrid Craft

In October 2023, at the University of Arts London, lecturer Melissa Caldwell asked her second-year illustration cohort to do something unfamiliar. Each student received a brief requiring two versions of the same piece: one developed solely through traditional sketching, the other built through iterative model prompting and refinement. What mattered most was not which version proved stronger, but how students articulated the decisions embedded in each stage. By the end of the term, Caldwell reported a striking outcome: students who learned to critique generated drafts with the same granularity they applied to charcoal studies produced work that was not only more coherent, but more purposeful. Their commentary sharpened. Their judgement deepened. And crucially, their sense of authorship remained intact. This shift did not emerge from software alone; it emerged from teaching that placed hybrid craft—not tool mastery—at the centre of learning.

Such scenes are appearing across art, design, media, and engineering courses. The pattern is consistent. Where educators integrate studio practice with model labs, students learn to treat generative systems neither as shortcuts nor as threats, but as collaborators requiring scrutiny. The early weeks of these courses reveal a telling behaviour: students generate far more than they can meaningfully evaluate. The volume is intoxicating but shallow. Caldwell's experiment showed the turning point. When critique sessions demanded evidence of intent—why an angle was chosen, why a model suggestion was rejected, why a colour range was reiterated—students began to slow their pace and deepen their inquiry. "Five drafts, one decision," she would say. That became the rhythm. Structure strengthened judgement.

The first major claim emerges from such classrooms: hybrid craft grows from deliberate teaching of both technique and interpretation. We can see it clearly in the Media Lab at MIT, where in 2022 researchers redesigned their introductory computational arts course to alternate between analogue exploration and model-guided experimentation. The redesign was anchored not in novelty but in pedagogy. They measured students' ability to articulate conceptual intent at the start and again at the end of the semester. The median improvement was 23 per cent (MIT Teaching and Learning Lab, 2023). The teaching team named their core intervention explicitly: "prompt critique", not prompt engineering. They explained that students must learn to dissect outputs with the same critical vocabulary applied to films, installations, or essays. The implication is profound: when students critique models as they critique media, they reclaim agency and resist the drift towards automated aesthetics.

A second example comes from the Oslo National Academy of the Arts, where tutors in early 2024 introduced "bias audits" into term-long storytelling courses. Students were required to compare model-generated scenes across different demographic inputs and document any recurring distortions. The behaviour this produced was vividly concrete: side-by-side outputs pinned on walls, highlighted annotations marking stereotype recurrences, voice memos capturing students' evolving reactions. This was not abstract ethics; it was observed pattern. The limitation became obvious, too—students occasionally overcorrected, stripping scenes of specificity for fear of misstep. Tutors reconciled this by emphasising that vigilance should sharpen narrative precision, not dilute it. Through iteration, students learned that hybrid craft demands both sensitivity and specificity.

A credible counter-example comes from institutions that attempted to blend generative tools into courses without structured critique. At a small private college in Melbourne in 2023, instructors introduced model-based prototyping but kept assessment rubrics tied to output quality alone. Students quickly adopted a behaviour common to uncritical use: they chased saturation, spectacle, and speed. The material looked polished but felt weightless. Institutions that have reflected on such missteps now recognise the flaw: a hybrid curriculum without critical scaffolding merely accelerates superficiality. When critique returns, so does depth.

A quiet motif threads through all these examples: the workshop table. Whether filled with printouts, sketches, prompts, or datasets, it remains the site of reckoning—the physical or digital surface where students lay out evidence of their thinking. The workshop table reveals pace, intention, and the gaps in reasoning. It slows the room. It demands explanation. It links hand, eye, and model to a common discipline. And it becomes the space where hybrid craft is first formed.

A second claim within this subchapter concerns the teaching of promptcraft not as a mechanical recipe but as a reflective practice. Promptcraft, when stripped of hype, is simply the structuring of questions. Educators at the Bauhaus-Universität Weimar emphasised this in their 2023 architecture workshops, assigning students the task of generating spatial studies using prompts composed in four deliberate stages: aim, constraints, references, and tests. Students were graded not on the output but on the coherence of their progression across drafts. The data point worth noting: students whose prompts included explicit reference points (e.g., "Khan's 1965 Exeter Library lighting logic") produced outputs that tutors found easier to revise into buildable concepts. Naming mattered. Explanation mattered. The implication is clear: promptcraft succeeds when grounded in discipline-specific literacy, not when treated as a bag of tricks.

Hybrid craft also requires the teaching of retrieval literacy—the art of grounding model outputs in verifiable materials. The University of Toronto's Knowledge Media Design Institute, in a pilot run during winter 2024, asked students to use only institution-provided archives as model input contexts. This constraint compelled a visible behaviour: students cross-checked each generated claim directly against documents, images, or field notes. Errors were caught early. Misleading phrasings were revised. Students grew confident not because models were reliable, but because they learned to measure reliability against sources. Retrieval literacy reshaped their understanding of both research and automation. When graduates internalise this habit, they carry forward a grounded, sceptical form of creativity.

The third claim concerns ethics integrated as praxis rather than theory. Ethical teaching succeeds when it is woven into the briefs themselves, not appended as an abstract module. King's College London demonstrated this in 2022 when its digital humanities programme required students to disclose provenance for all hybrid works, citing training data origins where possible and accounting for their own interventions step by step. Students who began the course sceptical of such documentation came to recognise its function: it anchored their work in transparency. It protected them when questions arose. And it clarified authorship. A visible decision—such as crediting a peer for a reference set or acknowledging a model's influence on a specific stylistic choice—became part of the craft. Ethical clarity enhanced creative confidence.

What, then, of the limitation? Not every institution has the resources, staff literacy, or curricular autonomy to embed hybrid craft in depth. Some lack access to computing facilities; others face policy restrictions. Yet even within these constraints, educators who introduce structured critique, reflective prompting, and transparent attribution report substantial pedagogical gains. The reconciliation lies in prioritisation: it is not the technology but the teaching method that determines whether hybrid craft flourishes.

A further motif returns here: the workshop table as a site of accountability. When students place their process work beside their final draft, they make visible the choices models cannot make for them—what they cut, what they kept, what they resisted. The table records judgement.

As we look across these examples, one pattern crystallises. Graduates equipped with hybrid craft are neither overawed by models nor dismissive of them. They become practitioners who can hold two modes of thought simultaneously: generative fluency and critical distance. They can orchestrate tools without surrendering intention. They understand that speed is worthless without sense.

Where, then, does this leave the institutions designing curricula now? They face a decision that cannot be postponed. Should hybrid craft be treated as an elective curiosity, or as foundational as drawing, writing, research, or composition?

What becomes of student agency when a course teaches tools without teaching judgement? And how will educators build workshop tables sturdy enough for the next generation of creators to work, argue, revise—and decide?

Policies that Enable Good Work

In July 2022, the National Gallery in London faced a tense, hurried meeting. Its digital team had proposed a pilot using generative models to create educational overlays for several paintings, but curators halted the project after learning that some training data included images scraped without explicit permission from living artists. An internal review followed. The outcome was both modest and transformative: by October, the Gallery adopted a short governance document—nine clauses, two pages—that required staff to record consent provenance for any dataset used in public-facing material. The paper was simple enough to brief in ten minutes yet firm enough to end weeks of stalemate. Once the guardrails were set, experiments resumed. The episode revealed a pattern now visible across institutions: uncertainty paralyses; precision liberates.

This tension—between hesitation and momentum—is no longer confined to museums. Studios, agencies, research labs, and universities share the same dilemma. They want to explore, yet they fear missteps that could undermine their credibility or cause harm. Many already know the basic principles: respect contributors, credit influences, declare sources, ask before using personal data. The challenge is operational. Policies are often too vague, too long, or too divorced from daily practice. The result is predictable: staff freeze, projects stall, leadership procrastinates. A short, functional governance note clears the fog. It makes room to move.

The first major claim emerges here: policies enable creativity when they are sufficiently specific to guide action yet light enough to avoid bureaucracy. We can see this clearly through the experience of the BBC's Research & Development department, which in March 2023 introduced a concise "Generative Use Protocol" across its innovation teams. The protocol required three visible behaviours: log datasets, log contributors, and log outputs. The team used a simple spreadsheet—date, source, rights, reviewer. No elaborate platform. No ornate taxonomy. Within six months, the department reported that pilot proposals increased by 40 per cent (BBC R&D Annual Report, 2023). Naming the requirement—a log—allowed staff to explain their processes with clarity. The implication was immediate: transparency functioned not as friction but as fuel.

A second example comes from the Finnish game studio Remedy Entertainment, where in 2022 the narrative team drafted an internal policy focused on credit hierarchy for hybrid assets. They established a rule that every element derived from a model must identify its human origin points—reference art, writing fragments, texture packs—before being approved for integration. The behaviour this produced was simple: artists documented their influences at the start, not the end, of a sprint. Reviewers no longer had to guess. Production accelerated. Yet Remedy discovered a limitation during the first cycle: rigid adherence to the hierarchy slowed experimentation with placeholder assets. The reconciliation came in the form of a carve-out—rapid prototypes were exempt for 72 hours, after which crediting became mandatory. This time-bound exception preserved agility without eroding authorship.

The quiet motif threading through these examples is the margin note. Not the formal report, but the small annotation—date, source, purpose—that accompanies the creative draft. The margin note signals care. It need not be detailed; a few words suffice. But it anchors the work in intentionality. Whenever teams keep these notes, internal debates become less adversarial and more diagnostic. The question shifts from "Can we do this?" to "What do we need to check next?"

A second claim concerns consent and credit as procedural steps, not philosophical abstractions. The Rijksmuseum in Amsterdam demonstrated this during its 2021 digitisation update, long before large-scale generative tools entered public use. When expanding its open-access image library, the museum published a clean rights table for each work: creator, date, reproduction rights, known restrictions. This table, later adapted for generative workflows in 2023, became a visible decision tool—staff could measure risk at a glance. When uncertainties arose, such as the status of recent restorations, they recorded questions directly alongside assets. The implication is clear: when institutions make rights legible, teams can move decisively.

Contrast this with a limitation observed at a mid-sized marketing agency in Toronto in 2023. Leadership drafted a sweeping AI policy spanning twenty-five pages, filled with risk categories, flowcharts, and ambiguous clauses. Staff, unsure which rules applied to which tasks, avoided models entirely. Creativity contracted. The document was technically comprehensive but socially ineffective. Months later, after client complaints about missed innovation opportunities, the agency replaced the policy with a two-page practical guide modelled on Creative Commons' rights labelling. Adoption surged. The reconciliation lies in simplicity: broad policies suffocate; succinct ones breathe.

A third claim sits at the heart of this subchapter: freedom flourishes when guardrails are visible, inspectable, and periodically reviewed. The Allen Institute for AI in Seattle exemplified this when, in January 2024, it introduced a "consent-first" charter for internal dataset creation. Researchers were required to record evidence of permission for any personal data, note uncertainty levels, and tag borderline cases for quarterly audit. The behaviour this triggered was constructive: researchers began planning dataset scope earlier, budgeting time for consent gathering, and restructuring their annotation strategies. Efficiency improved not because risk evaporated, but because teams could measure it. Quarterly audits forced reflection; reflection improved judgement.

The margin note returns here, again unobtrusive yet essential, as the mechanism through which guardrails remain proportionate. Every datapoint, every reference, every prompt iteration gains a trace. These traces help institutions explain their work clearly to collaborators, regulators, and the communities from which material is drawn. Traceability becomes part of the craft.

A fourth claim surfaces when we examine the role of governance in preventing gridlock. Consider the London-based design studio Pentagram, which in early 2024 quietly introduced a hybrid workflow policy: teams were allowed to experiment freely with generative tools during concept exploration, but no draft could move into client presentations without a provenance check signed by a designated reviewer. This single requirement—one reviewer's signature—streamlined an otherwise chaotic environment. Designers regained confidence. Clients trusted the process. The policy named the reviewer, explained the step, and implied the consequence: no provenance, no pitch. Work accelerated, not slowed.

Yet we must acknowledge a credible counter-example. Some organisations, particularly in fields with strict regulatory regimes, cannot adopt lightweight policies alone. Medical publishers, financial institutions, and public-sector agencies face compliance burdens that make two-page documents insufficient. For them, experimentation must be more constrained. But even here, reconciliation is possible. They can apply the same principle at a narrower scale: small team pilots with tight, reviewable scopes; localised governance before enterprise-wide adoption. Freedom with guardrails becomes freedom in pockets, expanding as confidence grows.

A fifth claim concerns the importance of involving practitioners—not only legal staff—in shaping policies. When the Metropolitan Museum of Art in New York began drafting internal guidelines for generative interpretation tools in late 2023, they convened not only digital managers and counsel but also educators, conservators, and public engagement staff. Each group annotated the draft—again the motif of the margin note—and those annotations revealed friction points that leadership alone would have missed: equity concerns about voice tone in generated descriptions, the risk of trivialising complex cultural objects, the need for rapid correction mechanisms when errors surfaced. The finished policy struck a balance: experimentation encouraged; sensitive objects flagged; revision pathways formalised. Because staff participated, trust increased. Policies written with practitioners hold.

Across all these cases, one truth stands out: institutions that draft policies early avoid future paralysis. Policies written after controversy tend to be punitive; policies written before controversy tend to be enabling. When teams define consent procedures, credit expectations, and documentation habits in advance, they give themselves the confidence to explore without fear of crossing invisible lines.

Where does this leave organisations now? They stand before a choice that will shape their creative capacity. Will they default to silence, hoping that informal norms suffice, or will they commit to short, useful structures that set boundaries without stifling invention? What language will they choose for their margin notes? And who will be responsible when new materials, new collaborators, or new tools challenge the assumptions embedded in those early drafts?

Personal Operating System

In February 2021, the Royal College of Art in London ran a quiet experiment. A cohort of twenty design postgraduates were asked to keep a single sheet of paper on their desks for the duration of a six-week studio module. On that sheet they recorded, daily, three things: one goal, one method, and one review note. No complex framework. No digital platform. Just a one-page checklist. When the module ended, instructors noticed a stark pattern: students who updated the sheet consistently produced work with clearer intent, tighter scope, and stronger reflective rationale. The students said something similar: the sheet made them feel less scattered. They could see their practice on the page. It grounded them.

That sheet is not a productivity hack. It marks a shift in how creative professionals organise their craft in hybrid environments where models can accelerate tasks but cannot supply judgement. When tools multiply, choice becomes the new constraint. Without a personal operating system—something stable, portable, self-authored—creative work risks drifting into repetition or fatigue. The RCA experiment shows the opposite: structure gives freedom shape. The motif of the single page reappears throughout this subchapter because that page represents a commitment. It shows that clarity is not an accident; it is a discipline.

A first claim follows directly: individuals who define their goals explicitly work with greater agency. Consider the example of the journalist and author Helen Lewis, who in 2022 documented her writing process while contributing a long-form series for *The Atlantic* from her base in London. She set one visible behaviour at the start of each week: a written brief for herself stating the story's desired outcomes, its emotional register, and its investigative limits. This brief became her internal compass. By naming her direction, she explained her choices, and the implication was clear: she avoided scope creep because she had defined the boundaries of inquiry.

Lewis later remarked in a public lecture at King's College London (2023) that these self-issued briefs were "insurance against distraction". They acted as a page-sized commitment to intent.

A second example comes from Pixar Animation Studios, whose story departments—in both Emeryville and Vancouver—introduced personal rubrics for story artists in 2020. Each artist assembled a short checklist before a pitch: clarity of motivation, emotional pivot, visual logic, narrative tension. These items were not dictated top-down; they were built collaboratively and refined individually. Artists then used their rubrics to measure drafts before presenting. The outcome, reported in the studio's internal workflow review that year, was a measurable reduction in late-stage revisions. Because artists had a personal operating system that aligned with shared standards, the human judgement remained prominent even as digital tools began generating more visual alternatives during ideation. The implication is worth noting: personal systems scale collaborative work.

The limitation is visible in a contrasting case. In 2023, a major European publishing house piloted an "author tool stack" for novelists, providing an array of writing assistants, version trackers, and model-based drafting tools. But the system failed to gain traction. Writers reported that the stack felt intrusive: too many screens, too many nudges, too many suggestions. Their individual operating systems—quiet, idiosyncratic, often analogue—were overwritten by corporate enthusiasm for uniform workflow. Productivity dipped. The reconciliation came when the house allowed writers to opt out, then repurposed the tools as optional kits rather than mandatory platforms. Agency returned when authors chose the tools that served their existing habits.

A second claim centres on the idea that effective personal operating systems integrate three components: kits, rubrics, and review loops. The kit is the curated set of tools—digital and physical—that supports the work. The rubric is the standard by which work is judged. The review loop is the practice of stepping back to evaluate progress. This triad appears in the work of composer Anna Meredith, who, during the creation of her 2019 album *FIBS* in Glasgow, kept her own hybrid system: a notebook for musical sketches, a set of digital patches she built herself, and a nightly audio review of fragments. The kit (her patches) constrained her palette; the rubric (her notes on emotional and rhythmic targets) shaped the direction; the review loop ensured she corrected course rather than accumulating unused material. Her process was hybrid, but her agency remained intact because her system was hers.

The page returns here as motif. Meredith used ruled pages, hand-drawn bars, arrows mapping energy shifts. The RCA students used a single sheet. Pixar's artists used index cards pinned beside monitors. These modest artefacts anchor judgement. They show that personal operating systems are not abstract frameworks; they are physical or digital surfaces that capture intent, direction, and reflection.

A third claim builds on this: review loops create momentum. The University of Helsinki's Information Studies faculty demonstrated this in a 2022 study examining how students used generative text tools during research design. The study, published in *First Monday* (June 2022), found that students who implemented weekly review sessions—where they audited the outputs they had accepted or rejected—developed stronger critical literacy. Their behaviour most strongly associated with improved performance was not tool selection but tool evaluation. By reviewing their decisions explicitly, they gained confidence and clarity. The implication is straightforward: reflection enhances agency. Without it, tools dictate the rhythm of work.

Yet review loops face a credible counter-example: in high-pressure environments, teams often sacrifice reflection for speed. When a Berlin-based editorial collective facing a tight deadline in January 2024 attempted to introduce daily review pauses while using generative tools for illustration, they found that the practice felt stressful, not strengthening. They were too rushed to think clearly. The reconciliation came when they shifted reviews to twice weekly, extending the sessions slightly and reducing the cognitive load. Reflection thrives when the cadence matches the project's tempo.

A fourth claim concerns risk and judgement. A personal operating system enables practitioners to decide when to use models, when to avoid them, and when to verify outputs manually. The choice is visible behaviour. One example comes from the BBC Visual Journalism unit, which in May 2023 issued internal guidance advising reporters to declare their personal thresholds for model use: when they would use summarisation, when they would avoid generated visuals, when they would switch to manual transcription. Each journalist created a personal "red lines" note. This visible act clarified risk appetite while preserving autonomy. Reporters could explain their processes to editors quickly and confidently. The implication is significant: clear personal boundaries reduce downstream disputes.

A contrasting case comes from a New York advertising boutique that in 2022 introduced strict rules around generative ideation without helping staff develop personal systems. Creatives were told to explore widely but avoid biases, stay original but use models fluently, take risks but preserve brand consistency. The contradictions were paralysing. Staff felt scrutinised without being equipped. The policy improved only after leadership asked each team member to craft a one-page operating system identifying goals, decision criteria, and review intervals. Clarity emerged. Critique became more consistent. Projects stabilised. A good personal system supports institutional expectations; a missing system leaves workers exposed.

A fifth claim: a personal operating system is adaptive. It is not carved in stone. It evolves as tools, contexts, and goals change. The London-based architecture studio Heatherwick Group provides a powerful example. When experimenting with generative concept models in 2023 for urban furniture prototypes, designers recorded their operating systems publicly on an internal wiki. They updated them as new methods emerged. They noted where tools helped, where they misled, and where judgement overruled automation. This documentation became a living record. It offered new designers a starting point while preserving room for individual divergence. The implication is hopeful: when personal systems are adaptive, organisations learn collectively from individual reflection.

The page returns yet again. A personal operating system does not require grandeur. A single sheet can hold a kit list, a rubric, and a review rhythm. And because it is concise, it encourages adherence. When systems become too ornate, they fail. When they remain modest, they invite use. The page becomes a companion rather than a constraint.

This subchapter must also consider the psychological dimension. Agency is not a slogan. It is a feeling, often fragile, and it grows through practice. When creators assemble their own systems, they assert authorship over their process, not just their outcomes. They know why they make certain decisions. They can defend their choices. They can revise thoughtfully. A personal operating system lifts the fog of experimentation by clarifying intention.

The unresolved tension sits with the reader: how will they choose to design their own operating system when tools evolve monthly? Which parts will remain stable—goals, values, review cadence—and which parts will flex? How will they balance structure with freedom? The page is waiting.

A Principles-Based Future

In July 2023, during tense contract negotiations in Los Angeles, SAG-AFTRA released a statement condemning a proposal from a group of studios that would have allowed background actors to be scanned once and reused indefinitely. The union argued that the plan would erase consent and distort the meaning of authorship. The proposal was withdrawn within days after public scrutiny. What mattered was not only the eventual outcome but the moral clarity driving the response. The dispute revealed a deeper truth: when technology accelerates faster than custom, the compass for creative work must rest on principles stable enough to guide decisions under pressure.

A smaller but equally telling moment unfolded in October 2021 at the National Gallery in London. Conservators unveiled findings from a research project combining multispectral imaging and generative modelling to study underdrawings in Renaissance works. The team went to great lengths to document their methods, disclosing which parts of the reconstructions were algorithmically inferred and which were directly observed. Their insistence on clarity—naming tools, steps, and assumptions—became part of the exhibition's integrity. Visitors were not asked to trust the image; they were invited to understand the process. This insistence on openness is a thread that runs through every serious conversation about creative work today. It grounds practice. It protects the human centre.

These scenes point to the same question, one that returns throughout this chapter: which principles stay steady as technical capacities shift monthly? The motif of a compass is apt here. A compass does not predict the terrain. It simply tells you where you stand and how to stay oriented. A principles-based future operates the same way. When the ground moves, the bearings matter more.

The first claim is straightforward: human purpose must come first. A visible example of this alignment appeared in the BBC's Editorial Guidelines update of July 2023, in which the corporation explicitly affirmed that generative tools "must support, not supplant, editorial judgement". Embedded within that sentence was an actionable behaviour: editors would sign off on any use of synthetic imagery for broadcast, identifying why it was appropriate for audience understanding. The explanation was precise. The implication was stronger: when leaders articulate human purpose openly, teams can measure decisions against shared values. The guideline was not a prohibition. It was a commitment to narrative clarity and audience respect.

A second example comes from the Rijksmuseum in Amsterdam, which in 2022 ran a collaborative project exploring digital reconstructions of damaged artworks. Technologists, historians, and the museum's own ethics team worked together to define a simple rule: no synthetic reconstruction could be displayed without an accompanying statement about what was real and what was generated. The behaviour was visible—every label named the status of each element. This transparency signalled purpose. The institution chose understanding over spectacle. The implication travelled beyond the galleries: provenance is a communication act, not a technical footnote.

A credible counter-example emerged in early 2023 when a global retailer released a promotional campaign featuring AI-generated portraits that unintentionally reproduced racial stereotypes. The company defended the campaign initially, citing "creative experimentation". The backlash intensified. Trust collapsed. What failed here was not the technology but the absence of principle: no articulated purpose, no consent-oriented workflow, no clarity around verification. The reconciliation came later, when the retailer withdrew the imagery and published a new framework for creative approvals, prioritising representation review and naming responsible decision-makers. Once principles were restored, practice stabilised.

A second major claim is that consent by default is not optional when creative work involves likeness, voice, or identifiable cultural material. The UNESCO Recommendation on the Ethics of Artificial Intelligence, adopted in November 2021 by 193 member states in Paris, made this explicit, urging institutions to ensure that individuals could meaningfully decide how their data and identity are used. The visible behaviour here was procedural: organisations were encouraged to record consent at the point of capture and at the point of reuse. This was not idealism. It was a practical safeguard. The implication is unmistakable: if creators cannot choose how their identity enters a system, the system is not worthy of their trust.

A concrete illustration comes from the European Commission's negotiations around the EU AI Act in December 2023. Draft provisions required developers of generative models to document the copyrighted materials used during training. This did not solve every question of ownership, but it created a trackable chain of responsibility. Once again, the behaviour—documentation—became the ethical backbone. Transparency is not a moral flourish; it is the infrastructure of consent.

The counter-example is well known: synthetic voice cloning performed without consent. In 2020, several public figures discovered models replicating their speech patterns in unauthorised commercial contexts. No amount of technical sophistication could redeem the absence of permission. The harm was not hypothetical. It was audible. What reconciles this case with the larger claim is the emergence of rights-clearing services—such as Veritone's digital voice licensing platform launched in 2021—which hinge on explicit agreements detailing scope, duration, and revocation. The principle survives when practice enforces it.

A third claim: clarity must outrank hype. The rise of generative methods invites grand promises, but clarity is measured through behaviour. One such behaviour is plain-language explanation. The Guardian's data journalism team, for example, began publishing methodological notes in February 2023 detailing when generative summarisation or classification had assisted research. These notes named each tool and described its role without exaggeration. The outcome was mutual respect: readers could judge the reliability of the work, and journalists could defend their process. The implication for creative industries is direct: clarity is a competitive advantage. Hype collapses under scrutiny; openness withstands it.

A second example surfaces in the UK Advertising Standards Authority's adjudications throughout 2022 and 2023, where campaigns that overstated AI capabilities were ruled misleading. One case involved a fintech company that implied its model could "predict market movement with certainty". The ASA required the claim be withdrawn. The behaviour—enforcement—signalled a principle: public communication must match demonstrable capacity. Creative professionals learned the quieter lesson: precision earns longevity.

A limitation appears in research labs where complex models cannot always be fully explained due to proprietary constraints. But reconciliation is possible. Increasingly, labs such as DeepMind provide model cards and evaluation reports naming limitations and uncertainty bands, as seen in their January 2024 release notes. This partial transparency upholds the principle: where full disclosure is impossible, contextual honesty still matters.

A fourth claim: quality must exceed novelty. A visible metric comes from the Cannes Lions International Festival of Creativity, which in 2023 tightened judging criteria after concerns that AI-driven submissions leaned on spectacle rather than craft. Juries were instructed to prioritise narrative coherence, cultural sensitivity, and execution fidelity over technical novelty. The behaviour change was small but symbolic. It realigned incentives. The implication is that industries gravitate towards what they reward; when juries reward quality, practitioners take notice.

The motif of the compass returns here. A compass does not thrill. It steadies. Principles function similarly. They orient creators towards purpose, consent, clarity, and quality when novelty dazzles or pressure accelerates decisions. The true test of a principles-based future is whether individuals and institutions can keep their bearings when convenience tempts shortcuts.

This brings us to the unresolved tension. As models become more capable, how will creators decide which principles to adapt and which to defend without compromise? Where will they draw their personal north lines? And when the easiest path conflicts with the most humane one, which direction will they choose? The compass rests in their hands.

About the Author

Jahan Vespari writes at the meeting point of technology and culture, helping readers separate durable shifts from passing fads. Having worked alongside creative teams across studios and start-ups, Jahan focuses on how tools change taste, craft, and the economics of making. A recurring thread in the work is stewardship: how communities preserve voice and credit as techniques evolve, much like printers safeguarded type foundries when moveable type transformed authorship. Jahan's essays and talks emphasise practical workflows, ethical clarity, and respect for lived experience. The mission is simple: keep human judgement at the centre while using machines to widen possibility. When not testing new tools, Jahan documents field-tested methods that help small teams ship work they are proud to sign.

www.ingramcontent.com/pod-product-compliance
Lightning Source LLC
Chambersburg PA
CBHW031338230926
51848CB00002B/291
9789374592786